My First Five Husbands

AND THE ONES WHO GOT AWAY

BROADWAY BOOKS NEW YORK

RUE McCLANAHAN

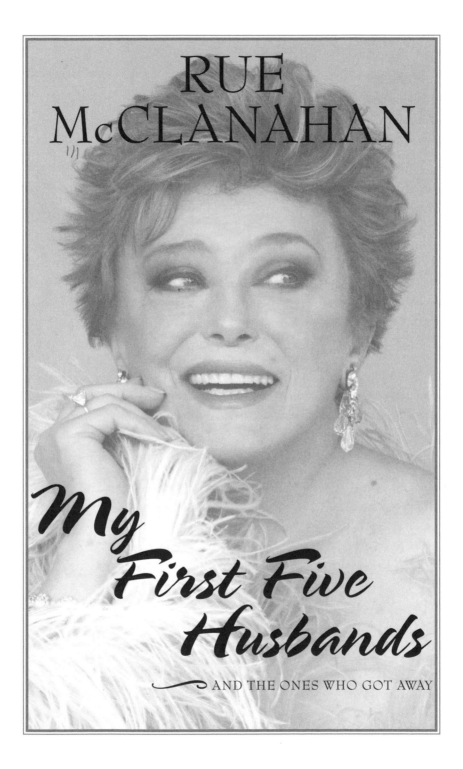

My First Five Husbands

AND THE ONES WHO GOT AWAY

B
mcClR

For photo permissions and credits, please turn to pages 337–38.

Book design by Fearn de Vicq

Library of Congress Cataloging-in-Publication Data

McClanahan, Rue.

My first five husbands — and the ones who got away / Rue McClanahan. — 1st ed.

p. cm.

1. McClanahan, Rue. 2. Actors—United States—Biography. I. Title.

PN4874.M483947A3 2007

792.02'8092—dc 22

[B]

2006102863

ISBN 978-0-7679-2676-8

Printed in the United States of America

10 9 8 7 6 5 4 3 2 1

First Edition

To Mark

Acknowledgments

*"I'd like to thank everyone who helped make this award possible.
The rest of you will be in the book."*
—Rue McClanahan, Emmy Awards, 1987

This book is about my life and experiences as I lived them, and anyone who doesn't like it can jolly well lump it. Others may have a different perception of events. I respect their right to render totally biased and self-serving commentary about their own lives, but only if sifted through long years and a few bourbons, dipped in forgiveness and wisdom, and salted with a sense of humor—because that's what I've done. But a word of caution: Writing a book is one hell of a lot of work. Let me assure you, I couldn't have done it without the love and support of the following people:

My erudite and sweet-smelling sixth husband, Morrow Wilson, whose advice always stopped short of interference; my beloved inimitable son, Mark Bish, and indefatigable sister, Dr. Melinda McClanahan, both of whom patiently endured uncounted phone calls to help with names and dates (and in my sister's case, repeated warnings: "Don't you say anything bad about him!"), as did my staunch and dear friends Andrew Greenhut, who had memories I'd forgotten, and Marty Jacobs, Curator of the Theatre Collections of the Museum of the City of New York; my friend and assistant, Kathy Salomone, who not only helped type the manuscript, but without whom I'd still be trapped in Computer Dysfunction Hell; my pal, Ed Kaczmarek, who took phone calls at his home and office in Chicago to get me out of the Computer Dysfunction Hells that even Kathy couldn't solve; my literary agent, Wendy Sherman, who shepherded me to Broadway Books; my editor at Broadway Books, Ann Campbell, who gently, firmly advised a better format while planning her wedding and never got the two confused; my memoir guru, Joni Rodgers, who, along with Ann, devised that better format, working hand-in-hand with me with unfailing enthusiasm; the design and production team at Broadway; all my friends who have been saying excitedly to me for over two years, "Oh, I can't wait to read it!" And finally, Saint Dymphna, patroness of insanity.

In a few instances, I've chosen, in spite of temptation, to refrain from using specific names and going into exquisite detail—not so much from fear of getting sued, although I might invite several lawsuits if I let it all hang out, but because, in spite of being a legal grown-up for some fifty-*ummph* years, like a good Southern girl, I respect my family elders, many of whom are still hale and hearty and possessed of clear eyesight. So some details have been altered, some events condensed, and some names changed to protect the innocent (me) and to discourage a few black-hearted scalawags.

My First Five Husbands

AND THE ONES WHO GOT AWAY

Prologue

I'm told the Esquimaux have a charming take on lovemaking.
They call it "laughing together." Working from that premise,
we could refer to the Laughing Together Quotient, or the LTQ. You
could have an LTQ from "snicker" to "guffaw" right up to "belly
laugh." But as I have yet to know an Esquimau under the walrus blankets, I'll stick to the Lower 48, and using our more familiar reference,
refer herein to certain gentlemen (and a couple of the other kind) in
regard to their FQ—that is, of course, as you undoubtedly surmise,
their Fun in Bed Quotient, or Fun Quotient, for short.

As every woman knows, it's possible for a man to have an FQ of
A+ and an IQ of Zip. Ah, yes, we know him well—he falls into the
Smoldering Handyman or Stanley Kowalski Category. Certainly right
up there at the top of *my* All-Time Hits List. But generally, high IQs
bestow upon their owners equally high FQs, since FQ is greatly
enhanced by imagination and wit. Two of the best lovers I've known
were psychoanalysts, both brilliant.

Loony, but brilliant.

And FQs of A+. Rare as a day in May? Let me tell you . . . which I
shall. This book is about men I have known, in both the platonic and

biblical senses. Some I knew only slightly, some quite well. Some I'll love always, some I no longer like very much, and there are a few I'd like to strip naked, tie to a maypole, smear with sweet syrup near a beehive, then stand back and watch. I'll describe a goodly number of these hot dudes—and *duds*—keeping the nicest man for last, because—if for nothing else—I'd like to leave you, dear reader, with a good taste in your mouth, and Hubbies #3 and #4 might make you want to rush to gargle. There were times I truly wondered, *Lord, will I EVER get it right?* Thank God I thrive on variety.

⁓

"Tomorrow's assignment: Bring in five scenes depicting five reasons to get married."

Barney Brown's acting class, Perry-Mansfield Dance-Drama Camp, Steamboat Springs, Colorado. Summer of 1955. I was twenty-one, my partner a year younger.

"There's only one reason to get married, and that's being in love," I told my scene partner. "I guess some people get married for money, but"—I frowned—"would you really get married for money if you weren't in love?"

"I dunno."

"Well, I wouldn't. Should we put it down anyway?"

"I guess so."

"Okay, we've got two reasons. What else?"

"Okay," he said. "See, maybe someone was run over by a car or something, and to keep from going to jail, he marries the girl he ran over."

"Hmm." I considered that. "No, that's not logical. Gosh, this is hard. Okay, look, let's say you're getting married, okay? So why are you marrying this girl?"

"Well," he squirmed, "I never really thought about getting married for any reason."

My Lord, he's gay.

"Oh, brother," I sighed. "We're gonna flop."

So we brought in two reasons: marrying for love and for money. But I simply couldn't imagine getting married without being in love, and up to that moment, my experience of love was . . . well, *lovely!* Pen is the first boy I remember being enamored of. I was five. We played house, imagining we were a married couple. In my mind, this meant "romance." In his mind, it meant "mud pies." (A dynamic that persists between many married couples.) My first really big heartthrob was Benny Frank Butler, from ages eight to fourteen. In junior high, Al Ringer and Johnny Brooks gave me fits of unrequited passion. And I liked my high school beau so much, I married him thirty-five years later. In college, there was dear Bill Bennett, and heck, I was still a virgin! So who's the first man I ever slept with? That's what everyone wants to hear. *Who was first? What was it like?* Let's make a game of it: "Erotic Mystery Maze! Follow the Hidden Clues to the Virgin Encounter! Three free spins to get it right!"

As I made my way in the world, my worldly ideas of love evolved. Over the next twenty-nine years I lived out five marriages that afforded me plenty of reasons why people get married, including a raft of reasons not to. In the pages that follow, you'll find my musings on my various attempts at the venerable institution of marriage. Each time, I believed the wedding would be the first day of a lifelong union. My suspicion that I'd possibly made a horrible mistake came later. Sometimes as late as—hmm . . . *the honeymoon!*

I'm not very lucky with honeymoons, and some of them were even in lovely places. Or at least, decent. But all in all, I'd rather go to Hawaii with a girlfriend and, as I'm being balmed by the balmy breeze and mooned by the melon moon, sigh, *Ah, if only I were here with a man in this romantic place!*—instead of being out there in the moonlight with a man, thinking, *Oh, no—another turd in the punch bowl.* Getting past the honeymoon requires mature judgment in mate selection, as well as luck, proper planetary alignment, and most important, burying an Irish potato in the dark of a new moon. I kept getting distracted by good looks and sex appeal (and occasionally desperation) and forgetting to bury that damned potato.

Now, every once in a while, as I float through the living room of my cozy Manhattan apartment, I run into my husband sitting there with one leg akimbo.

"I think you're marvelous," I sigh.

He looks up from his book, and says, "Why?"

But I don't have a list of reasons. There are too many. Or maybe I was right in the first place; there is only one reason. And it ain't mud pies.

"You will do foolish things," said the great writer Colette, "but do them with enthusiasm!" And that, my darlings, I have done!

So put your feet up, relax, and let me take you on one woman's journey through the beguiling, bewildering wilderness of romantic encounters, replete with puppy love, Latin love, smoldering lust, stardust, obsession, high comedy, high camp, and all manner of peccadilloes and misadventures. A rollicking, madcap ride through the wide-open countryside of love.

Just watch out for land mines.

CHAPTER ONE

"How the hell did we end up here?"

—Christopher Columbus

My mother, Rheua-Nell, was five feet and one half inch tall. She always included that one half inch. (Hey, if you got it, flaunt it.) Bright and talented in music and dance, she won a Charleston contest when she was sixteen. Had she been younger, I suspect, my grandfather, Pee-Paw, would've soundly whipped her with his razor strop. He raised his family in a strict Southern Baptist tradition; no dancing allowed. Shortly thereafter, still sixteen, she graduated valedictorian of her high school class and went off to Dallas to study cosmetology to become a beauty operator. Four years later, she was working in Mrs. Rose's beauty parlor on Main Street in Healdton, Oklahoma, when she met my father, Bill, who had hurt his back in the construction trade and was managing a billiards parlor a few doors down.

Six weeks later, they married. Ten months after that—February 21, 1934—I was born. The doctor nicknamed me "Frosty" because I had a full head of white-blond hair, but when Mother saw me, she burst into tears. I'd been taken with forceps after she labored (at home, of course) for thirty-some hours, so my head was elongated and blue and apparently quite alarming to behold. I soon rounded out and pinked

My Choctaw great-grandfather, Running Hawk, and Big Maw-Maw, holding my grandmother, Maw-Maw. We used to say chi-hullo-li, *which means "I love you" in Choctaw.*

My maternal grandparents, Ed and Allie Medaris, whom we called Pee-Paw and Maw-Maw.

Zebbin and Fannie McClanahan, my paternal grandparents. They say I have her Copeland eyes.

up to her satisfaction, however. Mother thought I was adorable and took photos like they were going out of style.

When she was pregnant, Mother had been approached by Aunt Wenonah Sue, my father's sister, begging to let her name the baby. Mother acquiesced, but only if she could name Wenonah's firstborn, to which Wenonah agreed. Frankly, I wouldn't let anyone name my first-born. But my mother was a sweet and compliant young lady of twenty, Wenonah's junior by a couple of years, and somewhat under the thrall of this enthusiastic and insistent sister-in-law. My father's name was William Edwin. So when, in the fullness of time, I was born, Wenonah brought forth her marvelous name: *Eddi-Rue,* a little composite of both my parents' names.

Everyone just loved it. It was so cute! It had a hyphen.

"Eddi-Rue," my aunt Nonie has been heard to say, "I think you have one of the prettiest names in the family."

Then Wenonah Sue married a fine fellow named Earl and had a daughter whom Mother dubbed Earla Sue—no hyphen—who wisely dropped the "Earla" when she was fourteen. Because of the "Eddi"— which people always misspelled "Eddie" like a boy—I was sent a man's handkerchief as a high school graduation gift from Daube's Department Store, along with the other male graduates. I also received a draft notice, inviting me to come down for a physical exam. I've always thought maybe I should've gone for that physical. Some childhood friends still call me "Eddi." People who knew me as a baby call me "Frosty." My friend Lette called me "Baby Roo," my friend Jim Whittle called me "Rutabaga," Betty White calls me "Roozie," and my friend Kathy Salomone calls me "Rue-Rue." The staff at Sloan-Kettering Cancer Center call me "Mrs. Wilson." And my husband calls me "Darling." I like them all. Each name brings forth its own era and memories.

When I was in my late twenties, I bought eight used dining room chairs for a dollar each (yes, a dollar!) and set about removing the old varnish. As I applied the varnish remover, a vivid visual memory flashed into my mind: I was almost eight months old, sidestepping along the front of the sofa, holding on for balance, looking up over my left shoulder at my mother and Aunt Irene standing in the doorway making vocal sounds.

"Iddle bongingferd da wondy," said Mother.

"Bid gerpa twack kelzenbluck," replied Aunt Irene.

"Ferndock bandy," Mother replied. "Critzputh." And they laughed.

I realized they were exchanging thoughts with those sounds. *Oh,* I thought, *I'm brand new here. Soon, they'll teach me to do that, too.* What an exciting thought!

Smells are strong memory-triggers. Mother and Irene must have been using varnish remover that day in 1934, and the odor of it in 1963 popped out this early memory, crystal clear. My next memory is of Christmas when I was ten months old: a circle of uncles and other adults winding up a little red rocket that chased me from one side of their circle to the other, everyone laughing. But I was truly terrified, running frantically from the noisy thing and wondering why they thought it was so funny.

Mother gave me my first perm when I was eleven months old, under one of those old stand-up octopus-armed permanent wave machines. Mother was movie-struck, you see. She kept the beauty shop stocked with current movie magazines, was nuts about Fred Astaire, Ginger Rogers, and Shirley Temple, and wanted me to have a full head of bouncy sausage curls, just like *Little Miss Broadway*. And I never existed without a perm until I was well into my forties.

"Why do you keep a perm in your hair?" my beautician asked me one day.

"Can you exist without one?" I responded, utterly amazed.

This revolutionary concept had never occurred to me. Wouldn't my hair just flail about wildly? Like Albert Einstein's? I gave it a try, and from that day to this, I've lived quite happily without a perm. And learned that I have a natural wave to boot.

Aunt Irene, my mother's seventeen-year-old sister, moved in to take care of me while Mother worked in the beauty parlor, but I wanted to be downstairs in the shop. It was lonely upstairs, and boring, and Irene was hot-tempered and brusque, while Mother was jolly fun. It's hard to remember her without a smile. I was allowed to play in the shop from time to time, as long as I sat under the counters and didn't ask too many questions. It was fun under the counters. Legs coming and going, chatter, things happening. To help keep me quiet, I was allowed to nurse my bottle until I was over three. It was bolstered with Eagle brand, a thick, sweet canned milk, because I'd been born a bit scrawny and, on doctor's orders, Mother was trying to fatten me up. She used to send me up the street to the five-and-ten store to buy my own rubber nipples. I remember standing at the cash register getting change.

Mother had also been taking me to the movies since I was a babe in arms, wearing PJs under my street clothes. One night as I sat in the row behind her, waiting for the picture to begin, I tapped on the back of her seat, saying, "Mama?"

She turned and said, "Eddi-Rue, you're too old now to call me 'Mama.' From now on, call me 'Mother.'"

Ooooh. I was so chagrined to be reprimanded in front of everyone, I wanted to crawl under my seat. I never called her Mama again. Mother and Bill expected me to behave like an adult, and I was dead set not to disappoint them. I never went through a rebellious period and was terribly stricken whenever I accidentally lost or broke something. They worked so hard for their money, and I knew this, though I don't recall being at all aware of the Depression. Mother had plenty of customers, we went to the movies every time we turned around, I had a new doll every Christmas, a new birthday dress every year, plus a birthday party. However, I do remember pinto beans every night for supper; I never ate a supper without pinto beans until I went to college, where I was astonished to learn that you didn't have to have them on the table. I'd assumed it was some sort of rule. On the rare nights Mother was too tired to cook a meal, we had corn bread crumbled in a glass of sweet milk, which I considered a big treat.

But it was probably because of the Depression that my father had to go off to the oil fields to get construction work. He was called "Bill" by everyone, including me. (Just in case an old girlfriend showed up, he joked.) He left before I woke in the morning, came home long after I was asleep, and didn't toss me around like my uncles did. He wasn't a hugger. His mother, Fanny, was the only daughter in a family of four boys, forbidden to have a doll (her father even burned a corncob dolly her mother made her, the old buzzard) or to show physical affection. She, in turn, didn't hug her four children. Still, she made me an adorable new outfit for every birthday and taught me to sew on her big treadle sewing machine. She was a loving, kind person—just not one for hugging. So my father never learned how, I guess.

One day when I was five, he came home from work earlier than usual. I was standing on the front porch as dusk settled over our neighborhood, and as Bill walked toward me, my arms and body ached so deeply for him to stop and hug me hello that my skin hurt. But he only said a weary, "Hello, Frosty," and I said, "Hi, Bill," as he trudged past me, leaving me feeling empty and alone. (Later, when I was in the ninth grade, I watched my friend Carol Ann Bristow hugging everybody and decided to learn to do it. It took courage the first few times, but I made it a habit. And it felt *good*! I'm a staunch advocate of hugging to this day.)

Aunt Wenonah always told me my father was a brilliant man.

"But strange," she always added. "Not like the rest of us kids."

Yep. That he was. A dry and hilarious storyteller, Bill wrote a dark play during his senior year in high school, exposing some ugly truths about the people in Healdton. The principal made him burn it after one performance. Bill was funny, poetic, and moody, while Mother was funny, musical, and feisty. Bill, six feet tall, had thick, slightly wavy ash-blond hair and big blue eyes. Mother had green eyes and dark auburn hair and was quite petite (even with that all-important half inch). Both were good-looking and popular, with plenty of friends, but Bill wouldn't sing if anyone was listening and couldn't dance worth a hoot, unlike Mother the enthusiastic Charleston champion. She played piano in an overripe, barroom style without having had lesson one. All her family sang, and she started teaching me songs before I could speak.

"Who's that comin' down the street with that organ grinder's beat? Da-dee-ah . . ." I sang for the ladies being primped and permed in the beauty parlor. *"He's the greatest rhythm king with that organ grinder swing! Da-dee-ah . . ."*

Mother enrolled me in tap-dancing lessons at the Armory when I was four, but I hated it. The only child in a class of adults, I was lost in a forest of legs wearing clickety-clackety tap shoes and wanted nothing to do with it. A year earlier, my first appearance in front of an audience had been a fiasco. I was supposed to be the ring bearer at a fancy Lebanese wedding, a big family whose sons were Bill's best friends. Decked out in an adorable dress, I sailed through the rehearsal in the empty church, but the next day, the music started, the church doors swung open, and—well, you remember the old nursery rhyme: Here is the church, here is the steeple, open the doors and *see all the people*! Nope. Not me, nohow. No matter how they cajoled.

But by kindergarten, I'd gotten over that and was cast as Mother Cat in "The Three Little Kittens." We all knew our lines and were ready to perform. But those three little kittens giggled instead of saying their lines, ruining the illusion. I was disgusted. "We're cats! We're not little girls! Stop that giggling!" Oh, it was all too childish. Someday, I'll do "The Three Little Kittens" again and do it *right*.

Even as a child, I was more than disenchanted with that sleepy Oklahoma town, which I assumed to be the whole world. No one spoke the same language as me, so to speak. One summer night, gazing down on Main Street from our apartment above the beauty parlor, I watched cars driving from one end of Main Street to the other (all of about a block and a half). They'd slowly cruise down the main drag, turn around, cruise back again. June bugs buzzed through the air, sticking to the grilles of the cars, crunching under the feet of people on their way to the movie theater. Monotony beyond bearing. I specifically remember realizing: *I've been born into the wrong world! A terrible mistake has been made!*

"I want to learn to read," I kept begging Mother. My friend, Emma Jane Irving, a year older, started school and shared her penmanship exercises with me on the beauty parlor floor. I learned the alphabet and was delighted to discover how letters fell together to form words.

This is Jane. This is Dick. See Jane run. See Dick run.

Thrilling! Action *and* romance!

In 1939, Mother was expecting, and for months I waited with bated breath for the new arrival, fervently wanting a baby sister. One day, in mid-August, when Mother was almost due to deliver, I was doing acrobatics and broke my arm. Aunt Irene whisked me up and ran lickety-split down the street to the doctor, followed by a waddling, distraught Rheua-Nell. I was given ether and promptly died right there on the table. Doc Cantrill revived me, set the arm, and sent me home. Quite a trauma for poor Mother, nine months pregnant, but wonderfully dramatic from my perspective. Just like a movie, only I was the star!

I awoke a couple of weeks later to find she'd been taken during the night to the Ardmore hospital twenty-five miles away. The wall phone rang, and Aunt Irene answered with me at her feet. Finally, she looked down and said, "Well, Frosty, the baby's here."

"Oh, Irene!" I was bursting with hope. "Is it a boy or a girl?"

"A girl."

Oh, joy! Trumpets blow! I had a baby sister, Melinda Lou! That night, Bill drove me to the hospital. I clambered onto Mother's bed with my broken arm.

"Frosty! Get down! Don't shake the bed!"

Oops. Big goof. Embarrassed, I climbed down. Mother smiled. The little bundle, face all squinched up and red, was a miracle to behold. I was bursting with happiness and didn't want to leave, but Bill took me to a rooming house to spend the night. I had never spent a night away from Mother, never slept away from home, except at grandparents' houses. And I had certainly never slept anywhere with just my dad! Bill turned off the light and rolled over to go to sleep. Feeling lonesome and scared, I said, "Bill? Can we talk for a while?"

"Frosty, this is not the time for talking, it's the time for sleeping."

Watching headlights sweep slowly across the faded wallpaper, I felt panicky, my chest tight with fear in that dreary, empty room.

In a few days, Mother and Melinda Lou came home and I was allowed to hold her, even with my arm in its sling. Melinda looked up blindly toward my face and scratched my forearm with her sharp little nails. I wondered if she liked me. I was certainly proud to pieces of her. But Melinda scratched a lot. She wasn't a terribly affectionate baby and didn't appreciate the tenderness I lavished on her.

"If Eddi-Rue had been the baby and Melinda had been born first," Bill has been heard to say, "Melinda would have killed her."

There was no jealousy or sibling rivalry. I simply and unabashedly adored her, and she was the best possible playmate. As we grew older, we became great pals and I never thought of her as "the baby." She was extraordinarily bright and able to grasp pragmatic things (as one might expect from a future Ph.D. in radiation biology). She was vivacious, flirtatious, and self-assured, but she could be stubborn. When she was two, she dropped something or other on the bedroom floor and created an all-out battle of wills with short-tempered Aunt Irene.

"Melinda Lou, pick that up and put it in the wastebasket this minute!" ordered Irene.

"No!" Melinda flatly refused, determined to defy Aunt Irene.

"I'll spank you!"

"No!"

Irene ended the standoff, seizing Melinda's hand and forcing her to put whatever it was in the wastebasket. And then she spanked Melinda—*pat! pat!*—on the bottom. *Oh, why wouldn't one of them just pick it up?* I fretted. Mother did not believe in physical punishment. She simply told us what was expected and, because we loved her so, we did it. About the harshest reprimand I remember receiving from Mother was for talking too much in the beauty parlor one day.

"Eddi-Rue," she finally said in exasperation, "go sit on that chair and be quiet for five minutes."

I obediently sat, eyes fixed on the clock, but I thought it was a minute between each number. After an eternity, the minute hand had traveled from twelve to five, and I said timidly to Mother, "It's been five minutes. Can I talk now?"

"Why, Eddi-Rue!" Mother exclaimed. "Are you still here? You were so quiet, I forgot all about you."

Not surprisingly, that was the day I learned to tell time.

⌒

An ambitious man, Bill was determined to find the best work he could, building derricks in the oil fields and later constructing "corduroy" roads in Louisiana through swamps to the drilling sites. Corduroy roads are made of logs, like log cabins, cheap and quick to construct. He drove us out one day to see his work—*bumpety bump bump!* What fun!

My first day of school in Lafayette, Louisiana, I lowered my head on my desk and bawled, unspeakably terrified to have been dropped off by Mother in a strange place with a strange accent. The one thing I remember is learning the verse "To market, to market to buy a fat pig." At home that afternoon, I asked, "Mother, what's a *mahkit?*" The second half of the first grade we moved to Bishop, Texas, just after they'd had a flood, which was more fun, because I got to walk to school in knee-deep water. We put on a recital in which I was supposed to deliver a patriotic speech. I memorized it while hanging upside down on the closet clothes rod while Mother was doing housework. But on The Day, I saw all those people looking at me, launched forth, and went stone blank. Maybe I should have tried it upside down. My teacher gently prompted me from the front row and I continued, but oh, I was embarrassed.

A year later, Bill landed a general contracting job in Houston with Mr. Curtis B. Kelly. It must have been a real step up. "Kelly" recognized Bill as unusually talented and intelligent; we were often at his home, a house I found fascinatingly big and spacious—and spent the next fifty years trying to duplicate. I spent the first semester of second grade in Houston, then skipped to the first semester of the third grade, having been double-promoted, along with my two boyfriends, Pat and Charles, who walked me home from school every day. Pat was tall and pudgy with a sweet, open face. Mischievous Charles had bright red hair and a most wonderful talent: He could fall straight backward to the ground, stiff as a stick. A remarkably brave, if foolhardy, thing to do. I don't know how he kept from killing himself, but it delighted me so, I guess the pain was worth it.

In Houston, I studied ballet for a year with Miss Emma Mae Horne. Oh, how I loved ballet class! For our recital, I was in a maypole dance with sixteen little girls weaving crepe paper streamers, all of us in striped dirndl skirts over gathered white net petticoats, flowers in our hair. I also danced a duet with another girl, a lyrical little tippy-toe piece of fluff done in short purple velvet tutus. Mother made my costumes, and I felt like a fairy princess. Nothing was more magical than dancing.

I won three contests that year in Houston. One was for the longest list of words made from the letters in "Constantinople"—on which Mother, Irene, and I labored for a week, and I felt secretly guilty for having had help. The *Houston Chronicle* held a contest for the best essay on *The Jungle Book,* and my prize was two tickets to the movie. For drawing the best Thanksgiving turkey—well, I tied with one of the boys. The winning boy and I were called up to Mrs. Butler's desk to receive a special lollipop each, and I was given first choice. One was a huge, jolly clown face, the other a small green Christmas tree. I very much wanted the clown, but I figured the boy would think the Christmas tree girlish and obviously second best, so I reluctantly took the tree—but dammit, it pissed me off to be so noble.

After Pearl Harbor, Bill enlisted in the CBs (the Construction Battalion branch of the military). I never asked why. Perhaps patriotism, perhaps a better salary. Thirty-four with a wife and two children to support, he moved our family to Durant, Oklahoma, and went off to serve his country, gone for three years, till the war in the Pacific was over. Mother worked all day, came home after dark, and went out "with the girls" several nights a week. During this time, I developed a daily panic that came on at dusk and plagued me well into my thirties. Other people would say, "Oh, isn't dusk a lovely time of day!" while my throat tightened and my chest ached. Many nights in high school, while my family was asleep, I got up and wandered around the house in the dark, touching furniture, trying to connect, going outside to traipse around the yard, looking at the moon, wondering why I felt so anxious and what on earth was wrong with me.

Getting double-promoted in Houston was wiped out the following September in Durant, which had just plain old third grade. It turned out to be a blessing, however, because we had the theatrical Cecil McKinney up front as our homeroom teacher, and sitting in the back was brown-eyed Benny Frank Butler, with whom I was smitten. Yvonne Mayberry and I were best friends right off the bat, inseparable until fifth grade, when her family moved to Pauls Valley, about eighty miles away. Other side of the moon. Yvonne and I wrote frequent letters, still thick as thieves, but she got married in the eleventh grade to a boy named Coy, and I never saw her again.

Mother sent us up the street to Mrs. Lemon's house for piano lessons, starting when I was eight and Melinda only three. I did well, but Melinda had a real knack. She can still play the heck out of any piece of music. I continued taking ballet, Melinda took tap, and Mother taught us to sing barbershop harmony. Every car trip was filled with "Lay That Pistol Down" and "White Cliffs of Dover" and other wonderful songs. We sang all the way to Dallas to shop for hats, gloves, and Easter getups and all the way to visit Mother's folks, strict "hard-shell" Southern Baptists. There was no swimming, cards, or checkers allowed on Sunday. Only Chinese checkers. Why? I don't know. But we played *a lot* of Chinese checkers. Pee-Paw and Maw-Maw owned the local telephone exchange in tiny Achille, Oklahoma, so all the children took turns running to get whoever had a phone call. Only the town doctor and a few other folks had a phone at home. Everyone else came to Maw-Maw's to take the call at the switchboard.

Our homeroom teacher in the fourth through sixth grades was Velma Moore, a stern-tempered redhead who lived in the duplex adjoining ours and kept a horse in her backyard. Many's the happy hour I spent pulling up clover to feed him through the back fence. Both Miss McKinney, a sweet-tempered little brunette, and fiery-haired Mrs. Moore were wonderful teachers who loved putting on shows. Cecil composed her own lyrics and music and dances, and every December, Mrs. Moore performed an entire chapter from the children's book *A Birds' Christmas Carol* for us, playing all the roles herself, from memory. And she was *good*!

"Mrs. Bird opened her eyes and drew the baby closer. It looked like a rose dipped in milk, she thought, this pink and white blossom of girlhood, or like a pink cherub, with its halo of pale yellow hair, finer than floss silk."

We were enrapt.

I played the fairy godmother in the *Cinderella* musical and Aunt Polly in *Tom Sawyer* (I can still sing my solo from that show, and am likely to, at the drop of a hat), using Mrs. Moore as my model for Aunt Polly: strict with a well-hidden heart of gold. A local radio station held a contest for kid singers, and I entered with "His Rockin' Horse Ran Away," one of those fast and furious Betty Hutton numbers with murderously tongue-twisting bim-bang lyrics. The only other contender was a pudgy young man who sang "Across the Alley from the Alamo." Well, I made short work of him. Rode my rockin' horse right up his alley, thank you very much, and won the contest hands down.

In February of 1945, my father got orders that he was shipping to the Pacific in May for parts undisclosed. Mother drove Melinda and me out to California to be with him for his last two months in the States. We left on my eleventh birthday in Mother's old car with bad tires, having flats all along the way. Tires for civilian use were strictly rationed, so Mother had to find black-market dealers to replace our blown-out ones. Bill's camp was in Oakland and we lived on the base, first in a trailer house (very exciting), then in a Quonset hut (even more exciting!). I was bussed off to Catholic School in Pleasanton, where I spent every recess hiding in abject terror from a gang of big, rowdy Filipino boys. I made no friends, since I was always hiding, but my teacher adored me, as I was the only well-behaved kid in her class. After Bill shipped out, we drove home. I'd put on a bit of prepubescent girth while I was gone, so three girls in my class taunted me unceasingly. "Roly-poly Eddi-Rue! How do you get home, roll down the hill?"

They wrote insulting sentences on the blackboard every morning before class. And Yvonne wasn't there to be on my side. I dreaded going to school. But by the beginning of the sixth grade, I was trim again and had a new best friend—Glenna Anderson, the principal's daughter. I turned twelve in February and, a few days later, got my period. Mother was getting ready to go out for the evening and hastily handed me a Kotex. "Here. Put this on."

My friend Skipper Edelen was spending the night, he and Melinda and I sleeping on pallets on the floor, and the two of them banded together, kidding and razzing me. I thought their behavior was unforgivably crass. I suddenly felt much older, having crossed the threshold out of childhood.

⟶

Halloween at Washington Irving Grade School in Durant was a spectacular event, with games, prizes, and cookies and candy for sale. A haunted house in the basement was reached by a slide down some narrow stairs. Mr. Bateman, the custodian, created it differently every year. All the events cost a dime ticket, except the spook house, which was fifteen cents and worth every penny. For the sixth-grade Halloween night, Mother made me a white satin hoop-skirted frock trimmed in black lace. I had just read *Gone with the Wind* and thought I was Scarlett O'Hara. Sashaying down the crowded hallway, I ran into Benny Frank Butler, on whom I'd harbored a secret crush since third grade.

I curtsied.

He bowed.

I almost fainted.

We ended each happy term in May with an all-school picnic at the city park, a huge, rambling acreage full of running space, trees, and a stream. Some people said the stream was the city sewage line, but it looked clear enough to us and just narrow enough to jump over in some places. (I only fell in once.) The picnic went on all day and we never got tired.

At the start of the seventh grade, my friend Don Knight was at my house one afternoon, and I revealed my long-held crush on Ben. Don jumped on his bike and bounded away, to return twenty minutes later with Ben in tow. Luckily, Ben was also smitten with me. Tall, with an understated, dry wit, Ben took me for rides on his horse, walking the stolid mare along with me sitting close behind him, my hands on his waist. Joy sublime? You better believe it.

One evening, Ben and I were sitting in Mother's Chevy in the front yard and he said, "Eddi-Rue, remember I told you I'd kiss you when you least expected it?"

"Yes."

"Well, do you expect it now?"

The outcome lay squarely in my lap. I took a breath and innocently said, "No."

And . . . oh, Lord . . . he kissed me.

That piece of acting ranks right up there with winning the Emmy.

⟋

After serving in the Army and dancing in ballet choruses in New York City, a certain Newcomb Rice returned to his hometown of Durant with his Scottish wife, Kitty, to settle down, have children, and establish the Oklahoma Dancing Academy. He was an excellent teacher, schooled in the Russian ballet system. Mother enrolled me in his classes in the fall of 1946, and I was enchanted from the get-go. Every Saturday morning, I walked up North Fifth Street to Southeastern College for a glorious hour of ballet instruction on the basketball court. (Basketball and ballet became forever entwined for me.) After a year, we were moved up to pink toe shoes. I found the technique difficult but the soul of dancing natural. Newcomb used to say we were "Pygmalion and Galatea," like the Greek legend about a statue brought to life by her mentor.

All through the seventh and eighth grades, we had wonderful parties at my house. We danced—and I mean to tell you, we *danced*! Mother had taught Melinda and me to jitterbug, Charleston, "sugar," foxtrot, and waltz, and many of the boys were good dancers. (Sadly, Ben was not among them, but maybe that would have made him too perfect.) We played Spin the Bottle and Post Office and other kissing games. In Go Fish, a girl was blindfolded and all the boys lined up and walked around her. Whomever was in front of her when she said, "Stop!"—well, she had to walk around the block with him.

Holding hands.

But who wants to walk around the block holding hands with some twerp? Ben and I worked out secret signals, a carefully timed sneeze, a little cough. He and I shared a sense of humor and a special romantic rapport. Moonlit Oklahoma nights, balmy or brisk, holding hands with Ben—sheer heaven! We went steady for two years, ages twelve to fourteen, with only one week off when we agreed to trade partners for a week with another steady couple, Tawana Lou Clark and Carol Roberts. Both Tawana Lou and Carol were awfully good-looking, but I didn't really have much to say to Carol, so when the week was up, Ben and I were both eager to change back. (Hey, maybe if married couples could take a week off and try another flavor . . . but then again, maybe not. It didn't work wonders with me and Husband #2.)

What a wonderful time junior high school was! Hayrides out at Joe Walter Colclazier's house, playing Kick the Can and Red Rover at my house after school, getting Miss McKinney back for our seventh- and eighth-grade homeroom teacher. All those shows she put on—even Ben joined the chorus. And—can you believe it?—I was elected cheerleader in the eighth grade, along with Tawana Lou Clark, who had the cutest figure in junior high. I was floored. I didn't think of myself as the cheerleading type. Of course, I was. A flat-chested cheerleading type.

But casting a shadow over those happy years was that deep, underlying panic I felt, along with the knowledge that we would be moving the summer after eighth grade. When Bill got back from the war, instead of settling in Durant or Houston, he went to Ardmore, Oklahoma, and hooked up with Mr. Leonard Hurst as Hurst and McClanahan, General Contractors, buying five acres north of town on which to start building our house, which he designed himself. Years later, I asked him why he chose to move us to Ardmore instead of back to Houston, which had obvious professional and cultural advantages, and he said, "Oh, honey, your mother's hay fever was so awful in Houston. I had to find a place where she'd be more comfortable."

He'd given up advancement in Houston so Mother would be more comfortable? Mother has always maintained that Bill had gotten a better offer from Mr. Hurst. Who knows what really happened? I do understand, however, knowing my father, why he chose to buy land outside town and build his own unique house, instead of competing with the Ardmore millionaires. Our house was truly one of a kind, not as expensive as the millionaires' swanky digs but ahead of them in many other ways. My father wasn't rich, but he more than made up for it in talent and ingenuity, a trait that runs in our family. (Cough, cough.)

We drove over every few weeks to see the house as it was a-building, practically by Bill's labors alone, assisted by his wonderful foreman, Lee. (Many's the time I heard Bill say, "Lee is the best Negra man I've ever met.") Walking over the floors of the house with more and more framework up was exciting. I didn't want to move away from my friends in Durant, but I was bursting with pride at what Bill was creating—a large, modern house unlike anything in Ardmore. Two stories, flat-roofed, with a door opening out onto the lower roof and a ladder (which we weren't supposed to climb, but did) to the top roof. There was an intercom system, a stairway with vertical silver poles instead of a regular banister, a secret panel in the fireplace where he kept a special bottle of booze. The second floor was one large rumpus room with a real soda fountain, big round mirrors on the ceiling, and a tiled floor designed like a shuffleboard. Later, he bought a used jukebox—a real one that played 78 records. *Wow*, huh?

It took until June of 1948 to get four rooms more or less finished and insulated: Bill and Mother's bedroom, the kitchen, the breakfast nook, and one bathroom. Melinda and I slept in the breakfast nook, barely big enough to hold a double bed. By fall, Bill had finished our bedroom and the hallway. He built in all the beds, with headboards balanced to swing forward so private things could be stored behind

*Sketch made of me in Greenwich Village,
1949. I didn't like it then. Love it now.*

them. Over the years, he was always adding new rooms, changing the interior, building, building, building. We ended up with four bathrooms. Mother's had an artfully designed mosaic floor, which Bill hand-laid himself. All this while building dozens of houses and public buildings in town.

Our house was situated "thirteen telephone poles past the standpipe north of town," as I used to instruct my high school dates, on a five-acre meadowland that my dad worked on incessantly, planting trees and flowers and raising large vegetable gardens of organic, composted, gorgeous produce. I spent my high school years exploring the wide meadow and the woods beyond, finding fossils and bleached-white tortoise shells, looking at the sky, gazing always northeast, dreaming of going to New York to make it big in show business.

The summer of 1949, Bill had driven us all to New York City for a week's vacation. On the way, we stopped at Four Corners, Illinois, to drop Grandmother Fannie at Wenonah and Earl's house, pulling in around eleven that night. The strangest feeling came over me as I got out of the car. I felt encased in an impenetrable glass cylinder. My cousin Sue and her friend were talking a blue streak, but I felt removed, isolated. It lasted until I went to sleep and was very scary. A most alarming state to be in. When we arrived in New York, however, we left our car in New Jersey and took a subway to Manhattan, and as I emerged from underground onto Forty-second Street, I felt with enormous joy and clarity: *This is home!*

We saw Joe DiMaggio hit a homer in a doubleheader at Yankee Stadium, climbed the Statue of Liberty, looked down from the top of the Empire State Building, ate at the Automat, walked through Greenwich Village (I still have the sketch of me made by a sidewalk artist). And then—oh, the *pièce de résistance*—we went to see Ray Bolger in a matinee of *Where's Charley?* on Broadway! I'd grown up loving the movies, knowing since sixth grade that performing was in my blood, but there in that balcony on Broadway, soaking up every second, I knew, "I have to do *this*. And I have to do it *here*—in New York." In Four Corners, I'd been shut off from the outside world. In Manhattan, I was part of it. This was my world, no bout a-doubt it!

I've felt that way about New York ever since.

CHAPTER TWO

⌒

"It's a shame that youth is wasted on the young."
—George Bernard Shaw

I sang second soprano in the chorus at Ardmore High, led by Mr. Elmo Pankratz, who told us that when he had knee surgery he brought home a bone fragment with some meat on it, which he fried up and ate. Said it tasted like chicken. Eccentrics are a rich natural resource below the Mason-Dixon line. Colorful idioms grow like kudzu. If you're not tighter than Dick's hatband, you're poor as Job's turkey. If you're not traipsing through town like Cox's army, you're awkward as a pig on ice, or so bucktoothed, you could eat corn through a picket fence. According to conventional Southern wisdom, a cow can be led up stairs but not down, and if you make your bed, you "lay" in it. Growing up with the eccentricities of Southerners prepared me for the eccentricities of theatre folk. The word "culture" means something very different down Oklahoma way.

God love my mother! She went out of her way to keep her country chicks informed in the arts. She joined a series presenting musical artists three times a winter (whee!) in Denton, Texas, and drove me sixty miles to Durant every Saturday morning to continue my ballet lessons. All through high school, I consumed dance magazines and biographies of Pavlova and Nijinsky, and my copy of *The Marx Brothers* was fingered to shreds.

Ardmore was very different from Durant. Uppity, cliquish. I was scared to death of those highfalutin kids, suffering the pangs of hell being outside the popular crowd. After six months, when my fifteenth birthday rolled around at the end of February, I summoned all my courage and told Mother, "I want to invite *everyone* to a picnic at Devil's Den."

I delivered handwritten invitations, and, to my astonishment, everyone accepted! Devil's Den is a great geological upheaval thirty miles east of Ardmore near Tishomingo. We piled into parents' cars and jammed into the back of Bill's pickup under a tarp, and the drizzly February day was a roaring success. I was accepted, one of the gang. They still thought I was a little offbeat, a bit of an outsider; I was the only ballet dancer for miles, and since our house was two miles north of town, I couldn't go for ice cream after school or drop in to kids' houses. Living in the country had its advantages, however. My classmates loved coming out to parties, especially slumber parties when we girls slept on the roof under the dazzling Oklahoma night skies. A friend gave me an astronomy book, and I learned to identify many constellations. I still have it, but the night sky over Manhattan does not easily reveal Orion and the Big Dipper.

Most of the gang were A students, ambitious and competitive. Some were funny. Several were kids of local millionaires. Ardmore's exclusive section was rampant with ranchers, oil moguls, old money. But most of the kids were from working middle-class families like mine. Carol Ann Bristow was pretty, petite, peppy, and made her own clothes. Gwynne Hann was beautiful, brainy, and a talented artist. Kenna Hudson's father was seriously insane, and Kenna was a bit odd herself, but in an endearing way, one of the few kids besides me who didn't cheat on tests in algebra II. Hilarious Lynn Pebbles kept us in stitches. I had a crush on basketball stars Al Ringer and Johnny Brooks, but neither gave me the time of day, so I was part of a terrific bunch but didn't get asked out by anyone interesting.

Then one day before class, our teacher said, "Give us a song, Sheridan."

Reluctantly, Sheridan Kinkade got to his feet and self-consciously started to sing.

"Oh, Danny Boy, the pipes the pipes are calling . . ."

Sheridan was a gorgeous thing with curly brown hair, a Botticelli angel face, and a lovely tenor voice, but he was terribly awkward socially. His father had been killed, leaving his mom and a gaggle of little ones in poverty. By the end of the haunting Irish melody, I was titillated by this strange creature. I let him take me to a Sea Scout cookout, at which he whipped up a pot of mulligan stew. Standing on my front stoop later, he offered a perfunctory goodnight, but I decided, "It's about time this guy started kissing." So I stepped up and kissed him, and he fled to his car.

Tom Keel, on the other hand, blew into the tenth grade at Ardmore High and was "in" right away, easy as pie. Keel rode a motorbike, wore a brown leather bomber jacket, smoked cigarettes—oh, I mean to tell you. A spunky stack of muscular libido; outgoing, handsome—*yummy*! But I was far too bashful to let on. Until one fateful night in October. At a home football game. Oh, autumn in Oklahoma! Small Southern towns are all about football. The crowds in the stands, the glare of the lights, the night air so fresh, so alive with promise! Well, by halftime no promises had come true, so I was headed home. As I left, Keel sauntered by.

"Hi!" Huge grin, pretty brown hair, laughing eyes. He radiated energy. "Leaving early?"

"Yep, that I am," I said, strolling backward, looking at him.

"Why don't you stay?"

"Aw, no, I better go. It's dangerous around here. You're too cute!" I laughed and walked away. That statement had taken all my courage.

I'd gone about eight steps when I heard, "Hey, Eddi-Rue!" I turned to see Keel standing in the middle of the dirt walk.

"What you said before," he asked, "did you *mean* that?"

I took a breath and with a big smile said, "Every word." Then I turned and walked away.

⸺

"I just want you to know one thing, Eddi-Rue, I'm not a sex fiend."

"A sex fiend?"

Our first date. On our way to a neighboring town for a football game. The bus was dark.

"You don't have to worry," Keel told me. "I won't take advantage of you."

I smiled to myself in the dark bus. Although I was only fifteen, I thought he was quaint. At the same time, I liked him for being quaint. And at the *same* time, I was pretty quaint myself, because I totally believed him, totally trusted him, and I guess the times must have been pretty quaint, because it turned out he totally meant it. We had a beautiful, sensual, off-and-on relationship for three years; he taught me a lot about the male sex, and I was still a virgin for years to come.

Newcomb Rice was now teaching in Ardmore twice a week, with me as class demonstrator. During my junior year, he moved to *Borger*, for God's sake, so I taught all the Ardmore classes and got half the profits. The previous summer, I had attended a seminar for dance teachers in Dallas led by Adolph Bolm, one of the elderly stars of the Ballet Russe, whom I'd read about in Vaslav Nijinsky's biography. Diaghilev, impresario of the Ballet Russe and Nijinsky's lover, made Nijinsky the most famous dancer of the 1920s, eclipsing Mr. Bolm's career. I was thrilled to meet and study with Bolm—second only to Nijinsky! Well-built, leathery-faced Mr. Bolm taught in casual clothes and sneakers, showing his superior technique, his beautiful movement. And he was God only knows how old. *Ancient*, I thought. He was probably pushing sixty.

My beloved car, Dynamite.

"What was it like to dance with Nijinsky?" I asked him, to which he shrugged and huffed, "Oh, Nijinsky—*puh!*"

The next summer, Maria Tallchief was our teacher. In her prime, this prima ballerina had formed what would become the New York City Ballet with her husband, George Balanchine. She was half Osage, half Scottish, honored with the title Wa-Xthe-Thomba, meaning "Woman of Two Worlds." (I know how that feels.)

During my senior year, I became the proud owner of the Oklahoma Dancing Academy at Ardmore, teaching kids from age three to eighteen. That year, I choreographed an ambitious recital piece, set to Gershwin's *An American in Paris.* Melinda danced the principal role: a country girl who comes to the fair, falls in love, has her heart broken by some glamour pusses, and does one hell of a lot of dancing. That same year, Gwynne Hann and I codirected *The Red Feather Frontier Frolics,* an evening of comedy, song, and dance, featuring our talented classmates. I was constantly on the go, tooling around in "Dynamite," my black 1930 Chevy, painted with the kids' names and quotes like "Twenty-three Skidoo!" and other scintillating witticisms. My grades were down from straight As, but I really didn't care anymore. I was doing what I loved, about to graduate and get the hell out of Ardmore. I began plotting my course and decided to major in drama at the University of Tulsa.

At the end of my senior year, I was voted "Most Likely to Succeed."

⌁

Jacob's Pillow was a prestigious summer dance camp outside Lee, Massachusetts. After graduation, Mother—God love her!—sent me there for six glorious weeks. It was quite primitive, bunking five or six girls in each unheated cabin. I told my cabin mates I was sixteen, not eighteen, figuring they'd undoubtedly be ahead of me in technique. They enthralled me with their accents from Europe and New York, pushy and brash. We had group showers in cold water, and a mess hall where I tasted (and hated) mutton stew for the first time. I trained and trained for six weeks in the woods, learning castanets and Spanish heel work and basic Indian dance with its side-to-side neck movement, rib undulations, and sixteen positions of the eye. Myra Craske, ballet mistress of the Metropolitan School of Ballet in Manhattan, taught ballet. After the first day of lessons, I could barely hobble but reported for ballet barre the next morning.

The guru of Jacob's Pillow, Ted Shawn of the famed Denishawn dance team, appeared to be in his sixties but was still performing his famous "Whirling Dervish" presentation. Mr. Shawn liked me. Coming from the wilds of Oklahoma, I was different, a little blond anomaly. Each week, we saw famous dancers who no longer appeared professionally. Mia Slavenska, who could hold an on-point arabesque for impossible eons. Breathtaking Marina Svetlova, Antony Tudor, Danilova—still on point at sixty! I was lucky to experience the early years of Jacob's Pillow, the declining years of Ted Shawn, and I'm proud to be an alumna of that remarkable place.

Every life includes a cast of thousands. Some are principal players, others have walk-on roles, and extras are always coming and going in the background. Theatre may seem strange to those who've never been backstage. For one thing, theatre people know that "theatre" is the art of actors on stage, and "theater" is the place where you go to see a movie and hopefully get kissed between previews. As in real life, you get hams and clowns, comedy and tragedy, seasonal relationships that end all too soon but are no less sweet to remember. In theatre, we work in an intense group dynamic for the run of the show, then say "Ta-ta!" Do we weep at the parting? I certainly do! But we add some people to our permanent repertory company. In my case, the journey is of paramount importance, a powerful, unbreakable trip, a golden lifeline, if I may wax melodramatic. And I don't allow the truly important people to get away. Friends are crucially important to me in theatre and in life.

Every year, summer stock theatre companies spring up in small town and country settings, rehearsing and performing shows that run in tight rotation from June through August. Thousands of young actors apply, and the summer after my sophomore year in college, I landed my first summer stock job with the Jatoma Players, a little company in Alpena, Michigan. There I met dear, fascinating Norman Hartweg, who became a major player in my life. Norman had a whale of a crush on fifteen-year-old Melinda, who came with Mother on vacation and effortlessly threw all the boys into a dither. Unlike me, Melinda did go through a rebellious stage, sneaking out and doing all manner of things I never would have dared. Gorgeous, self-assured, and sex on wheels, she proceeded to break Norm's heart. I nursed him through his misery, doing eight plays in nine weeks, including two with dancing, which I choreographed and taught to the cast, all for the magnificent sum of $50 a week.

All summer long, I exchanged frequent letters with my college sweetheart, Bill Bennett, a tall, good-looking engineering major who was both brainy and musically inclined, with big brown eyes and a wonderfully quirky sense of humor. I was overboard about him and foaming at the mouth to see him my first night back at school. He pulled up in front of my rooming house, and I flew out to jump into his car.

"Eddi-Rue," he said, "my mother says I shouldn't see you anymore. You want to be an actress. She says you're a dreamer. So I'm afraid this is it. I'm sorry."

Heartbroken, I stepped out of his car into a deep, dark hole. That old childhood panic gripped me for weeks, subsiding only during play rehearsals. I threw myself into classes and theatre activities, but I eventually came down with bronchial pneumonia and became so ill my landlady called Mother, who came the next morning. I confided in her for the first time about the panic that had plagued me since I was eight. She took me to an M.D., who did nothing, but then she took me to a pet shop and bought me a parakeet. Caring for that little budgie and having another living creature with me in the dark brought me enormous comfort, and in a few weeks I was well again.

As an amusing footnote to Bill Bennett's truncated role in my passion play: Years later, his younger sister went off to New York to become an actress. Mrs. B must have shit a brick.

Meanwhile, Norman and I wrote voluminous, witty (we thought) letters back and forth over the next year. He was the smartest person I'd ever met, and a wonderful writer. Mother, Melinda, and I went to the Jatoma Players reunion in Ann Arbor in February of 1955 and stayed with the Hartweg family at their comfortable, welcoming home. I adored the intelligent, affectionate Hartwegs and instantly wanted to be one of them. We saw everyone from the Jatoma Players and filmed much of our visit with Mother's Super 8 camera.

One night, after everyone had gone to bed, I found Norm standing in the corner of the dark living room, the glow of his cigarette marking his presence, obviously creating a dramatic moment right out of a 1940s movie. Playing my assigned role, Lana Turner or perhaps Ingrid Bergman, I walked over to him, and he, in the role of Stewart Granger or perhaps Humphrey Bogart, took me in his arms and kissed me. Then we said goodnight and went to our separate bedrooms. This was our first awkward attempt to move our friendship into the romantic arena.

I spent the following summer at the Perry-Mansfield Dance-Drama Camp in Steamboat Springs, Colorado, with Mother, Melinda, and good ol' Skipper Edelen, along for the ride, and late in the season, Norman showed up to round out the motley crew. Skipper got a job washing dishes in a restaurant, but after a few days of dirty plates, he announced, "I can't deal with vulgar tradesmen." He got a far more prestigious job delivering clothes hangers for a cleaner's. Norm just hung out. Melinda, her hair bleached platinum blond, kept herself busy vamping a troupe of love-blinded swains.

The Colorado camp's *marvelous* modern dance teacher, Harriet Ann Gray from Hunter College in New York, offered me a full dance scholarship with an offer to join her professional dance troupe after graduation. I had also been offered a full scholarship in the German Department at TU. If I took the latter, I'd get to play all the leads in the plays, since I'd be a senior. But if I took the dance scholarship, I'd become a professional modern dancer. I agonized over the decision for days. Am I a dancer who can act or an actress who can dance? I wanted to express myself with my voice as well as my body, so I decided to return to TU and head toward a theatrical career.

My freshman year at TU, I entered Varsity Nite with five fellow Kappa Alpha Theta apprentices in a little dance. Ordinary stuff. My sophomore year, I codirected the entire program. My junior year, I conceived a modern dance piece I intended to call "Three Embryos in Search of a Womb," but Mother wouldn't hear of it, so the piece became "Three Eggs in Search of a Beater," danced and sung by a funny character actress named Mary Ann Cooper, a big, dreamy blonde, Carol Carter, and me—three barefooted nymphs in pink, yellow, and lavender leotards with white tulle streamers. My senior year, I entered "Revelations of the Female Subconscious," a musical examination of five different types of female, and what they do to get a man, for which I wrote the words and music, accompanied by my dear friend J. Martene Pettypool. Carol, Mary Ann, and I also did "Sur la Plage," a number from the Broadway hit *The Boy Friend*. We won lovely gold cups for Best Individual and Best Sorority, and if I'd had one more year to enter, we could have retired the cups.

In the fall, Norman transferred to TU for our senior year, rooming with Skipper until Skipper's fastidiousness and Norm's sloppiness drove them both crazy. The Odd Couple, 1955. Norman and I played the leads in most of the plays, including Macbeth and Lady Macbeth. We spent a lot of time together and were terribly fond of each other, but we made no more attempts to ignite a fire that just didn't seem to have the proper matches. Something essential was missing.

"I'm just not in love with Norman. There's no sexual thing there," I told a girlfriend. "Maybe when I'm forty, and that sex stuff is all behind me, maybe then I can marry him." And hey, folks, I truly believed that! Forty seemed *exceedingly* old and awfully far away.

Meanwhile, Marino Grimaldi, a handsome, intelligent grad student from Massachusetts, transferred to our theatre department and instantly took a shine to me. He played piano, sang, cooked, and was unfailingly cheerful. We cut up and wrassled like two kids. I hadn't dated anyone since Bill Bennett took a powder, but Marino was so jolly and uncomplicated. And so *persistent*. He took me dancing and camping, and I took him to visit Ardmore, where everyone loved him. One night, he drove me out to Swan Lake in Tulsa. The moon was out. There was a balmy spring breeze. Marino, looking utterly heartstruck, reached in his pocket and drew out . . . oh, no.

"It's an engagement ring," he said. "I love you, Eddi-Rue."

"Oh . . . well . . . my goodness, Marino. I, um . . . what a surprise."

He was a swell guy, but I wasn't in love with him. And he was Catholic, which meant (Mother of God!) I would have to become Catholic, too.

"Please, wear it, Eddi-Rue. I'd be honored."

"Marino . . . I don't know," I said.

"Please," he said, his soulful eyes full of emotion. "Wear it for me."

Promise me that if you take one thing away from this little journey of mine, it will be to henceforth and forevermore always summon the wit to say, "Let me think it over." Repeat after me: *Let me think it over.* If only those words had come out of my mouth! But I couldn't bring myself to break Marino's heart. He tenderly slipped the ring on my finger, and like a fool—for the first time, but unfortunately not the last—I allowed myself to be stampeded into an ill-fated engagement.

I began Catholic instructions under Monsignor McGuldrich, and *oooh, my Gawd,* those four months of instructions were painful. I tried to be a good little convert, but I could have more easily turned myself into a duck-billed platypus. I didn't believe a word of it. It struck me as a way to keep people in awe and keep the church all-powerful. I was confirmed the day before graduation from college and tried to be a good Catholic, attending mass every Sunday, but I never did learn to quack. The dogma, incense, confessions—it all made me sick as a dog. Physically sick at my stomach.

∽

The summer of 1956, Marino and I were accepted as summer apprentices at the Fitchburg Playhouse in Fitchburg, Massachusetts, and encountered big-time showbiz personalities for the first time. I roomed with a nice Irish Catholic girl from New York, Eileen Brennan. I arrived a day ahead of her and the third female apprentice, and a young male apprentice showed me to our cabin, warning, "The pipe under the sink is sawed off, so the water empties into this bucket." I unpacked, washed my hands in the sink, then emptied the bucket—into the sink. As water gushed through onto the floor, I fell back onto the bed laughing. What a ninny!

That summer, I was in three of the plays, all negligible roles, but it was a bang-up introduction to New York theatre. Eight different stars passed through on one-week stock tours. The first week, Henry Morgan, a famous New York personality, played a fellow who daydreamed of beautiful young women, we apprentices being the delicious apparitions he conjured up. At the start of each performance, I crouched out of sight behind the sofa, waiting onstage with Mr. Morgan for the curtain to rise.

"So, Mr. Morgan," I said one night, "you must find Fitchburg pretty boring. What do you do all day?"

"Masturbate," he replied, and up went the curtain!

Guy Palmerton, the owner of the playhouse, was under a lot of stress or going through menopause or something that summer. He bashed his fist through a window in his house and came to the theatre roaring drunk on opening nights, reeling down the aisle, shouting that the play stunk, the star stunk, the playhouse stunk, and show business stunk, until the strong, young male apprentices forcibly extricated him. He had all the female stars in tears. Four male apprentices left right away, two more a week later. Marino stayed, and Guy liked him, though he hated almost everyone else. He also liked Eileen, who went out drinking with him nearly every night. She didn't go regularly to mass or confession. I figured lifelong Irish Catholics must be more lax about the rules and regulations.

"You'll be a superb actress when you get over that Camille fixation," Palmerton said to me one day. I guess he thought I should have Eileen Brennan's spunk. Maybe I should've gone out drinking with him. Then I, too, could have slept through the morning yard work instead of whitewashing the rocks that lined the driveway.

Gypsy Rose Lee came through and was a darling. She spent mornings in our cabin, hair in curlers, chatting over coffee, advising us on the care and tending of the mama cat and kittens we'd acquired. Of course, Guy had her in tears. More male apprentices left. Spirits were low. Then along came Tallulah Bankhead, playing Peter Pan in stilettos and tights with James Kirkwood as her Captain Hook. From the wings, I shot about fifteen seconds of her opening number on Mother's 8mm camera and later had it transferred to video so I'd always have it. This giant personality impressed me with her every move. Ain't nobody gonna reduce *that* lady to tears! Hearing her tell off Guy Palmerton was music to our ears. She had *him* in hysterics. Coulda floored him with one rabbit punch.

Over the summer, it became increasingly clear that I simply couldn't marry Marino, and in September I returned his ring. It hurt him and I felt terrible, but we remained friends, and I was relieved to give up the whole Catholic charade for good. With a degree in theatre and three summers of stock to my credit, I was chomping at the bit to attack the Real World of Professional Theatre in New York, and I persuaded my high school pal, Lynn Pebbles, who wanted to be a journalist, that she should head north, too. Everyone at home was aghast. Leave Ardmore? It made no sense—not common, not book, not horse! Damn foolishness! When I left, Lynn still seemed a little stunned herself.

I arrived in New York in January of 1957 with one suitcase and enough money to see me through two frugal weeks. I checked into the YWCA on Eighth Avenue for a week, then found a large one-room studio in a brownstone at 27 West Seventy-fourth Street. The rent was $97 a month. Lynn and I could swing it. The strange room had once been the dining room at the end of the dark hall on the ground floor of a Victorian mansion, all polished mahogany, with winged wooden cherubs peering down from all four corners of the high ceiling. (Oh! The things those cherubs saw! No wonder there was a slight blush on those chubby cheeks!) In a small alcove was a high double bed. Two tall chifforobe closets flanked the overstuffed chairs and sofa. Heavy drapes shrouded the windows. I'd never seen such a place in Okla-homa—so dramatic and thrilling! I moved in and wrote Lynn that she should come at once.

I didn't know a soul in the city except a few fellow would-be actors from college and summer stock, including Norman, Marino, and Jim Broadhurst, who'd had a crush on me when we were in the Jatoma Players. These three aspiring actors, all of whom had some sort of romantic history with me, had found quarters together in Murray Hill with a fellow who took in roommates. The original guy slept in the bedroom, and my three friends rotated between a sofa, a thin mattress on the floor, and only a quilt for the unlucky third guy. I spent the night there twice, sleeping on the floor on another quilt. I wasn't about to commandeer the sofa or the pallet. It was all good fun. Eating beans, sleeping on the floor.

Lynn arrived and, walking from the bus station, had a harrowing experience that almost convinced her to run right back to Oklahoma. She was distraught: She'd seen a couple walking down the street hold-ing hands, one white person and one black.

"Don't make up your mind yet. I have a welcoming party all set up for you. Try it a few days," I begged her, and she reluctantly agreed.

I had invited Norman, Marino, Jim, and some people I'd met in acting class, including a delightful guy I'd met at Perry-Mansfield. Bill Smith, an exuberant dancer from New York, was not only gay but black, and astonishingly, my mother had gotten a huge kick out of him that summer we were all in Colorado. I had seen a lovely new side of my southern Oklahoma mama. The party was bouncing along nicely when the doorbell rang just as I was getting more hors d'oeuvres. Lynn opened the door to find Bill and a friend—a tall, handsome black actor who was beginning to make a name for himself—and she turned away, ashen and shocked.

"Oh, Bill!" I called. "Get in here, you little skink, and meet my friend, Lynn."

Mr. Personality bubbled in. "Hey, Eddi-Rue! This is my friend, Jacques."

"Lynn, this is the dancer who became such good friends with my mother," I told her. "What would you guys like to drink? Lynn, would you find a vase for these flowers?"

We played show tunes on the turntable, everyone jabbering away, eating, drinking. About an hour later, I looked over and saw Lynn on the lap of the handsome black actor, chatting away, happy as a clam. After that, she took to New York rather quickly and never mentioned leaving. In fact, Miss Pebbles had herself a high-heeled time.

Norm, Marino, and I auditioned for the renowned acting coach Uta Hagen at the Berghof Studio and were accepted as first-level students in her eight-week course. Her classes were notoriously difficult to get into, so I was ecstatic. I enrolled in dance classes with the phenomenal modern jazz teacher Matt Mattox, Hanya Holm for classical modern, *and* at the Metropolitan School of Ballet with Myra Craske, the ballet mistress from Jacob's Pillow. I also worked for Brown's Steno Service as a part-time file clerk, which paid just enough (with a twenty from Mother now and then) for living expenses, classes, and even an occasional beer.

I felt particularly close to Norman. We'd meet near my apartment on West Seventy-fourth and spend hours in a nearby bar, talking philosophy and theatre and God knows what over beers into the wee hours. Once we talked all night, and then I got dressed in my conservative suit and went, bleary-eyed, to do the loathsome filing for eight hours. Norman walked me to work, all the way from West Seventy-fourth to the forties, as the pinkish dawn broke over mid-Manhattan.

What the heck, I thought, *I'm in New York and this is Show Business!*

CHAPTER THREE

～

"I only like two kinds of men—foreign and domestic."

—MAE WEST

*U*ta Hagen was a force to be reckoned with. The exercises in her first course were primarily sense memories: carry an imaginary cup of hot coffee across a room without spilling it, rush to do something important with a broken arm, eat a formal dinner with a badly dripping nose. Then we began working on partner scenes from well-known plays. Meticulous and somewhat abrasive, Hagen did not suffer sloppy work gladly and was as tough as her reputation. After eight weeks, Norman and Marino had had enough and opted not to reenroll, but I thrived on that demanding regimen. Cast as Gwendolyn in *The Importance of Being Earnest*—the scene in which Gwendolyn comes to tea in Cecily Cardew's garden—I finished what I thought was a damned good presentation, then got a critique from Uta that let me know I didn't know squat about professional acting. Four years of college acting hadn't given me an inkling.

"Tell me, Eddi-Rue," she began, "what kind of ground were you walking on? Grass? Cobblestones? Where was the sun? In your eyes? You had a parasol. Why didn't you use it? Was there a breeze? Where had you just come from? Did you have a toothache? A headache?

What, in other words, was really going on? You must enter a scene with total preparation and react moment to moment!" A brilliant revelation! She pulled the veil from my eyes.

⌐

Lynn had taken to staying at a friend's apartment overnight from time to time, and on one of those nights when I had the apartment to myself, Norman spent the night with me. It was my first sexual . . . I mean, I lost my . . . how best to say this?

We had sex.

I was still a Goody Two-Shoes, but I was interested in growing up, and Norman was a trusted friend, so we plunged in. Okay, maybe "plunged" is not the right word. It wasn't exciting or amazing or anything else I'd heard. Where was the blood? The big virgin experience? Had dance training broken my hymen without my ever knowing it? The fact is, I loved him like crazy from the neck up, but we simply didn't fit each other down below. Damned unfortunate engineering. Norman, however, seemed pretty excited by me.

"I'll never get married, Eddi-Rue," he told me, "unless I marry you."

Newcomb Rice had founded a summer arts camp near Terrero, New Mexico, in the Sangre de Christos mountains and offered me a job teaching modern dance the summer of 1957. I suggested Norman as drama teacher, J. Martene Pettypool as accompanist, and an art major friend to teach pottery. That glorious month in the mountains was a creative joyride with my friends. Norman composed irresistibly witty piano music for Rudyard Kipling's "The Sing-Song of Old Man Kangaroo," and I created whimsical choreography to fit it. We were decades ahead of *Cats*! I waded chest-deep in the ice-cold Pecos River, sometimes sharing the river with water snakes. We drove to Santa Fe and saw an excellent *Così fan tutte* that actually made me like opera for the first time. J. Martene Pettypool got monumentally drunk and lost a shoe as we carried him to the car, and we got back to camp very tired and very happy.

While I was out west, a college friend, Mac Forrester, who was teaching English to challenged third-grade boys in Denver, invited me to spend a few weeks with him in Estes Park, Colorado, square-dancing, mountain-climbing, and getting better acquainted. Bill Bennett and I had double-dated with Mac and his girl a few times at Spring Creek, floating on inner tubes, sleeping in sleeping bags, roasting wieners and marshmallows, singing songs, and playing Lummi Sticks, an old Indian game. (Back then, the phrase "gone wild" still meant nature!) He was vivacious and hilarious, with a big grin and an easy laugh. The night I arrived, he parked outside his friend's house and, before I knew it, we were doing things I hadn't thought possible in such a small car. Right there at the curb, streetlights on, people likely to pass by any minute! The most daring thing I'd ever done. We spent a night on a steep mountainside in the Rockies. Who felt any rocks? Not me. So *this* was what the fuss was all about! Fun Quotient? A big ol' A!

I'd gotten a job as a chambermaid—three jobs, actually, in three motels—making beds and running vacuum sweepers. My eyes and nose ran like faucets. Dust aggravated the gargantuan hay fever I'd developed in that clean-air capital of the USA. But I was a top-notch chambermaid. One day, as I folded the bedsheet corners in an expert Army-grade crease, my supervisor observed, "My, my, you are going to make some man a wonderful wife!" And I thought, *Is that what you think it takes? Guess again, sister.* But in his practical way, Mac also saw me as a fitting life companion. I could square-dance and hike. I was a willing, if untalented, cook. We were terrific in bed. I even wrote and illustrated a book for his students, *A Pig in a Pit.* The fact is, we *were* excellently suited, but when he asked me to marry him, he said, "Eddi-Rue, I told my girlfriend I was going to ask you first, and if you turned me down, I'd marry her, and she said okay."

Excuse me? Girlfriend? *Okay?* That is one understanding girl!

But I didn't want to be a mountain-climbing schoolteacher's wife. I *had to be* an actress. I had to get back to New York! So I sent Mac back to that astonishingly patient girl, and I've been told they did get married. He was a marvelous guy, well worth waiting for. We all did the right thing.

Some decisions actors have to make along the way are gut-wrenching. The only thing that makes them possible is when the compulsion to become an actor is unshakable. Like an edict from God. I don't understand it, myself, but I experience it every time I walk out onto a bare stage in a dark, empty theatre. It's a religious experience for me. I stand on that stage and I feel complete, blessed, at home, where I belong.

Melinda was only seventeen, but she was madly in love with none other than that strange, angel-faced tenor Sheridan Kinkade, and they got married late that summer. I was maid of honor, resplendent in a gathered chiffon frock that made me look like an exploded peach. I remember sobbing to Norman, "Oh, they're going to have such beautiful children!" And they did. Four of them. My beloved nieces and nephews, Marcia, Brendan, Sean, and Amelia.

A few weeks later, I boarded a train for Pennsylvania. The Erie Playhouse had offered me a job, beginning in September: a full season as the ingénue/leading lady. Not exactly New York, but I'd be acting my trim little ass off for a steady paycheck, putting into practice everything I'd learned from Uta Hagen and hopefully making some good East Coast theatre connections.

Back in Estes Park, Mac had told me, "Eddi-Rue, if you're going to be an actress, you have to do something about that name of yours."

"I know!" I said. "But I can't find a last name to go with Eddi-Rue!"

"Your last name isn't the problem," he said. "It's the Eddi. Drop it. Become Rue."

"Rue?" I said. "Just . . . *Rue?*"

What a revelation! Well, well, just Rue. I liked it! So as Rue McClanahan, I arrived in Erie, Pennsylvania, on September 14, 1957, to begin a brand-new adventure at the Erie Playhouse.

And, as fate would have it, to meet . . . take a big breath . . . Husband #1.

CHAPTER FOUR

"Good manners make any man a pleasure to be with."
—British author Peter Mayle

"Dreary Erie, the Mistake on the Lake."
This unfortunate appellation was due to the weather in Erie from September to April: rain, sleet, snow, or ice. Or heavy overcast *threatening* rain, sleet, snow, or ice. The sun took a bow at the autumn solstice and made his next appearance around the Ides of April. This didn't bother me a bit. I was happy to be in a winter stock company, performing six nights a week, rehearsing six days a week, and enjoying a steady paycheck of $55 a week—$42 after deductions. *Cha-ching!* I even put $20 a week in savings. I ended up sharing a one-room apartment with a pull-out sofa with another actress. One of many one-room apartments, at least three of which had pull-out sofas, that I shared with roommates over the next seven years.

Don't put your daughter on the stage, Mrs. Worthington.

The company consisted of a core of three women and six men, with other actors coming in occasionally for a role or two. Jean Tarrant, the temperamental but talented wife of Newell Tarrant, the managing director, was on hand to play leads and character roles. I was a little scared of her. A tall, taciturn character actress named Nora handled supporting roles, and here came Rue McClanahan for the ingénues and younger leads. The adolescent roles were played by Robin, a talented little bundle of energy with an irrepressible personality and colorful expressions like "Oh, for crying out tears!" She always made me laugh.

Years later, Robin came to see me at a theatre in New Jersey. In her midtwenties now, all married and settled down, she was still adorable.

"You got me through some pretty rough patches there in the Erie dressing room," I told her. "I don't know what I would've done without you."

And she said, "Oh, Rue . . . for crying out tears!"

In October, a beautiful, voluptuous blonde came in from New York to play the role that made Jayne Mansfield in *Will Success Spoil Rock Hunter?* Since her name eludes me, I'll call her Va-voom. She was jaded, well acquainted with the hard facts of life, but Va-voom loved to tell ghost stories in the dressing room, and curiously, they always made her cry. Looking like a *Playboy* centerfold, she'd relate some spooky tale, tears running down her cheeks, always apologizing, "I'm sorry, I'm sorry. I can't help it." I found it unique. Endearing, if a bit odd.

Of the six male actors in the company, I immediately developed a crush on not one, but two—both out of the question. Jack Shapira, a fine actor from New York, was solid, loving, and good-tempered, but married, and I liked his wife fully as much as I liked him. Southerner Jason Crane was hilarious and talented, but seemed possibly gay. (In hindsight, it was only my Okie naiveté that allowed any "possibly" about it.) He'd been around the block. There was a mean streak in his humor, but oh, my, he could make me laugh. A very good actor named Bob took on the "older" parts (as in *over thirty*). Joey Phelps, from Montreal, was very blond and very gay. (No doubt even in this little Oklahoman's head.) He was the first Canadian I'd ever known, so I found him terribly exotic. Tall, dark, and handsome Corbin Willis built the sets and played bit parts, and a few years later, he and Jason Crane formed a business (and more) partnership, building sets in Hawaii. Who'da thunk? My naiveté always dismays me. Bea Arthur always thought I was faking, but I wasn't. I was sheltered as a child. What can I say? Maybe *duh*.

Rounding out our merry troupe was Thomas Lloyd Bish, a handsome musician who'd moved to Erie from Jamestown, New York, after being discharged from the Army. He was an apprentice, hired at half-salary because his experience was not in acting. He'd played trombone and sung in an army band and was charming enough, courteous, up to the task of his first small role. But he didn't grab my fancy. In *Will Success Spoil Rock Hunter?* however, he played a reporter coming to interview the blond bombshell, and every night he invented a new name to introduce himself. And every night he got funnier.

"Hello, I'm Ferd Raffleholder."

"Hello, I'm Jerkin M. Smurt."

I suspect he was doing it more for Va-voom than for me, but one night during the usual dressing room gossip, Va-voom said, "I don't like that Tom Bish."

"Why?" I asked, but she just smiled ruefully and shook her head.

It bothered me, because that sense of humor, that bit of improvisational derring-do had piqued my interest. Suddenly, I noticed the smoldering good looks and army-built body I'd somehow overlooked, and . . . hey, this guy was *yummy*.

I played Rachel in *Inherit the Wind,* the sweetheart of the schoolteacher on trial for teaching Darwin. There was a scene with a chimpanzee, who was kept in a cage in the prop basement. One day, I went to the basement to put some props in order and the male chimp started banging and rattling his cage, creating quite a ruckus. His screams got louder, more insistent, and I started to get nervous. I fled upstairs, and Newel assigned one of the men to put props in order until the chimp left. Apparently, male chimps get excited when a female human comes around them during her monthly period.

Terrific. The chimp was the first male to show any interest in me since I got there.

In November, I learned that a pain I'd been feeling at the base of my spine was from a pilo nidal cyst. *A pilo nidal who?* Apparently, soldiers get pilo nidal cysts from bouncing around on unpadded jeep seats. The doctor asked if I'd ever landed hard on my coccyx, and yes, in sixth grade, I'd come down the slide at recess, missed my footing, and landed with a wham on my—what do they call that? The sits bone? The sitz bone? Well, where you *sits*. So now—gloriosky—I had this pilo nidal cyst that required surgery. We had no understudies; during an earlier production, I'd played several nights with the flu, delivering comedy lines with a fever of 102, so dizzy I couldn't stand up straight. And now I had to have an operation. Well, *fudge*.

I told Newell Tarrant I'd need a week off, wrote to my parents, and on a cold, gray Sunday morning, packed to check into the hospital. I'd never been a patient in a hospital before and I was scared, but my new roommate, an actress who'd arrived from New York a few days before, sensed my terrified state and kicked into an extemporaneous comedy routine that had me howling. What a gift she was giving me! The gift of laughter.

"Okay, toots," she said after twenty minutes of clowning, "get over to the hospital."

I picked up my suitcase and set forth across town, feeling blessed. It would have been nice if someone had offered to take me, but it never occurred to me to ask. I'd never hired a cab in my life, or considered the possibility. I had driven myself since I was sixteen. Without a car, all I thought of was *walk*.

The operation was, shall we say, less than pleasant. A day or two later, I had my first visitor. There in the doorway stood Tom Bish with flowers, smiling sheepishly. I was astounded to see him. And touched. The Shapiras brought me the book *The Road to Miltown* by S. J. Perelman, and I still have it. It's moved with me across the country, put up in innumerable bookshelves, for almost fifty years. It's showing signs of wear. (Hell, so am I, but we're both still good to take to bed.)

Mother came to Erie to be with her recuperating daughter and meet everyone, and she said, "If you take up with any of these actors, I hope it's Tom Bish. He's the most courteous."

And he was. He opened doors for ladies and displayed a very well-brought-up demeanor. He had nice manners. But there was a hidden side—the side Va-voom had hinted at, a side I didn't meet until after we were married—a selfish, terrified little boy, rattling to get away from anything that confined him.

Not unlike that unruly chimp.

Tom and I started going together to the pub where all us actors convened after the shows to drink beer and watch TV—*The Treasure of the Sierra Madre* with Humphrey Bogart, *The African Queen* with Bogart and Katharine Hepburn—and then he'd walk me home. One night, as we stood on my door stoop, chatting, I remember thinking, *It's getting time for me to get married.* Melinda was married. And pregnant. Women my age were *supposed* to be married, weren't they? As a mature, sophisticated woman, shouldn't I have a life partner by now?

He kissed me goodnight and I went in. And pretty soon, Tom went in with me.

We made love, and it was a sweeter, deeper, more thoughtful experience than any I'd ever had. It touched a different place in me, and moved by the moment, I said, "So this is what it's like." I was aware he might think I was implying he was my first. He was, by the numbers, my third, but it was the first time *like that,* and I wasn't making a literal statement, I was just—oh, all right, I was fudging. What—you never did that? Not even *once?* Well, bully for you. It's very dumb. A Crime of Omission. And it can get you into mighty hot water.

One night shortly afterward, Tom was drunk and got ugly about it.

"Did you think you were fooling me? You liar!" he belittled and baited me. "Who was the first? How many have there been?"

"It doesn't make any difference in how I feel about you," I said, squirming with guilt, but he demanded I tell him, chapter and verse. "It's none of your business. Unless you want to tell me all about *your* sexual history!"

"I was thirteen the first time," he said grudgingly.

"*Thirteen?*" I was amazed. "With whom?"

"A red-haired movie star."

"Oh, my God, that's . . . that's absolutely *fabulous*."

Dying to hear the whole fascinating story, I begged for details. It was in Florida. That's all I got out of him, darn it. After that, every time I saw a 1940s movie star with flaming red locks, I wondered, *Was it her?* Of course, I have a prime suspect, and I wonder if I'll ever meet her—and if I'll be tipsy enough to ask her if she was in Florida in 1947.

This was the first—and least important—of the many things he never told me. As it turned out, Tom was a young man full of dark secrets.

During December, we dated, slept together a few more times, and even talked of getting married. We performed one play at night, rehearsed another during the day, did a kids' show on Saturdays, and toured high schools with *The Miser* two afternoons a week, carting sets from school to school, getting into costumes in empty classrooms, trying to interest teenagers in Molière. There was a good bit of horseplay from Tom and others onstage, which grated on my serious Uta Hagen nerves. Rehearsals are the time for joking around. I didn't (still don't!) find it funny when people fall out of character, giggling like—well, like those three silly little kittens.

Tom bought me something feminine and pretty for Christmas, and I bought him a pair of Levi's. All the boys in Oklahoma wore Levi's; I thought Tom would look sexy in them and hoped he'd think it funny to get them as a Christmas gift. He didn't. He was insulted, and he let me know it. That was my first Christmas away from my family.

Mother sent me a box full of white things—a fluffy white scarf, a white evening bag with rhinestones, white gloves, everything white. I thought that was awfully clever, and the tenderness of the gesture made me homesick. I still have the evening bag.

Erie was unrelentingly overcast and bitterly cold. But hey! I was a *working actress!*

Norman Hartweg came by Erie for New Year's Eve, opening night of *The Desk Set*. Afterward, there was pizza (actors are always fed pizza, because it's cheap) with champagne (also cheap) and music at the theatre. Actors were dancing in the aisles, and I was itching to tango. Norman didn't fancy himself a dancer, but Tom squired me up and down the aisles until just before midnight, when we all headed for a party at a patron's house. I was already woozy from champagne, but off we went. Tom and I wandered around but didn't see Norman. Later, we tumbled into someone's car. I vaguely recall climbing the stairs with Tom, my head reeling . . . and the next thing I knew, I woke up in my sofa bed with a sizable lump under the quilt next to me. I was in my slip. And I was sure I'd worn a dress to that party.

While I was making coffee, the lump woke up.

It was Norman.

The car he was in had ended up at someone else's party, and later he'd arrived at my apartment to find me passed out and Tom about to leave. Tom said I'd fainted as we entered the apartment, so he carried me to bed and undressed me down to my slip. I was intrigued.

Passed out? How Carole Lombard.

And a man undressed me? How Doris Day.

And I spent the night in bed with someone else? How *deliciously* theatrical!

There had been nothing sexual, so I wasn't feeling guilty. Just awfully Noël Coward. But when Norm went back to Michigan later that day, Tom started badgering me.

"Was he the first? *Confess!*" Tom demanded. "It was Norman, wasn't it? *Wasn't it?*"

He wouldn't let up. Frightened, I finally took a long breath and whispered, "Yes."

I hadn't been raised to deal with angry people, never even seen anyone in a rage like that. I was a naive small-town girl from a loving family. I was taught The Golden Rule. Be kind. Return goodness for goodness. Perhaps not the best preparation for professional theatre. Or for a frighteningly dysfunctional relationship. Up to then, Tom and I had laughed a lot, sharing our common interests and attitudes. He'd brought lunches from home that his sweet mother packed, and shared them with me. There had been many good times, and more would follow, but now an undercurrent of strain had been added to the mix.

In mid-January, I missed my period and knew at once I was pregnant.

I wasn't sure I wanted to marry Tom. Or that Tom wanted to marry me. Could I give up Norman forever? But I couldn't marry Norman . . . could I? Terrified and confused, I wrote a letter to Norman, but before I worked up the nerve to send it, I got one from him. Sitting at the counter in a diner, I opened it. He said he might have gotten a girl pregnant back in Ann Arbor. If she was, he was going to marry her. She would know in a few weeks. I sat frozen for a long moment, knowing my next move would have a profound effect on the lives of several people. I was deeply afraid of making a terrible mistake.

I slowly tore my letter to Norm in half, then quarters. My fate was sealed.

CHAPTER FIVE

~⟋

"Entrances are wide; exits are narrow."
—JEWISH PROVERB

*I*n the quaint 1940s, Saturday cinema matinees included short features starring such invincible heroes as Captain Midnight and Captain Marvel. In one Agent 99 cliffhanger, our hero was fighting the Black Widow, a buxom alien beauty determined to subjugate Earth at the behest of her nefarious father, king of a distant planet. Magically conjured from the bowels of a low-budget set, he appeared on a tinseled plywood throne flanked by diapered Nubian standard-bearers. Temporarily bested by Agent 99 in one deliciously cornball episode, the king narrows his eyes and solemnly declares, "This will set my plans for world domination back a week!"

I hate it when that happens.

~⟋

Tom and I were crossing a busy street in Erie when I told him, "I missed my period."

"A friend of mine got someone pregnant," he said. "And he left town."

"Oh . . ." I digested that chilling tidbit.

Was Tom the kind of guy who would skip out on me? How would I survive if he did? Now, I suppose some will throw the *Let me think it over!* thing back in my face, but folks, this was 1958. I was pregnant. There was nothing to think over. I needed this man to stand by me.

"I think we should get married next weekend," I said, and crossing that street, he agreed.

We made the mistake of telling Newell Tarrant, who told Ken, the publicity guy, who wanted a couple of weeks to set up newspaper coverage, a cute angle to promote the playhouse, and we foolishly agreed. The wedding date was set for Sunday, February 2. My grandmother Fanny's birthday. Groundhog's Day. A nice coincidence, I thought. A good omen.

Word to the wise: Never trust omens! Omens don't mean bloody squat.

I wrote to my parents and Norman to tell them I was marrying Tom. No details. Why not? Because, my dears, I was monumentally stupid. Why would I ask anyone for *advice*? That would have been as outrageous as calling a cab for a ride to the hospital. I picked out an affordable white eyelet wedding dress with all the fixings, including fake pearl earrings and white net gloves with the fingers cut out. I still have the dress, though it's beige now and would fit my foot. Tom and I shopped for wedding rings and settled on small gold bands with silver etchings. Things seemed to be working out. Tom was taking it all in stride and our sex life hadn't faltered. I wanted this man. I *needed* him. I loved him. He commented one night that he hated blondes, which hurt my feelings, but rather than say so, I dyed my hair dark red to please him and bought a slinky black nightgown to give me courage for the honeymoon.

My parents flew up to Erie with Melinda, now six months pregnant. I walked down the aisle with my father and stood before the minister with my knees shaking so badly, I was sure it must show beneath the full skirt of my princess-length wedding gown. (That means calf-length, men and young-uns.) Mother filmed the festive little reception with her Super 8 and had photos made for the newspapers, so Ken was happy. I wasn't exactly happy, but I was hopeful.

We spent our one-night honeymoon in a motel in Jamestown, New York. When I opened my suitcase, out fell tons of rice and a pair of oversized flannel pajamas. Tomato red with white polka dots. I dug around in the rice but found no black nightgown. For decades, I blamed my sister, but a few years ago, she told me, "Nope. It was Mother." Fortunately for all concerned, I learned this after Mother had died. (I mean, *really*, Mother, what were you thinking?) Some honeymoon. I sat there with my sullen spouse in that dumb little double bed in that dumb little motel, watching *Your Show of Shows* on TV, feeling like a large red and white polka-dotted turd.

⟶

Norman wrote that his girlfriend had turned out not to be pregnant. Swell news, huh?

"I married Tom," I wrote back, no reasons given.

Tom and I moved into a gloomy little one-bedroom apartment and continued the spring season at the playhouse. As a wedding gift, Newell upped Tom's apprentice salary from $27.50 a week to the actor's level of $55 a week, which really was decent of him.

Two weeks later, Tom and I walked over to a party about ten blocks from our apartment. The house was full of guests, the buffet table groaning with food, and anywhere there's free food, you'll find a line of actors eagerly picking up plates. (They don't call us starving artists for nothing.) A gangly, acne-pocked apprentice stood at the end of the line, alone and awkward, and I stepped in line behind him and chatted him up, expecting Tom to fall in line behind me. I filled my plate and looked for Tom, but I didn't see him, so the boy and I found empty chairs among a group of playhouse personnel. A few minutes later, Tom strode up.

"Hey, Tom, where've you been?" I smiled up at him. "I've been looking for you."

"It was plain you already had your dinner companion," he said—and stalked off.

"Tom?" I ran after him. "Hey, that kid's just one of the apprentices. C'mon and join us."

"Forget it! Obviously, you don't want to be with me."

He disappeared into the crowd, and for the rest of the evening, I dogged his tracks, trying to get him to talk to me, but he wouldn't acknowledge my presence. *Good grief,* I thought, if I'd latched on to some handsome guy our age, he'd have a case, but that pimply-faced, tongue-tied kid? Tom got thoroughly drunk, and we left early to walk home in the bitter cold. Walking thirty paces ahead of me, he stopped to bang his head against a tree.

"Tom! What on earth?" I cried, alarmed (to say the least!) by this bizarre behavior.

He trudged a few paces down the block, stopping at the next tree. *Bang.*

"Tom! Stop that! You're going to injure yourself!"

"Ooooh," he moaned in anguish, and trudged a few more paces. *Bang.*

"Tom! Please!"

"Oooooh." *Bang.* All the way back to the apartment, where he fell asleep, dead drunk.

All I got out of him the next day was that I had betrayed him, and he remained distant. Except in bed. Sadly, I soon had morning sickness that would kill Sabu. And it wasn't just in the morning, it was all the damned time. Tom was unsympathetic. He kept trying to make love, but the slightest movement of the bed and—*whooooa, Nelly*—I was running for the john. It felt like the "car sickness" I'd had as a child. By mid-April, my dark red hair had faded to the color of a Florida orange and I was still throwing up, three months pregnant, big as a house. I came down with a serious respiratory infection, and the high fever left me too weak to get out of bed. I looked and felt about as sexy as a tree sloth. With orange hair.

"My wife is pregnant," I heard Tom tell Newell one day. "She's too sick to continue here. I'm taking her to Oklahoma."

My wife, I remember thinking. *He called me his wife!*

The feeling that swept through me was like the fever that had left me weak, like a virus that infiltrated my system and altered my biology. And my psychology. Tom was my *husband.* I was his *wife,* carrying his precious baby. For better or worse, in sickness and in health, I adored him.

⟶

Tom bought an old car with the $600 I had saved from my salary, and off we went to Oklahoma. (Oh, goody, now I could have car sickness for real!) Actually, I should say, off we went *toward* Oklahoma. Somewhere in mid-America, the car began barking and wheezing. Tom took it to a mechanic and came back with the news that our buggy needed a few hundred dollars' worth of work. We didn't have *any* hundred dollars. Chagrined, I called my parents, who wired the money, and Tom and I spent the night in a cheap hotel, not shaking the bed.

We stopped in Edmond to see Melinda and brand-new baby Marcia Ann. Melinda was keeping house in a tiny silver trailer while Sheridan went to college, and they were bustin' their buttons over their new little miracle. Marcia was adorable. And in only six months, I'd have my own baby! None of my skirts would fasten anymore, so I was grateful for Melinda's hand-me-down maternity clothes. They were ridiculously fifties—pleated and gathered tops over skirts. I looked like a . . . oh, name a fruit. A cantaloupe. A ruffled yellow cantaloupe. A pleated pink cantaloupe, a gathered blue cantaloupe, a beige—well, you get the idea.

Tom and I moved into Melinda's and my old bedroom in Ardmore. Bill found some odd jobs for Tom on his construction site, though Tom wasn't really one for physical labor. I bought a little booklet, *How to Crochet* (yep, I still have it) and spent my days crocheting booties and bonnets in pink, blue, and yellow, since we didn't know which sex was coming. I had a powerful feeling the baby was a boy, though. Tom had told me he wanted only a boy. No girls! *At least,* I thought, *I'll have that on my side.*

Mother took me to the beauty parlor and bleached the orange from my hair, so I was my old blond self again. I felt almost attractive, but Tom was indifferent. At that point, he probably wouldn't have cared if I'd shaved my head into a Mohawk. I made lunches for him every day and dreamed up every variety of milk shake and ice cream sundae imaginable, concocting flavors nobody ever heard of, while he became more and more withdrawn.

"What's making you so miserable? Is it being married? Being married to *me*?" I asked, but he wouldn't discuss it.

Too pregnant to work as an actress, I put my nose to the grindstone, typing letters and helping Tom apply for summer stock jobs all over the country, finally striking pay dirt. He was offered the small role of a handsome swain in *The Merry Widow* at Casa Mañana in Fort Worth, and the Alley Theatre in Houston offered him a summer apprenticeship, which didn't pay but opened the door at that prestigious regional theatre, which had a full-year program.

"It *could* lead to an offer to join the company," I encouraged.

He drove down to Fort Worth in our old jalopy to rehearse *The Merry Widow,* and Mother drove me down later for the weeklong run of the show. We stayed in a very modern, very chic hotel, and the heady fragrance that lingered in the rooms and hallway haunted me for years. Even now, a trace of that scent catapults me back to that place and time. Every night I stood at the back of the darkened auditorium, my pregnant body full of longing, waiting for Tom to appear in his few scenes. He was so dashing and handsome, my love for him leapt out of me and flew to the stage. The gorgeous song "Delia, the Witch

of the Wood" came just before his first entrance. It moved me to tears
every night—and every time I heard it for the next thirty years.

⁓

When the show at Casa Mañana closed, we drove to Houston and
checked into a tacky motel while we looked for an apartment. Houston
in the summer is as hot and humid as a steer's mouth. Every step outside is like slogging through sorghum. On the bright side, my morning
sickness had finally passed, and I was ready to shake the ol' bed again.
But Tom was more withdrawn than ever. Lying next to him in that
motel, aching for him, my heart in my throat, I finally found the
courage to ask, "Tom, is something wrong?"

He lay silent for a few moments. Then—

"I love you," he replied tightly, "but I'm no longer in love with you."

"Oh, my God!" I rolled out of bed, crying. "Oh, my God, oh, my
God."

"Jesus, Rue, don't make such a big deal out of it," he said.

I stood staring out the screen door, sobbing, "Oh, God, what if he
looks like you?"

I was too terrified to sleep. What would become of the baby and
me? How could I live without Tom? I was trapped in this huge, pregnant body; no way out, no remedy. A horribly evolved form of that old
childhood panic seized hold of me and didn't let up for the rest of my
pregnancy. Tom went to bed every night around midnight, but I sat on
the floor of the bathroom, the door shut to keep the light from bother-
ing him. Drinking black coffee, smoking cigarettes, writing in my
diary, I waited for dawn to creep through the window.

"For Christ's sake, Rue, come to bed!" Tom raged. "Stop acting like
an idiot."

"I'm sorry," I wept. "I don't mean to interfere with your schedule,
but I can't help it."

"You stupid bitch! You fucking cunt!"

I wasn't sure what "cunt" meant. This was the first time I'd heard the word. But it sounded worse than "bitch."

Just to be among people, I walked over to the theatre in the evenings and watched the actors moving through their performance like a little match girl watching a grand party through someone's parlor window. One night, a friendly young apprentice invited me into the office and taught me to play a word game, which helped keep my panic down to a dull roar until Tom was free to go home. But after the show, Tom came into the office and announced, "I'm going out with some of the cast. I'm taking the car."

It was after eleven, and we lived ten blocks away.

"Can I give you a lift?" the apprentice offered. He didn't ask Tom, "Aren't you going to take your wife home?" I didn't either. I spent a lot of nights in that office, playing word games with that kid and letting him take me home, and I doubt he'll ever know what it meant to me to have two hours of relative peace and a sane person to talk to.

One night, Tom got home from his after-hours whatever with whomever and, to my profound relief, seemed to want to connect with me for the first time in months. God only knows whose idea it was, but we started playing strip poker, taking off one article of clothing every time we lost a hand. It was the scariest performance I could imagine giving just then—monumentally pregnant, doing a striptease for a man who didn't want me anymore—but I made it a comedy routine, loving his laughter. As I threw off the next-to-last garment with a funny remark, Tom blurted out, "Oh, Rue, I'm starting to love you all over again."

"Oh, my God! How wonderful!" I cried. This miraculously amazing and extremely welcome expression of interest triggered a sudden gush of tears.

"Well, hell," he responded. "Now you've ruined everything!"

And he walked out of the room, leaving me on my knees on the bed, down to my scanties, with no idea what had just happened.

Back to the bathroom and waiting for dawn. I didn't confide in my parents. I felt it was my problem. And I didn't confide in Tom's parents, because I didn't want to betray him, but I wrote Tom's sister, Pat, asking for advice, and she wrote back, "We always thought Tom was an alien, not like any of our family. You have to try harder, Rue. After all, it takes two to make a marriage work."

Thanks, Pat. And this "two" would be me and who else? Captain Marvel?

During the day, I started visiting speech and exercise classes at the theatre. I was able to do stretch exercises, even with my big belly, and the speech classes gave Tom and me something we could share and laugh about. Some of the people had Texas accents too thick to drip through a slotted spoon. The teacher would say, in impeccable British, "*Hah-oo nah-oo, braah-oon cah-oo?*" and someone right off the ranch Texan would drawl, "*Hay-ow nay-ow, bray-oon cay-ow?*" which afforded Tom and me a certain deal of delight. Somebody suggested we put together a scene from *A Hatful of Rain* with me as Celia, the pregnant wife, Tom as the estranged husband Johnny, and another apprentice, Pete Masterson, playing Polo, who was sympathetic to Celia's plight. Mighty close to home, I thought, but maybe it would bring Tom and me closer—if it didn't alienate him further. We performed the scene and got raves from our audience. But it made no difference between Tom and me.

Pete was only eighteen, but he and his girlfriend, Carlin, had become good friends with me and Tom. One afternoon, at their apartment, I confided I'd been suffering back pain and blood in my urine for two or three days.

"My God, Rue. You need to see a doctor," said Pete.

Tom just stood there, so Pete took me to a doctor, who gave me medication for a severe bladder infection. What a good feeling, having a man take care of me. I was ashamed for Pete and Carlin to see that Tom didn't care, but Pete (who was just a kid!) reminded me how a real man behaves. Years later, I saw Pete's production of *The Best Little Whorehouse in Texas* on Broadway, with Carlin, now his wife, in the lead, and when I was in Hollywood working on a TV series, Pete and I had lunch at The Farmers' Market. When I reminded him of that day he had come to my aid, he made light of it. He and Carlin are superior people. And wasn't their beautiful daughter, Mary Stuart Masterson, wonderful in the movie *Fried Green Tomatoes?*

· Summer drew to a close. We went back to Ardmore, but the Alley offered Tom a year's Equity contract as a member of the company, so he whisked back to Houston. Alone. It was late August. I was eight months pregnant. I hadn't told Mother what was going on, but it was consuming me. She took me to the drive-in to see *The Ten Commandments,* and even husky Charlton Heston—who couldn't act his way out of a paper bag—didn't distract me. As he stomped his sandaled way down Mount Sinai, all I could think was, *Rue, thou art abandoned.*

Pacing my parents' house in turmoil, I decided, "I should be with my husband!" Taking the bit between my teeth, I joined Tom in Houston. He let me know I was about as welcome as a bullfrog in the pickle barrel. He was living with another couple in cramped quarters, so I was assigned a sofa to sleep on. The first night, Tom made love to me on that sofa and I fell asleep feeling bittersweet. The next night, I crept over to him, kneeling on the floor in all my hugeness.

"Tom, what is it you want?" I asked. "Please tell me."

Looking up at the ceiling, he said quietly, "I want a career and lots of money."

Well, you damn fool, I thought. *That's exactly what I can provide.* But I didn't say that.

Instead, I said, "Okay. I'll call Mother to pick me up in Dallas tomorrow."

I spent the last month of my pregnancy on tranquilizers, alone in that house thirteen telephone poles past the standpipe north of town. While Mother and Bill worked, I walked and walked, around the house, around the yard, talking to the baby in my belly, telling him how much I loved him, singing to him, saying, "Daddy loves you. He'll come to his senses." I crocheted more booties, jackets, and caps. I also developed a persistent ache in my right side, which remained a mystery until 1982, when I almost died from undiagnosed gallbladder deterioration.

⌒

Tuesday, October 1, opening day of the 1958 World Series, my aunt Peggy stopped by Ardmore on a car trip with her two little daughters. I'd been having labor cramps since nine in the morning, and around five in the afternoon, I was sitting on a stool at the kitchen counter when I felt a strange sensation.

"Oh, great grannies, Eddi-Rue!" cried Aunt Peggy. "Your water's broken!"

Oh. *Well . . . goodness,* I thought. Now *what do I do?* Peggy left. Mother came home from work, we had dinner, and I went to bed, but around nine, I woke Mother and told her the cramps were unbearable. She took me to the hospital, where they said I was in the second stage of labor.

"I want to call Tom," I told Mother around eleven. "The curtain must be down by now."

I went to a pay phone in the hallway, filled with emotion. Oh, God, his voice.

"Tom?" I said. "I'm at the hospital. The baby's coming."

A little pause on the other end of the line. Then: "No kidding."

I went back to the labor room, but they made Mother stay in the lobby. The nurses said they couldn't give me any medication because (wink, wink, nudge, nudge) I wasn't yet nine months pregnant, right? I tried using the breathing technique I'd been practicing, but it didn't help. At one in the morning, a nurse came in and gave me a shot of something in my hip. For the next six hours, I writhed in agony, trying to get away from that excruciating, unbearable pain, begging the nurses who stood guard on either side of the bed, "Please, kill me!"

"Now, now, don't act like that. Lie down! Be a good girl!" They kept pushing me down until—*finally*—after what seemed a lifetime, someone said, "Roll over. You're going to delivery. The doctor's on his way."

I obediently rolled over. Then I was in another room with very bright lights, where I fell unconscious. That was a little after seven in the morning. They tell me that my son, my darling baby, made his appearance at 7:25 A.M. on Wednesday, October 2. I woke up in yet another room, the pain gone, everything looking white and swimmy. Someone placed a bundle in my arms and, with my blurred eyesight, I vaguely made out a little white face with a bright red triangular nose. *Oh, my God,* I thought. *I've given birth to a freak, and they're afraid to tell me.*

After they took him away, I began to cry and I couldn't stop. All that day, all that night, all the next day, I kept crying. My eyesight cleared, and I could see that I had a beautiful little boy whom the entire nursing staff praised as the prettiest baby in the place, and I loved him completely. But I couldn't stop crying. And I couldn't fall asleep.

"You've got to get control of yourself," the worried doctor told me.

"Doctor," I confided through tears, "I want to nurse my baby, but there's—"

"Oh, I already gave you a shot to dry up the milk," he said. "Nursing ruins the shape of the breasts."

How 'bout them good ol' days, huh? The tears kept flooding. At eleven o'clock Thursday night—some forty hours after Mark was born—I was told that my husband wanted to see me. Mother had driven him up from Dallas, and through my tears I saw her standing in the doorway as Tom rushed in and threw himself over me.

"Oh, Rue! I made a terrible mistake!" he cried. "Can you ever forgive me? I love you!"

"Tom . . . *of course!* Of course I forgive you. I love you, too."

I decided to name my beautiful new baby Mark Thomas Bish, and I fell asleep, thinking, *It's like a fairy tale! A miracle! I can't believe it!* The next morning, Tom came by early. Mother was going to drive him to Dallas to catch a plane back to Houston. But then I noticed . . .

"Tom, why aren't you wearing your wedding band?" I asked.

"Oh, baby," he said, turning to the window, his back to me. "Don't be a drag."

CHAPTER SIX

⸏

"When tumbling down a mountainside,
endeavor not to land on your head."

—DAME EDITH EVANS

I recently read a fascinating book about sociopaths, who are a lot more common in our society than we'd like to think. They're regular butcher, baker, candlestick maker types who walk through life with a sort of emotional color blindness that renders them incapable of compassion. It's estimated that one in twenty-five people suffers from this congenital inability to empathize or otherwise give a flea fart about anyone other than themselves. One in five people in prison, which is like a day spa for sociopaths who need to work on their methodology.

My God, I thought when I read that, *maybe Tom was a sociopath.* Then again, maybe he was just a putz. But if he was, he was a putz of pathological proportions.

During my "lying in" week at the hospital and over the next five weeks or so at my parents' house, I sent Tom photos of Mark and letters chronicling our baby's remarkable progress and asking Tom when we could join him in Houston. Nary a word back. I did, however, receive a letter from Norman. He'd been drafted and was stationed at Fitzsimmons Army Hospital in Denver. What a gift that letter was! I was truly a wreck, my self-esteem down around my ankles, way too pale and thin. (Hard to imagine being *too* thin.) But someone still found me worthwhile. And not just any someone! Remarkable, eccentric, inimitable Norman Hartweg.

Sitting there on the bed, watching Mark sleep, I suddenly realized what a zombie I'd been, and between caring for Mark, Norm's letters, and the natural recalibration of hormones, I started to feel human again, thinking, *Oh—why, this is me! I'd forgotten this person.* After six weeks of not hearing from Tom, I wrote him, saying if he wanted Mark and me to join him, he should keep the snapshots of Mark, and if he wanted a divorce, he could simply return the snapshots. Those snapshots came flying up to Ardmore like cannonballs. No letter. Not even a bar or two of "So Long, So Long." Nothing.

I started divorce proceedings with Judge Caldwell, who advised me to sever all claims Tom could possibly have in any future custody disputes by cutting him loose with no monetary demands. Mother—who'd once lobbied for that *courteous* Tom Bish—urged me to take this advice. I'd never intended to ask Tom for help anyway, and of course, Tom jumped on the "no joint custody, no support" deal. The divorce would be final in six months, in mid-May. So there I was. Broke. Wildly in love with my miraculous baby boy but stuck living with my parents in Ardmore, Oklahoma. None of this had in any way derailed my burning resolve to launch an acting career in New York, but my plans for world domination were set back more than a week.

I decided to set up a dancing and acting school that would include African-American kids, who weren't allowed in any other dance school in segregated Ardmore. I went to the black high school and invited everyone to a demo class at their community center. About a dozen kids signed up for dance. I did the same at the white community center and got five for dance, six for acting. Bill put up a ballet barre in the living room of a rental house. I couldn't afford a pianist, but I had classical, jazz, and pop records and a turntable. I was in business!

Sadly, as soon as white parents learned their kids were in a dance class with black kids, they pulled their children out. Oh, well. I still had some talented students and was enjoying teaching.

This was the year of the movie *The Defiant Ones,* starring Sidney Poitier and Tony Curtis as two escaped convicts who were handcuffed together. When I went to the Tivoli Theater to see it, there was a sign in the lobby, COLORED UPSTAIRS, with a big arrow pointing up the stairs. So up the stairs I went and settled into an aisle seat. Pretty soon, a little usherette came over and said, "Miss, you can't sit up here."

"I have to sit up here," I replied. "I'll get sick if I sit downstairs."

She argued a few minutes, then went away. People coughed uncomfortably and turned to look at me. An assistant manager came and firmly told me I had to sit downstairs, but I stuck to my guns. I wasn't lying. It truly would've made me sick to go along with that segregation shit. But a few months later, when my little group of dancers appeared on a program my mother hosted for a beauticians' convention, I took them to the soda bar for refreshments afterward and the counterman wouldn't serve them. Try as I might, I couldn't get the manager to listen to reason, and my kids had to go home without their after-performance treat.

That was Ardmore, Oklahoma, 1958.

For the dancing and acting school recital, I rented the YMCA auditorium, and parents, white and black, came in and rather self-consciously sat down at random. I peeked through the curtain, saw a salt-and-pepper audience, and felt great. After the recital, the black mothers gave me a handkerchief shower backstage. I still have most of those lovely hankies neatly folded in a wooden box.

"Miss Rue," they told me, "we never thought it would work, but it did, thanks to you."

I don't know when I've been more touched. And not one of those families owed me a single penny. Three white families stiffed me for the last month's classes. I even drove to their houses to collect but never got a red cent.

⌁

By Christmas, Mark was eating baby food like a trouper. Everyone found him adorable. I danced and sang with him and loved him so much it hurt. I saved every penny I was earning, eager for the two of us to have a place of our own. My parents had their own ideas about how he should be raised, and it bothered me when Mother picked him up, saying, "Come to Mother, sweetheart." I chronicled each amazing accomplishment in Mark's baby book and in long letters to Norman. We wrote to each other almost daily, and his letters were saving my sanity.

Another word to the wise: Don't fall in love with someone through the mail! We write with our left brain but feel emotion with our right. Nonetheless, Norman and I proceeded to rush in where angels fear to tiptoe. He came to Ardmore on Christmas leave. Army training had buffed up his slight build to go with his warm brown eyes and quick grin. He looked great. And he was terrific with Mark. He'd always gotten on well with kids, doing magic tricks, making them laugh. We decided we wanted to be together. I wrote the Xavier Cugat ballroom studio in Denver, applying for a job, and they said I could start teaching in April.

"Eddi-Rue," said Mother, taking me aside one day, "if you're going to live in the same city as Norman, I want you to marry him."

"We've been talking about it, Mother," I said, embarrassed by her implication.

When the doctor who delivered Mark fitted me with a diaphragm, I realized it was an open secret that there were only eight months between my wedding and Mark's birth, but we didn't talk about such things. This was the fifties. Repressed, uptight, *Father Knows Best*. The prevailing ideology was: Nice girls don't have sex before marriage. And Mother was brought up twenty years *ahead* of that by strict Southern Baptists, so you can imagine what she thought.

"I want you to marry him," she said firmly.

Wait! What are those magic words? Oh, yes. *Let me think it over!*

"All right, Mother," I said.

Late in April, I loaded up an old car that my folks gave me (what, to be honest, would I have done without them?) and, leaving Mark with Mother, drove thirteen hours straight to a little house Norm had rented in Aurora, a Denver suburb. Although my divorce from Tom wouldn't be final for another month, Norm and I were married (sort of) within a day or two by a justice of the peace, with the justice's wife as our only witness. We didn't have a wedding band. We borrowed hers. I wore a fitted gray suit, and the lady took a Polaroid of us. I still have it.

We look happy.

Much like smiling travelers waving from the deck of the departing *Titanic*.

CHAPTER SEVEN

"The curtain rises. A frog is on the center of the stage.
Frog: I don't think I'll go to school today.
Curtain."

—BENNET CERF'S SON, JONATHAN, AGE EIGHT

*J*onathan had the right idea. But since I set myself this task, I reckon I have to go to school today—though I must say, I did consider quoting Lady Macbeth, Act V, Scene 1, descending the stair with her taper: "All the perfumes of Arabia will not sweeten this little hand." It's much easier to write about the dastardly things done to you than the dastardly things you did to others. And I was about to become Queen of the Dastards. If I can get through this episode without turning to drink, I'll deserve . . . well, I'll deserve a drink! You might deserve one, too.

Mother brought Mark to Aurora. It was springtime. Birds were chirping. Mark was happy, Norm was happy, and I was—well, I was "The Wreck of the Hesperus." I couldn't stop thinking about Tom. I was married to my dearest friend, whom I loved, but I was still infected with that old virus, weak with that fever.

One day I went to a pay phone and called Tom's mother.

"Forget him," she told me right off the bat.

He'd gone off to Mexico and married somebody he'd met in—oh, God, I think she said *Las Vegas*. Devastating. The end of the world. One would think I'd get the message.

Earth to Rue: *You married an asshole!*

Rue to Earth*: Sorry, all circuits are busy. Please, hang up and dial again in thirty years.*

And then the "Gotcha!" Devil played an awful trick on Norm and me. Married less than a week, dear Private Hartweg was walking along, passed a general, and neglected to salute. *A general!* He was restricted to base for a month. Couldn't come home at all. We needed this like a hog needs a sidesaddle. I was allowed to visit Norm at the recreation center, where he was in charge of entertainment, and I occasionally took Mark along, but we didn't dare interrupt his duties. He was in enough hot water. We just watched him pass by from time to time, carrying things.

Norman got his pal Darren Rogers, a gifted poet and short-story writer, to babysit in exchange for the use of a typewriter. Darren was tall, slender, blond, with a sharp, focused brain and articulate tongue. Before he was drafted, he had been part of the Beat Generation of writers and painters in Venice, California. Their illustrious leader, Lawrence Lipton, whose best-selling book *The Beat Generation* truly defined that place and time, thought Darren was an especially promising writer. So did I. And he was so gentle with Mark, I felt secure leaving my precious son in his care. I'd come home after two or three hours at the rec hall, and Darren would read me what he'd written that night. I found him fascinating. I'd never met anyone like him.

Are you thinking, *Uh-oh*? You should be. Can you bear with me? Can *I* bear with me? This is the really hard-to-tell part, so I'm just going to plow ahead, devil take the hindmost.

"I believe in open marriages," Norman had always told me. "If one of the partners finds someone else desirable, it should be okay to explore that."

"I disagree," I always told him. "Married partners should remain faithful."

But to my alarm, I began to feel something more than friendship for Darren. One night, I came home to find Darren asleep on our bed.

He woke up and said, "Why are you looking at me like that?"

I hesitantly confessed my feelings. He admitted he was interested in me, too. But I was his friend's wife. For half an hour, we struggled with it, our desire sparking, glowing, growing.

Norm thinks it's all right, I told myself.

But I don't think it's all right, myself told me.

What if the Baptists are right, and I'm thrown in a lake of fire?

So what? I'm already hot as a firecracker!

I moved in like a cat. Norm had speculated I might fall for a hunky buddy of his on base, but he never suspected *Darren,* whose sibilant voice and poetic demeanor were hardly the answer to a maiden's prayer. And frankly, he was no great shakes in bed. I can only give him a C. (Which still beats a D, the damn best I can come up with for Norman. I dearly loved the man, but as Dorothy says in *Golden Girls* about her ex-husband, Stan, "It always seemed to be over before he got into the room.") About a week later, Darren got word that he was being sent to Korea. He told me he was leaving immediately for California to visit Lawrence Lipton, then his parents.

So there I was, yearning for Tom, who held me in his thrall despite his undeniable dark side; but married to dear, devoted, loving Norman, who was pretty mixed up himself; and sleeping with poetic Darren, who I suspected had one foot in the closet, if you get my meaning.

Another World was not my first soap opera.

I kept cooking, doing the laundry, caring for Mark, but I was in emotional splinters, electric bolts shooting through my head all the time—never mind my heart. I couldn't pull myself together. So what did I do? If you guessed "Rue did the mature, responsible thing"— please, pay closer attention. You're obviously not following this. If you guessed that I went to California with Darren, thus ripping good-hearted Norman's life apart—well, you get a gold star.

Norman didn't try to talk me out of it, and I have to wonder now, *Why not?*

Oh, why didn't he have me thrown in the loony bin? Did he *want* me to go? Did he subscribe to that butterfly BS about "if you love something, set it free"? The afternoon we left, Norm was completely blitzed, drunk as a hoot owl. I was devastated for him, but desperate to get away from the electric splinters. Darren and I drove to Ardmore, left Mark with my astonished parents, and continued to Los Angeles. My folks must have been appalled, but they never said so. In their repressed, non-expressive Oklahoma 1950s way, they probably surmised I'd been driven a little crazy by what I'd been through with Tom. I had always been so reliable. As a teenager, I had behaved maturely. Even as a little girl, I'd always behaved like a "grown-up." They'd made it clear to me from early childhood that I was expected to be a little lady, do as I was told. "Never dispute your elders!" I followed their rules, because I wanted their love. But now I was acting like a nutcase, running amok. And, children, run amok I did. Powerful, painful forces ruled my feelings, and the only relief came from running away. Run from the pain!

Frog: "I don't think I'll go to school today." Curtain.

But of course, Frog School followed me, as it always does.

⁓

In the spring of 1959, Venice, California, was at the heart of the Beatnik movement sweeping the country, and Lawrence Lipton's home was at the heart of the Venice Beatnik crowd, peopled with creatures I'd never imagined existed. Painters in torn T-shirts, writers in torn T-shirts, musicians in torn T-shirts, paint on their Levi's, all living in crumbling one-room digs, sleeping on mattresses on the floor, some with sheets, some without. Graffiti covered the walls. Disjointed jumbles of free-hand art. A lot of "Bird Lives!" and quotations from writers I'd never heard of. These lost souls had big aspirations, no clear direction, were primarily without talent, and undoubtedly on drugs. Eight or ten of the more promising ones showed up at Lawrence and

Nettie Lipton's large table for dinner every night, where they argued for hours over writing and art and ate everything in sight. It was probably their only real meal of the day.

Lawrence and Nettie kindly welcomed Darren and me. Fresh from an appearance on *The Tonight Show with Johnny Carson,* Lawrence was riding the huge success of his recent book. Darren fit right in with this heady crowd, apparently Lawrence's pet. Larry and Nettie had the beautiful custom of calling each other by double endearments. Sweetheart Darling, Lovey Precious, Baby Dear. Bright and upbeat, they held sway over this unruly coterie of loud, bumptious beatniks who obviously adored them. I quickly came to adore them, as well, but felt like a trout in a koi pond. All these artists, but not an actor in sight. Where were the theatre buffs and playhouses? Nobody ever mentioned theatre, but they argued writers at the top of their lungs. I couldn't discuss anything these fellows were all passionate about. I sat at dinner, wondering what they were talking about, and why Larry and Nettie fed and encouraged them.

I went with Darren to say good-bye to his parents, quiet, kind, normal folk who lived in Ojai, an artsy, academic town surrounded by orange groves, a big sky, and lovely mountains. A Shangri-la where rich people sent their kids. Darren had been accepted into an exclusive private school there because they expected him to become a force in the literary world. He was a gentle intellectual, hardly battleground material. Nevertheless, off he went to Korea.

I knew by then I wasn't in love with him, so after he left, I wasn't sure what to do. Larry and Nettie invited me to stay on while I decided, for which I was grateful and relieved. But I wanted to get out of their hair as soon as possible, and I was determined to find my way in the theatrical world (was there one?) in Los Angeles. The Yellow Pages yielded four playhouses worth checking into. The first three were not for me, but the Pasadena Playhouse was about to start its "Summer Talent-Finder Course," four weeks of training culminating in a pro-

duction of Noël Coward's *Present Laughter* in the Patio Theatre. I
scheduled an interview, looked up Pasadena on the map, and somehow
found my way there. (I have a terrible sense of direction, but I can read
maps like a champ, thanks to my fourth-grade geography teacher.)
The powers that be talked to me for an hour, had me read a couple of
scenes, and accepted me.

"Lots of film and television movers and shakers attend our plays," I
was told. And they'd had some major stars in the program. Barbara
Rush was discovered there. So were Victor Mature, Gig Young, William
Holden, Eve Arden, Robert Preston, Eleanor Parker, and later, both
Gene Hackman and Dustin Hoffman. The Playhouse had been out of
commission for a while, and the building had fallen into serious disre-
pair, but it was now being renovated, gearing up for a new era. I didn't
care much about all that. I just wanted a good part in a good play with
my own kind—actors, directors, and a stage to work on. But it would
be on my dime. And I had only a few dimes left and only four weeks to
make some money. But where? And how?

A falling-down old hotel on the beach in Venice provided a haven
for artists. In the once-elaborate lobby—proud in the 1930s, now
decrepit and probably unsafe—art students gathered by the dozens to
sketch and paint, earnestly soaking up the expertise of their guru du
jour, a guy named Randy. He was looking for new models. *Nude* models.
The pay was twice the minimum wage: two dollars an hour. A fortune!
Two dollars an hour! But nude, you see.

But *two dollars*!

But nude.

As in *NAKED*.

I brought it up at dinner, and the crowd around the table couldn't
comprehend why I wasn't jumping at this easy money. Two bucks an
hour! Oh, for—*for crying out tears!*

"What's the matter with you, Oklahoma? Jesus, man, get with it!"

"Wow, can you believe this chick? What are you, honey, from outer
space?"

Nettie said in her soft voice, "It's all right, Rue. Sweetheart Darling, it's *art*."

Then they all went back to discussing Jack Kerouac.

Ah. It's all right, it's *art*. I take off all my clothes, climb onto a platform, and pose *butt naked* for an hour. And I get two dollars. And it's *art*. An actress is required to expose her innermost being, raw emotions, nothing hidden, I reasoned. This is only exposing my body in front of a group of fifty art students . . . for two dollars an hour. I visited the art class and watched the proceedings, hoping the ancient ceiling wouldn't fall in on me. The students were intent on their work, focusing on sketching, while the models, some not in the greatest shape, were supremely matter-of-fact as they shed their robes, took center stage, and tried to strike interesting poses, perfectly immobile for twenty minutes, three poses an hour. As I watched, I thought, *I can do better than that.* After all that dancing, I was graceful, imaginative, and could hold a pose for twenty minutes without tiring. Heck, I figured I'd be a natural. Randy told me I could start the next day and, if I was satisfactory, work two or three sessions a week. And it was a very well-paying gig, he reminded me, to be paid in cash, on the spot.

Ah, that next day is forever etched in my memory. In Nettie's old beige chenille bathrobe, I climbed the steps onto the stage and slipped off my sandals. I dropped the robe nonchalantly off my shoulders, strode center stage, naked as a jaybird, and struck a pose. The students bent intently over their sketch pads. Attempting to relax, I breathed lightly, not moving a muscle, and tried not to wonder if they were all noticing how small my breasts were.

"Okay, everyone cool it a few," said Randy, walking through the standing artists, pointing out this and that. I didn't know whether to put my robe on or not. Everyone ignored me. I might as well have been a bowl of fruit. After two more twenty-minute sessions, Randy called an end to the class and I went over to put on my robe.

"You're good, honey," Randy told me. "Come back Wednesday at three."

And he gave me two crisp, lovely one-dollar bills.

I'd been searching the paper for real jobs and saw that the Harlequin Supper Club in Azusa was looking for "singing and dancing waitresses to present musical material." Fifteen miles east of Pasadena. A bit of a shlep. But I could dance, I could sing passably, I was a choreographer, and although I was never a waitress (at least, not yet), the owner felt I could swing it. All the meals were to be served from a rolling cart, after which we three servers—me, another girl, and George Kelley, who happened to be the current Mr. Pasadena—would perform floor shows at eight, nine, and ten, each night featuring food, songs, and dances from a different country. Monday was England, Tuesday France, Wednesday Spain, Saturday Hawaii—you get the idea. Pay? One dollar an hour, plus tips. We had to come up with costumes, but the owner (who was also the chef) would foot the bill, provided it was modest. We were paid twenty bucks a week for the rehearsals, and it worked out that we'd end the daytime rehearsals and open the restaurant the very night before the Pasadena Playhouse was to begin *its* daytime rehearsals. Unbelievably good timing! I'd have seven weeks of employment. I was desperate to get Mark out to California, and I still wanted keenly to go to New York, but that would take a lot more moola than I was earning now—with or without clothing.

After posing the following Wednesday, I told Randy I'd found a steady job and wouldn't be available anymore. It had been stressful for me standing there nude, even if they did see me as a bowl of fruit.

"I'm sorry to lose you," he said. "Will you at least share a farewell glass of wine with me this evening? The lobby won't be available. Come to my room in the basement of the hotel."

"Your room?" says I.

"Third cubicle on the left," says he.

Hmm, farewell glass of wine, huh? He'd always behaved professionally, so . . . oh, who am I kidding? This had all the earmarks of a real Beatnik experience. A one-time, far-out, unheard-of piece of audacity: strictly sex. But dare I? *Dare I? Did I dare?*

Oh, I daresay, I did.

That evening, I descended those basement stairs, trembling like a leaf, wondering who exactly I thought I was and what exactly I thought I was doing. On the floor of the third cubicle on the left was a mattress surrounded by candles. Randy appeared, drained his last swallow of wine, said "Hi!," and jumped me. Was this Beatnik foreplay? I'd never been jumped before. And never had sex like that before. It was athletic. Like, *wild,* man. And I liked it. I didn't feel guilty. In fact, I felt liberated. I was getting a fast course in a brand-new area. Pure sex!

One night about two months later, there came a knocking at my chamber door and there stood a haggard Randy, flanked by two skeezy pals.

"Can I borrow three dollars?" he asked.

Well, hell, I thought, embarrassed. *You only paid me four total!*

I gave him the three bucks and never saw him again (more's the blessing!), but I figured the education had been worth it. I'd not only learned to hurtle myself enthusiastically into boisterous sex but had found the courage to pose nude. And I was still one dollar to the good.

So what the heck. I'd still give Randy a solid A.

⌒

English Night at the Harlequin meant donning green leotards for "Robin Hood." America was "Steam Heat," a Bob Fosse number in white shirts and black derbies. For Spain, we did a mean flamenco—implementing the castanet technique I'd learned at Jacob's Pillow. France was a cancan. Italy was "Finiculi, Finicula." Hawaii was our blockbuster. We two gals did a hula, then George burst forth in a short feathered skirt and huge headdress, his Mr. Pasadena muscles bulging, and did a thrilling frenzy number. And *oh, my,* could he frenzy! Attendance was sparse, but we performed as if we had a full house, six nights a week. We closed at eleven, but George and I always spent an hour or more talking and laughing in the parking lot. Then I left for Venice in my station wagon and he took off on his Harley. He was fun, but too rich for my blood. Older, experienced, and way too good-looking.

Early every morning, I drove from Venice to Pasadena and rehearsed *Present Laughter* from ten to five. Exhilarating! I was acting! Then I was off to Azusa to be a singing-dancing waitress for four hours, then back to Venice for a few hours' sleep. I had no idea where I would go after the closing of the play. I yearned for New York, but how could I do it with Mark? I ached for him every minute of every day. The Harlequin fed us dinner with enough leftovers to take to the Playhouse for lunch, I was living rent-free at Nettie's, so I'd saved enough to pay the Playhouse summer tuition and get by a few months. Just before the play opened, I gave notice at the Harlequin and trained my replacement, who—bless her heart!—learned the routines in jig time so I could begin evening dress rehearsals on the play just before opening night.

Present Laughter was a hit. Toward the end of its short run, the Playhouse folks asked if I'd sit in the audience of a television show called *It Could Be You!*, saying they wanted some students in the balcony to publicize our new season. Then Mother called and said she was bringing Mark out for a visit! I was overjoyed. She arrived with a rawboned, redheaded country girl named Ruthie Mae Henry, who'd been babysitting Mark. Ruthie Mae had never been out of Oklahoma, and Mother said this trip was a bonus for the good care she'd given my baby. Nettie and Larry welcomed the whole crew into their home, immediately enchanted with Mark—as was everyone. I showed Mother and Ruthie Mae around Venice Beach, which they found as far out and groovy as I had. That afternoon, the sophisticated Larry Lipton sat chatting with my little Oklahoma mama, and I listened in amazement as Mother not only held her own with him but had him in stitches. Where did she get such *savoir-faire*? Heavenly days!

The next morning, at the studio in Hollywood, *It Could Be You!* started with two surprised recipients being called to the stage for prizes. Then they broke for a commercial.

"Our final prize," the MC announced when the show resumed, "will be awarded by a star of screen and stage, Mr. Lee J. Cobb!"

Mr. Cobb, who'd played opposite Marlon Brando in *On the Waterfront,* took center stage.

"I'm here to give a full third-year scholarship, the first of its kind, to a performer at the Pasadena Playhouse," he said. And then he boomed, "It Could Be You . . . Rue McClanahan!"

Mother beamed from ear to ear as ushers squired my stunned self onto the stage and Mr. Cobb read some very complimentary remarks about my acting and handed me a framed award.

Plus, the MC added, "this handsome set of Samsonite luggage!" And someone brought out two white suitcases and an overnight case. What next? A year's supply of Ivory soap? But hey—I didn't care if it was cornball, I used that luggage for the next fourteen years!

It had been a conspiracy. The Playhouse and Mother and Nettie and Larry had been planning it for a while. The scholarship would cover my tuition for nine months, and Mother would pay Ruthie Mae to stay with Mark while I rehearsed and performed. I was duly appreciative. But I wanted to be doing real theatre—the kind where *they* paid *me,* instead of the other way around. I wanted to be in New York! But in New York, I'd have no money, no prospects, and most important—no way to keep Mark.

So. New York would have to wait.

CHAPTER EIGHT

～～～

"Hand me his hammer and chisel!
There's a statue in this marble crying for release!"
— Bippo Spumoni, Michelangelo's apprentice from 1612 to 1612

On Mark's first birthday, I baked a white cake with white icing. He was walking—well, sort of lurching. I put the cake outside on the grass and made snapshots of him proudly toddling toward his cake . . . and then stepping in it. We both thought that was hilarious, but it turned out to be a parable of sorts for much of what lay ahead. Just when everything seemed to be coming up sugar frosting roses—ker-*plop*. I'm an optimist by nature, though. I tend to laugh off most missteps, even when things get a little messy.

Ruthie Mae, Mark, and I moved into a tiny two-bedroom apartment six blocks from the Pasadena Playhouse. Ruthie Mae slept in one bedroom on a real bed. Mark and I were in the other bedroom, he in his port-o-crib, I on a mattress on the floor. Since the scholarship didn't cover any living expenses, I'd started looking for a day job, when out of the blue, Norman wrote that the Army was going to send me a monthly spousal check for a little over two hundred dollars! This would make his personal paycheck less, but dear, generous Norm wanted me to have this stipend, which made it possible for me to be with Mark when I wasn't performing or in class.

I also got a letter from Darren, saying he'd been medically discharged with a nervous breakdown, would be back in the States in a week or two, and wanted to see me.

Oh, dear.

I dreaded telling him I couldn't continue a romantic relationship with him, especially in his state of mind, but when I spoke with him, he seemed more disturbed from his experience in Korea than from my news. He went home to Ojai, saying he hoped to see me again someday. He never did. Many years later, I heard he had become a Buddhist monk in France, and I like to think of him there, happily writing his poems and stories. Perhaps in French.

I signed up for only two classes at the Playhouse, because I didn't want to be away from Mark more than a few hours a day. In dialect class we learned the International Phonetic Alphabet, as well as Scottish, Irish, upper-crust British, Cockney, New Yorkese, and a limited but useful roster of other accents. Dance class was more like gym class. I was the lone female in third year. It was hard to find plays for five men and one little egg in search of a beater, so second-year girls sometimes rounded out our casts. The first show ran with good reviews. In the second play, I was cast as a raucous, drunken troublemaker. An exciting challenge! I was happy. Mark was happy. At last, life was working out.

Oh . . . *really?*

"I'm just too homesick to stay," Ruthie Mae announced in October.

She wanted to leave the following week, but I persuaded her to hang on for a week beyond that while I searched desperately for a nanny who could be trusted to care for Mark for a price I could afford. After ten days of fruitless interviews, I called Mother, who came and got Ruthie Mae and Mark. To say my heart sank is an understatement. Parting with my baby again! The last thing I wanted. But that's what happened. After Mother and that damn Ruthie Mae left for Oklahoma with my precious boy, I moved into a cheap one-bedroom apartment by myself.

⁓

Sexy, scrappy Troy Sanders was one of two particularly talented third-year actors.

"Come up to my place after rehearsal tonight," he said. "We'll have wine and run lines."

But of course, he had something else in mind.

I found him attractive but said, "No, Troy, I don't think so."

"It's perfectly safe. I'm medically unable to sire children," he assured me, and under his persistent blandishments, the wine and I succumbed. Rating: B. (Twelve years later, while I was doing *Maude,* a former Pasadena Playhouse pal looked me up and, in the course of conversation, mentioned that Troy was married and living in the Valley with his wife—and three children. Hmm. Must have found a miraculous cure. I felt such a fool. But *oooh,* such a lucky fool!)

Bill McKinney, a blond hunk from Arkansas, was the other gifted third-year actor. He was Troy's buddy, so I felt a little strange when Bill started coming on to me, but he was loaded with personality and very funny, despite his reputation for getting into bar fights. He was built like a bull with a lot of pent-up steam to blow off. After rehearsals, I always went home, but Bill and Troy often went out. Troy, who was only about five feet six, would pick a fight with some big guy in a bar, inviting the furious fellow to "step outside," forcing Bill to come to his rescue. Troy was a lover not a fighter, and Bill was both, so together, they were like Mickey Rooney on steroids.

One night during our brief but very active affair, Bill and I were in bed at my apartment when a loud fracas began outside.

"McKinney!" someone was yelling. "Get out here!"

"That's Troy!" Bill cried, leaping out of bed stark naked. He threw on a shirt and stomped outside to beat up whomever Troy had in tow, and I decided these two were just too much for me. No more shenanigans with either of them. Bill went on to a successful movie career—

usually typecast as a threatening, dangerous redneck, with his thick Arkansas accent. He used to say to me, "That's *RAT!*" Meaning "right." He played the southern bully who tied Ned Beatty to a tree and ravaged him in *Deliverance,* and I don't know about you, but that scene scared *me*! In fact, *Maxim* recently did a "50 Greatest Movie Villains" issue, and the #1 scariest guy of all time was—*that's rat!*—Bill McKinney. I see him occasionally on late-night television reruns. Usually in fight scenes. That man was a brawler.

Matthew, on the other hand, was a charming first-year actor from New Jersey. Tall, brunet, handsome as all get-out. He said he was twenty-four, so I told him I was twenty-four, too (I was actually twenty-five). He was a real gentleman. And may I say, terrific in bed—a solid A.

That Thanksgiving, I made turkey and fixin's for a bunch of friends. I was just serving everyone, wondering where Matthew was, when a knock came at my front door. There he stood, very agitated. He thrust a folded letter into my hand, made me promise I wouldn't open it until he was out of sight, then took off running across the vacant lot next door.

Dear Rue, the letter read, *I cannot go on with this deception. I lied. I am not twenty-four. I am eighteen, and it's tearing me apart. I can't see you anymore. Good luck. Love, Matthew.*

I stood there, thinking, *Good grief! I've been shtupping a teenager!*

He was awfully sweet, though. I've often wished to look him up, but I can't remember his last name, and I can't very well advertise: "Seeking Matthew: a solid A!"

I went home for Christmas, a whole week with Mark, who had grown so much! He called me "Little Mama" and Mother "Big Mama." Mother was spoiling him, and he missed me, which broke my heart. I determined then and there—in the final days of 1959—that I would get into a union show in 1960. Enough racing my engine and getting nowhere! By God and little green apples, I was going to become a bona fide Working Actress! And I would get Mark back!

Sure enough, just after New Year's, I got a call to read for *Malibu Run,* a popular TV series starring Ron Ely. I went in to read on January 6, 1960, and—can you believe it?—was hired to play a waitress. (I had some experience at that by then.) Only one day's shoot, but one of my two small scenes was with the guest star, Peter Falk. *Wow!* Now I could join Screen Actors Guild, which opened the door to jobs I couldn't get before. My salary barely covered the cost of joining SAG. But having broken that union barrier over the next few years, I got cast as a waitress in a cowboy bar in a popular Western, as a waitress in a few other series, and as an actress in *The People's Court.* These little jobs were few and far between, however, so I had to keep waiting tables in real life to make ends meet. I began to wonder if I was an actress playing waitresses, or a waitress sometimes playing an actress.

Also in January, we started rehearsals on *Roadside* by Lynn Riggs. I was cast in the marvelous role of Hannie, a bigger-than-life country gal. Our terrific director, Barney Brown, taught me a valuable piece of technique: "You have to be brave enough to go further than you feel safe. Let it all hang out. Go beyond your limits."

Good advice in art and life.

Sir Laurence Olivier once said: "The first rehearsal, think of jumping into an ice-cold pool of water." I rehearsed Hannie with all the gusto and guts I had in me. What a role! But one bleak morning, six days before *Roadside* was to open, Barney announced that Lynn Riggs's estate had put a stop on any performance of *Roadside.* Stunned and dismayed, we had to come up with another play, rehearse it, and open in less than a week! Barney found a science-fiction one-act for the men, and for me he selected *Before Breakfast,* a bitter little one-act pill by Eugene O'Neill, in which a woman shuffles around a kitchen in a shapeless blouse and skirt, haranguing her unseen husband. For twenty-five merciless minutes. He never replies. Finally, she exits to the bedroom, lets out a bloodcurdling scream, staggers back on, and slumps onto the table. Curtain.

A real laugh riot.

"Can you learn it in five days?" asked the director who'd been brought in.

"Sure," I said. "If I can find someone to drill me on lines for a few hours every day."

I called George Kelley, who said he'd be glad to cue me. With his help, I learned the lines. With the director's help, I created the character. With God's help, we opened on time. The men's play was a little shaky, but mine went flawlessly. George drove me home after the show, and I said, "George, I owe you a lot for the evening's success. I wish I knew a way to repay you."

He said he had a way. I liked him a lot, and he was gorgeous, but still . . .

I said, "Is that really what you want in return?"

He said, "It's the only thing I want."

So I gave it to him. Great sex, but I kept wishing he wanted me because he found me irresistible, instead of payment for a favor. I never saw George again, but that was some spectacular swan song. He deserved the title of Mr. Pasadena, ooh my, yes. A, A, A!

⌐

One night, a pair of important agents—husband and wife—who had just seen *Before Breakfast* came backstage and said they were terribly impressed with my performance. I took my pictures and résumés to their office on Sunset Strip the next day, and they said they wanted to see how I looked on camera and had arranged for me to judge a dance contest on an afternoon show. No lines, just walking around looking at the contestants. So a few days later, I put on my prettiest bib and tucker and went walking around looking at the couples dancing, feeling somewhat foolish. The show was live, so I didn't get to see it, but

Mother, who'd brought Mark out for a short visit, said I looked pretty, of course. Days went by. I didn't hear a word from the agents. They were never there when I called. *Finally,* they called me back to their office, and Mother, Mark, and I drove into Hollywood.

A receptionist in the outer office told me to have a seat, then got very, very busy.

I sat.

The wife was at the next desk, head down, also very, very busy. She finally glanced up and said, "My husband will see you in his office."

I went in.

He also kept his head down—very, very busy. Finally, he looked up and said, "You don't come across on camera. You're not photogenic. You have no future in television. Here are your pictures and résumés. Thank you for coming in."

Stunned and heartbroken, I stumbled down the stairs and got into the car in tears.

"Oh, Eddi-Rue. Honey, don't feel bad," Mother struggled to console me. "Remember, every kick's a boost!"

That made me laugh. In fact, I used that quote in my acceptance speech when I won the Emmy in 1987. (Memo to Mr. and Mrs. No Future in Television: Fall in a hole.)

After Mother and Mark returned to Oklahoma, I was thrilled to hear that my cousin Sue and her family were moving to L.A. and would be glad to share a house with Mark and me! Well, *hallelujah!* I went to Oklahoma and fetched Mark back on the train, along with his little kitten, Grice, and we all moved into a large house in Glendale, which was . . . well, Glendale. Blandsville. But heck, it was half an hour from the Playhouse, with a fenced yard where the kids could play. Sue took care of the kids while I was at the Playhouse, and I spent hours on the patio and in the sandbox with Mark. Once again, everything was happy, happy, happy . . . uh-oh.

In February, Mark started crying and didn't stop all day. He couldn't talk enough to tell me what was wrong, and Sue had no idea.

Frightened, I called Mother, who said to check his throat. I checked. White bumps. She said it was strep throat. I missed rehearsal and classes so I could be with him and swab his throat with medicine for a few days. It was miserable for poor Mark and scared me silly.

We were rehearsing the William Inge play *Bus Stop,* in which I played Cherie, the Kansas City chanteuse ("at the Blue Dragon nightclub, down by the stockyards") abducted by love-struck rodeo daredevil Bo (played by Troy Sanders, with Bill McKinney as his gentle sidekick, Virgil). A snowstorm has forced the bus to stop at a café along the way to Topeka. Of course, Bo turns out to be a dear and Cherie falls in love with him. During the long night, she stands on a chair and sings "That Old Black Magic" quite badly. I loved my tacky costume—an abbreviated, black, sequined getup with black fishnet stockings, my long hair piled on top of my head with a flower over one ear. It is a delicious role in a delicious play. And something happened during one particular performance that was pure bliss. For a few seconds—perhaps fifteen or twenty—I found Rue gone and only Cherie there. I was completely inside her. Actors pray for an experience like that.

Just after we opened, I was at a restaurant Playhouse students frequented when someone stopped by my table and said, "Oh, Rue, I met your ex-husband, Tom Lloyd, the other day."

The proverbial ton of bricks fell on my head.

"But . . . he used to be Tom Bish," I said. "Are you sure it was my ex-husband?"

"Yes, that's what he said. He's living in Hollywood. You want his number?"

Well, one would think that I already had this guy's number, but the moment I heard his name, my head was spinning with that old virus. I went unsteadily to a pay phone, and needless to say, he was surprised to hear my voice. We hadn't seen or spoken to each other since that day at the hospital when he'd given what was apparently the best acting performance of his life.

"I was wondering . . . ," I said, my heart in my throat. "Would you like to meet Mark?"

"Sure, babe," he said as casually as if I'd offered him a bag of peanuts.

That Saturday, I picked him up at his Hollywood apartment. Out he sailed, dressed in dazzling white.

"Hi, lady." He slid me a sideways smile. "I didn't think you'd ever speak to me again."

Deep breath, Rue. Deep breath . . .

I drove him to Glendale to meet his seventeen-month-old son.

"Mark, this is Tom. Your daddy."

We took Mark to the zoo and had a lovely time together. *Breathe, Rue, breathe . . .*

"Would you like to stay and see the closing performance of the play?" I asked, and he said, "Oh, yeah, baby. Cool."

"You were great," he said to me after the performance. "Hey, it's late, and you're tired. Why don't I stay over, and you can take me home tomorrow?"

"Okay," I said. That made sense. *Just keep breathing.* "Mark can sleep with me on the sofa. You can take his bed."

We had a glass of wine and talked, he going on about trying to get his career started but needing an agent, me telling him wonderful things about our son.

"My mother never forgave me for leaving you until the day she died," he said.

After another glass of wine, he fell into bed, instantly asleep. I lay awake for hours, acutely aware of him there in the dark. God almighty—who *could* breathe? In the morning, after breakfast, we played with Mark on the patio, like any little family out in the California sunshine.

"Thanks, babe. Mark's a great kid," Tom said when I dropped him off in Hollywood.

When I returned to Glendale, Mark started crying for "Daddy." I told him Tom would visit him again, but he kept crying for "Daddy" off and on all day until he fell asleep. I called Tom repeatedly over that week and left messages, but got no reply. Then I got an idea.

"Hi, Tom," I told his answering machine. "My agents are interested in seeing you."

He called back lightning fast. "Hey, babe. So when can I meet them?"

"You know, they *were* interested," I said tightly, "but the time has passed."

And I hung up. He never called back. Mark stopped crying for him. And twenty-eight years later, so did I.

The third-year class started rehearsing *A Streetcar Named Desire,* with me as Blanche DuBois—a plum role I had always wanted to tackle.

So where's that other shoe . . . isn't it about to drop? Oh, yes. Here it comes.

"We aren't happy in Glendale," Sue announced. "We're moving back to the Midwest."

Well, dadblast the fladderapp! Determined to keep Mark this time, I hit the Glendale papers and found an ad: "Single mother with child to complete household of three mothers with children." I'd have an upstairs bedroom and we'd all pay a lady to watch the children. With no alternative, I moved in, but I was shocked to learn that the kids were not allowed in the house during the day! They stayed in the backyard. All day. Bad enough for the five older children, but Mark was only eighteen months old! A toddler not allowed in the house? All bets off!

"This does not work for me," I told them. "I'll be out in a day or two."

I scoured the papers again, increasingly desperate. No apartments I could afford. No nanny I could—or would—hire. Then I got a letter from Norman. He was coming out for a three-day leave. I found a tiny trailer house (ooh-la-la). Two trips with the station wagon and I had us moved in. After Tom's latest rejection, Sue's sudden departure, those three cold Glendale bitches, I was all but beaten down. Norm arrived the next day, and being with this cheerful, devoted guy was like coming up for air. We decided to give our marriage a second try. It about killed me to drop out of *Streetcar,* but I did it. Good-bye Blanche DuBois, hello U-Haul. Norm helped me load the rented trailer, then flew back to base.

"We're going to see Norman!" I told Mark as we set out for Denver the next morning.

I figured we could make the trip in two days. It was warm in Los Angeles, so I wore shorts. I popped Mark into his port-o-crib in the backseat with his kitten, Grice, singing, "We're off to see the wizard!" We careened along the highway, dragging the weaving trailer with my station wagon. Mark enjoyed the whole thing mightily, but late the first day, a patrolman pulled me over.

"You sure you know how to handle the trailer, miss?"

"It's my first time," I told him demurely.

"Well, take it slow."

He gave me a few more pointers—and didn't ticket me, bless his heart. We checked into a motel in Arizona, sneaking Grice in. Early the next morning, we set out again. I was still in shorts, but I put a little sweater on Mark and he cuddled down in his crib with blankets. The steep Rockies now loomed ahead of us. We struggled slowly up Wolf's Head Pass, reached the snowy top, and started the sharply winding descent. It began snowing as we struggled down the treacherous pass, my heart pounding all the way, and by the time we reached Denver at dusk, it was colder than a witch's . . . nose. I was half frozen (the half in shorts) and woozy from fatigue, but grateful to be there in one piece. After dinner, I got Mark settled and fell groggily into bed. Norman began to make love to me. I was really too tired, and I wasn't protected. For some reason, I expected him to pull out before coming to climax.

He didn't.

"Oh, my God, Norm," I blurted out, "we've just gotten me pregnant!"

I had no doubt whatsoever. And God help us, I was right.

CHAPTER NINE

⁓

"The variation of light is remarkable."
—Henrietta Leavitt, measurer of Cepheid variable stars

T he female characters in film noir are of two types: the dutiful, chaste, and devoted good girl, or the gorgeous but dangerous dame, who lures men to rack and ruin. The twisting story lines are full of morally ambiguous choices and tragic consequences. Terse dialogue is growled over foreboding background music. The sets are mean streets slick with rain, abandoned warehouses, seedy rooms with neon lights flashing beyond the battered window blinds. Soap opera is like Film Noir Lite, with plots involving lost loves, amnesia, sexual peccadilloes, babies born out of wedlock, double-crossings. Pure-hearted heroines are duped by scoundrels, and vamps stir up romance-based conflicts. I created the soap in my own opera by being dumb as a damn booby and careless as a well-meaning twit.

I tried hard to be a good wife to Norm and a devoted mother for twenty-month-old Mark, cooking, cleaning, washing, and keeping an eye on Mark from the kitchen as he played outdoors. Norm's mother sent Mark a memory game, and the two of them played it every night, laying out the picture cards facedown in a grid on the living room floor. The trick was to turn up two cards that matched, so you had to remember where you'd put down the first one when you turned up its mate. I still have that game, timeworn but intact. Mark was as good as I was, Norm even better. But Norm was staggeringly brilliant, a walking encyclopedia, a gifted writer and artist. He sang and played guitar. Watching him with Mark, I felt such appreciation and joy. If all had been well, I would have eagerly had his baby. But Norm and I were never really husband and wife. No matter how hard I tried to feel that kind of love for him, it just wasn't there.

We were like that matching game. If you turn up a card and it doesn't match—well, damn it, it doesn't match! I quickly realized it had been wholly unrealistic for me to turn Norm up again, thinking we'd be better suited this time. And having a baby come along just then was unthinkable carelessness. Norm, who was emotionally repressed in the best of circumstances, wouldn't discuss it. We bantered about music, culture, and art for hours but didn't have heart-to-heart talks about our feelings or our future. Being a natural slob, adhering to Army regulations was a terrible strain on him, and the route our marriage had traveled thus far added to his tension-filled life. He tried to quit smoking but was always patting one foot or tapping his fingers, and finally he just exploded one night, shouting at me, the veins bulging on his forehead.

"To hell with it," he said after the eruption. "I'm smoking."

God knows, we tried to make this marriage work, with our meager emotional resources, but we were both terribly unhappy and scared with this unwanted pregnancy to cope with. I was terrified I'd end up on my own with two babies and didn't feel remotely capable of handling that. Abortion was illegal at that time, but as our desperation grew, I called a girl I'd met at the Playhouse—we'll call her Toula—who had confided in me that she'd had several abortions.

"I can take you to the doctor in Tijuana," she said. "It'll cost five hundred in cash."

Dear God! Tijuana? Horrible. Unthinkable. Even if we could come up with the money, I would be risking my life! But in those days, there was no place, no way for me to get a safe abortion. I was past two months pregnant, gripped by morning sickness. Time was of the essence. Then I got a call from a Hollywood agent who'd seen me at the Pasadena Playhouse.

"I've got an independent film you'd be ideal for," she told me.

Principal photography was to start in a week. In Hollywood. A three-hour drive from Tijuana. I called Toula. Her Tijuana doctor said he couldn't possibly fit me in for another month.

"But I'll be over three months along by then!" But he wouldn't take me any sooner.

"I'll get the money," Norm said grimly.

⁓

I took Mark and Grice to Ardmore on my way to L.A., where I moved in with Toula and her roommate, two gorgeously dangerous dames living in a flat in Westwood Village.

The movie's producer, Paul Lewis, introduced me to writer/director John Patrick Hayes, a big, handsome Irish guy from New York City. His short film *The Kiss* had been nominated for an Oscar the year before. John loved my reading of the role—an aspiring actress earning money as a stripper. It was a dark story, full of drama, titled *Walk the Angry Beach*. There would be no pay. It was non-union, being financed on a shoestring. I had to provide my own costumes, including one for the striptease sequence. With Rit dye and trimmings, I concocted a bikini brief and bra getup with dangling beads that swung furiously as I gyrated. Humiliated at having to strip for a living, the aspiring actress dances more and more frantically and rips off her bra. (Calm down, the camera was behind me, and my breasts were covered with duct tape.) We see in close-up that tears are streaming down her face. John cleared the crew out, all but the cameraman and sound crew and a couple of grips. I had to cry twice in that film. All I had to do was think about Mark, far away in Ardmore, and the tears flowed.

Workdays sometimes went on for eighteen or even a full twenty-four hours. Someone asked John if we ever fell asleep on our feet, and he replied, "No, but we do faint a lot." Actually, the cameraman did fall asleep once, with his eye against the eyepiece of the camera. After two grueling weeks, we shot a long tracking shot of me walking along Santa Monica Beach in a skimpy turquoise bikini and full-body makeup. I was three months pregnant and horribly insecure, but John was happy with the scene. The next day, however, we learned that the film had come out black. John was using "short ends"—cheap film strips he bought from a guy named Fouat Said. We had to shoot the whole bikini scene over again, and this time it was a cold, miserable day in Santa Monica. As I stood shivering on the clammy sand, I looked up to a bridge over the beach and there stood Norman. He came down and presented me with five hundred dollars he'd borrowed from friends.

"Grice was diagnosed with rabies," he told me. "We had to put him to sleep."

"Oh, my God!" I cried. "What about Mark?"

"He has to have rabies shots to be safe. In his stomach. Twice a day for two weeks."

"Oh, God, my poor baby," I anguished. "And that poor little kitten. Mark loved him so."

Norm returned to Denver, and I had three desperately needed days off before shooting the major love scene. Toula gave a party one of those evenings, and while she was serving drinks, she called over her shoulder, "Rue, be a dear and turn on the oven."

Opening the oven door, I struck a match. Before I could blink, I was blown back several feet against the wall. That vapid little idiot had turned on the gas without lighting it! My face and hands were scorched, my eyebrows almost gone, my lashes sparse and spiky. In shock and searing pain, I waited two hours in the ER while the medics dealt with a little boy who had fallen through a glass door. They treated my first- and second-degree burns, trimmed away the loose skin, and sent me home with painkillers and ointment—and an intimate love scene to shoot in three days. A sexy scene in which my character gets tipsy, dances with the leading man, and ends up in a clench with him on the sofa.

Shooting the scene took most of the night. We covered my peeling red face with makeup, and John arranged to shoot me from angles that masked the damage. When it was over, I told John, "I need a few days off to attend to personal business."

Then Toula, her roommate, and I drove down to Tijuana.

"You're past three months," the doctor said. "You'll need two procedures. One tonight. Then come back tomorrow morning."

As he muzzled my face with the anesthetic mask, a whole new dimension of panic separated me from everything I knew. I felt myself shooting far away from earth, spinning out into the cosmos, farther and farther into unending blackness. After what seemed an eternity, the doctor woke me and I trudged in incredible pain back to the hotel to lie down. Toula and her roommate went out on the town, and I lay on the bed next to an open window overlooking downtown Tijuana. Outside, a lone, loud trumpet played the same song over and over: "There's No Business Like Show Business."

Even in my tossing agony, I appreciated the irony.

The next morning, I returned for another horrifying trip into outer space, then we drove back to Westwood, where I rested for a day and tried to set the whole nightmare aside.

I have deeply regretted having that abortion. But at the time, I felt I had no choice. Occasionally, I add up the years, figuring how old he or she would be. I don't know if I'll ever forgive myself. It's the one true tragedy in my life. I still mourn that lost child.

Norman's child.

⁓

With only a few more scenes to shoot, I found myself a one-room place in Hollywood. John Hayes and I had been growing increasingly warm under the collar for each other. He was easygoing, blond, blue-eyed, funny, and talented both as a writer and director. I think he liked that I was such a trouper. I went to his apartment to discuss upcoming scenes after work one night, and we talked for hours about the movie, my role, our backgrounds and aspirations. As he saw me to the door, I said, "You know, John, I didn't really come over tonight to talk about work."

He smiled and said, "Why did you come over?"

I said, "To see you."

He closed the door. And opened the door on a serious involvement that would last four years. We had a bit of an engineering problem to overcome. John was six-four and built accordingly, and I'm a petite five-four, but with patience and goodwill—and we had both in abundance—with love, in fact, our spark of desire set off truckloads of Roman candles. We did something I'd never done before. It's a little embarrassing to relate, but . . . we sucked each other's toes. And it was damn sexy. Don't knock it till you've tried it.

One night, after making love, John got up to leave and panic welled up in me, and for only the second time in my life, I found the courage to confess the dusk panic I'd felt for years.

"Why are you scared?" he asked.

"Because," I told him, "I just need to know that you're here."

And he asked a very insightful question: "Do you need to know I'm here, or do you need *me* to know that *you're* here?"

I realized at once that he was right. That really was my problem and always had been. My father passing me on the porch, Bill Bennett dumping me for being a "dreamer," Tom abandoning me for whatever reason—as if my existence hinged on their wanting me.

"I'll be with you tomorrow, Rue," John told me. "Good night, sweet face."

And somehow it was all right. I wasn't scared. A small miracle.

In November, John was offered a job directing a kids' movie in Tulsa. He cast me in the small role of the mother. No pay, but he could get me fifty bucks a week as script supervisor if I learned to work a stopwatch and make proper script girl notes. We would finish the movie in mid-December, and—joy to the world!—I could spend Christmas with Mark in Ardmore!

We arrived in Tulsa, and John came into my room the next day.

"They fired me," he said. "I have to go back to L.A."

"*Wh-what?*" Shaken and dismayed, I stood there gaping at him.

Then he laughed. "I was only joking, Rue!"

I slapped him. The one and only time I ever slapped anyone. It just flew out of me.

"That. Was not. Funny," I told him, and he quickly apologized. I consider myself to have a pretty darn good sense of humor, but after the wringer I'd been put through in the last year?

I was in no mood.

Mark had grown by leaps and bounds and was now talking a blue streak. We had a wonderful Christmas together. Another New Year. Now it was 1961, and I was still too woefully short of funds to rent my own place and pay a full-time sitter. John spent Christmas in New York, then dropped by Ardmore with his mother, Kate—a jolly, outgoing Hell's Kitchen character with a thick New York Irish accent.

John had persuaded Kate to come with him to California, and they offered to share a house with me. But not with Mark. That was my big problem with John. He had two little girls who lived with their mother, and when they visited him, he wasn't very fatherly. He had a lot of issues from his childhood. Kate had farmed him out to his uncle and grandmother when he was a kid, and at seventeen he'd joined the Navy. When he returned, Kate pointed out a place across the street from her apartment and said, "Why don't you go see what they're doing? They seem to be having fun." It was Irwin Piscator's acting workshop. John checked it out and hooked up with Ben Gazzara, Tony Franciosa, Shelley Winters, Harry Guardino, and that bunch. He played Cheech on the road in *A Hat Full of Rain,* then a small role of a cop in the Broadway production of *West Side Story,* during which time backstage he wrote his movie *The Kiss.*

I loved John but couldn't commit to any kind of future with him. If he didn't want Mark, he couldn't have me. But I wasn't financially able to get to New York with Mark, and I sure as hell wasn't staying in Ardmore. So what to do? After much soul-wringing, I decided to go where I could most likely get work, leaving Mark with Mother.

John, Kate, and I set up housekeeping in a large ranch house in North Hollywood, and I hooked up the latest of my multitudinous waitress jobs. But Kate hated California. She missed her home in Hell's Kitchen, with the loo in the hallway and boisterous neighbors to gossip with. After four months of too much sunshine, she gave me her recipe for eggplant lasagna and fled back to Manhattan. John and I finished the six-month lease without her, then moved to a little cottage in Beverly Glen Canyon. There was an unheated bedroom built on out back, which we rented for $25 a month to my dear college friend, J. Martene Pettypool. Remember the guy who lost his shoe at *Così fan tutte?* He was now an escrow real estate officer in Los Angeles. (Where else would you find a one-shoed, piano-playing escrow real estate officer?)

That year I waitressed at four different places, and I don't know which I hated the most. I hated them all the most. One was a busy restaurant in North Hollywood from which I got fired after working one lunch. "Lack of experience," the man said. I felt like a fool in that uniform and hairnet, anyway, and I looked like Shelley Winters in *A Place in the Sun.* Next I worked at Chez Paulette, a coffeehouse on Sunset Strip. Max, the owner, played recorded Israeli folk music and hired only actresses to wait tables. The girl I replaced—Sally Kellerman, as I recall—had just gotten a movie role. Everyone in the place was very cool. Hollywood cool. Movieland cool. Max combed his hair like Napoleon and strode around with one hand tucked inside his vest—I swear to God! His mother, Paulette, a volatile Hungarian, was the chef. Once she dropped a fish entrée on the floor, picked it up, angrily slapped it back on the plate, and handed it to me to serve.

While waiting tables at Chez Paulette, I met Mervyn Nelson, a bright, funny New Yorker who had put together revues in the Big Apple and founded Theatre East, an actors' workshop, in Hollywood. He invited me to join, which I eagerly did. We presented scenes for other members to critique—strictly for our growth and experience as actors, no public audience allowed. It was a great place to keep my acting chops up, and Mervyn and I quickly became fast friends.

One night, J. Martene Pettypool came into Chez Paulette with a friend and stayed to closing. During the course of the evening, they ordered about twelve beers but he whispered to me to charge him only for nine, and I nervously did. Max fired me the next day, which I felt only appropriate. I was embarrassed for cheating but didn't mind losing the job. Paulette's patrons were so terribly cool they followed through with minuscule tips. I looked for a bigger, busier place and was hired at the Largo, a huge, popular strip joint on Sunset.

Down, boys—I was hired as a cocktail waitress.

We all had to wear fishnet stockings, dangling earrings, and a strapless leotard with a plunging neckline—as if I had much to plunge for. After four months of racing between the dining room and kitchen in high-heeled stiletto pumps on concrete floors, my feet felt like a six-toed cat with hangnails. I never really learned the difference between a Manhattan and a pink lady, and I loathed the butt-pinching, whiskey sour–swilling atmosphere of the strip house. The patrons weren't supposed to fondle us cocktail waitresses, but it was an unending battle.

All the while, I ached for Mark and for a family life. John and I were together most of the time, but he never said he loved me. He kept himself conveniently unavailable, blaming his estranged wife for refusing to begin divorce proceedings. Whenever I saw how distant he was with his little girls, I was sad for them. And not a little heartsick for myself.

Having been honorably discharged from the army, Norm was now living beneath a club on Sunset Boulevard. And I mean, *beneath* it. In a crawl space about five feet high, with a mattress to sleep on, books stacked harum-scarum all over the dirt floor. Once when Mark was visiting, I took him there and they were thrilled to see each other.

"Would you like to live with Norman again?" I asked Mark on the way home.

He said, "Oh, no, Little Mama. His place is too wrecked up."

Norm wanted us to get back together. We were still married, after all, and he was great with Mark.

"Quit that job at the Largo," he said to me. "I can't stand to see you demeaning yourself."

Boy, no need to preach to this choir!

I boomeranged between sexy, masculine John and intellectual, loving Norm—back and forth like a loony bird. But the deciding factor was all too clear. John said that if I brought Mark to live with me, he'd move out. So be it. Mark needed me, and I needed him. And I couldn't do it alone. John was out. Norm was in.

"But this is my last attempt," Norm made it clear. "No more getting jerked around. If it doesn't work this time, that's it."

I quit the Largo job and went home to soak my feet, then to Ardmore to get Mark. Norm left his "wrecked-up" crawl space and, just before New Year's 1962, he moved in and John moved out. Our friend J. Martene Pettypool was still renting the unheated spare room out back. Mark and I had a fine time racing around with Tiki, his curly-haired puppy, taking him on excursions to the nearby park, away from the heavy traffic that flowed through the San Fernando Valley, and to a larger park in Beverly Hills, where we flew kites. Or tried to. One day as I was running along in shorts, trying to get the kite to catch the air, a passing male motorist who was watching me appreciatively cruised headlong into a tree.

Norm didn't take part in these trips to the parks. He slept every day until after four, when the sun was going down behind the mountains of Beverly Glen. For the first few weeks, he had a job in a Westwood bookstore, but he overslept so many times, he was fired. His father, Kibe, wrote to him, saying that just as fathers in the old days gave their firstborn sons farms when they got married, he was sending Norm a hundred dollars a month until he got on his feet. It was a big help, but not enough to pay rent, utilities and phone, gasoline, and buy groceries. Norm halfheartedly looked for work, but sleeping past four limited his success.

It was lonely for me having no adult to talk to all day. Mark was a great kid, but he was just past three and I grew very hungry for adult conversation. Evenings, on the other hand, were great fun, with Mark and Norman drawing, and J. and I playing double solitaire, a lightning-fast game at which J. was a whiz. Sometimes we all played "I Doubt It"—a card game in which each player proclaims the winning cards he's holding. If the other players think he's lying, they say, "I Doubt It!"

But Norm—ever the man of integrity—always lost. Every time he tried to lie, he unconsciously brushed his hair back with his hand.

I liked that about him.

CHAPTER TEN

"Those who didn't care to wait would tend to drift off, stoned or
otherwise, and the Test would settle down to the pudding."
—Tom Wolfe, *The Electric Kool-Aid Acid Test*

Mark astonished me with his vocabulary, his perception, his beauty, his . . . *everything*. I was happy
beyond belief to have him with me again and did my best to keep up
with his unbridled energy. The fence around our backyard was made
of redwood planks, spaced just right for his small feet to climb up. I
warned him repeatedly not to go too high and came running from the
kitchen a few times to grab him just before he toppled over. I wasn't
big on discipline or "tough love," but one day I saw him going up and
thought, *I'll let him learn from experience*. Sure enough, he went ass over
teakettle and started howling. I went around to the sidewalk and
rescued him, scared but unhurt.

"Li'l Mama," he said to me, "dat wan't fun." And he never did it
again.

Life and gravity have a way of teaching us what we need to know,
and in those years, I scaled a few forbidden fences and took a few hard
falls myself. And it wan't fun.

Mervyn Nelson was directing *The Crawling Arnold Revue*—Jules
Pfeiffer's one-act, followed by a musical revue—at a large Hollywood

theatre, and I asked if I could try out. He had no inkling I could sing or dance but reluctantly agreed to let me come make a fool of myself. Well, I blew his ears off, if I do say so, and he cast me as Miss Sympathy, a social worker hired by snooty parents to cure their maladjusted son, Arnold, who comes home from work every day, puts down his briefcase, falls to all fours, and starts crawling. Miss Sympathy opts to crawl along with him, and of course, love blossoms. The second half of the show featured songs and sketches from the famous New York club Upstairs at the Downstairs, several numbers by the very clever Portia Nelson. A great show with two extra perks: I got to join the stage actors union, Actors' Equity Association, which was a big deal, and I lost seven pounds just from dancing! The costumer put Miss Sympathy in a beautiful blue silk frock—size six! I was so small, my head looked like a pumpkin on a stalk. But stunning! On the downside, both I and Jered Barclay, who was playing Arnold, got water on the knee from crawling and had to wear knee pads.

Many days I took Mark to rehearsal because Norm was still sleeping. Mark sat in the wings on a high stool, watching the proceedings, until our lunch break, when I'd take him home to Norm, who would watch him until I came home at six. I was earning enough to keep the household functioning and having more fun than I'd had in years. We opened with high hopes for the show. The next morning, a review in the *L.A. Times* began: "Intimations of disaster played like summer lightning around last night's opening of *The Crawling Arnold Review,* as the curtain was delayed twenty, then thirty, then almost forty minutes."

Alas, I've forgotten why we were so late with the curtain. Some last-minute trouble. And Hollywood wasn't ready for such an offbeat evening. A short play followed by a revue? What was *this*? Neither fish nor fowl. We ran only a few weeks and then I was out of a job again. But hey, I was a size six! For a while. My next job was another waitressing gig at Wil Wright's Ice Cream Parlor. Forty flavors. Twenty toppings. Two little macaroons with each order. One dollar an hour plus tips and all the ice cream I could eat. I sampled every variation of sundae possible, my favorite being black walnut with raspberry topping. After two weeks, I advanced from a size six red-and-white-striped Wil Wright's pinafore to a size eight. Then to a size ten. Then a twelve. I was heading for a size thirteen when I quit. The tips weren't good enough and the ice cream was *too* good. One night, I was the only waitress serving a private birthday party with twenty mothers and their children that lasted over two hours. The bill was over two hundred dollars, and they didn't leave a tip. Not a red cent! Now, that can hurt a hardworking waitress's feelings. Make her feel bad. Make her cry. Make her want to dump them in the cream vat.

I played the mother of the drowned boy in *The Bad Seed,* for which I received a glowing review saying I had a range that "covered a gamut of emotions from pleading to crowing" or something edifying like that. Then I played a tipsy wife in another John Hayes and Paul Lewis film, *The Grass Eater,* and then I played Poochie, a deranged girl who lives in a junkyard, prostituted by the yard's owner, who sends men to her little wreck of a trailer.

"Why not?" she says when asked to service them. "It only takes five minutes."

At last, I was no longer playing a waitress. I was playing a crazy whore! Hurrah!

John cast Norman as a lost soul who also lives in the wrecking yard, and he had several difficult, excellently acted scenes. This strange independent film is now called *Five Minutes to Love,* and *Walk the Angry Beach* is now called *Hollywood after Dark*. They can both be found on Netflix.com and in Hollywood at Sinister Cinema, along with *Angel's Flight*—the film noir performance I'm most proud of—which is often included in those wonderfully gritty film noir retrospectives.

And speaking of things getting gritty . . .

Norman had altogether stopped bathing, brushing his teeth, and shampooing his hair. I was baffled by this. He'd always been a slob, but this was way beyond normal slovenliness. We'd had sex exactly twice since getting back together, and now I couldn't stand to be in the same bed with him. He slept in the living room, leaving a brown smudge on the arm of the sofa. That man went eight months without bathing, shampooing, or brushing his teeth! J. Martene Pettypool moved out, unable to deal with the inescapable odor. An actor I was working with at Theatre East dropped out of our scene when he learned I was married to "Pig Pen."

"Norm, why are you doing this?" I asked. "Why would you go out of your way to make yourself so physically repulsive?"

"I want to find out who values me for my inner self," he said, "no matter what my exterior is like."

Well, I valued him for his inner self, but who could get close to it, for God's sake?

"What is it you want?" I asked. "Do you need to go off by yourself for a while?"

"I don't know," he told me, his eyes dull and bleak. "I can't think straight."

Now, there's a news flash. Clearly, he was suffering some sort of breakdown and our marriage was circling the drain again. It broke my heart to see him with Mark, who accepted him inside and out. During those difficult months, Norman created a marvelous cartoon painting on a huge piece of hardboard, an extravaganza of nursery-rhyme characters, and Mark adored it. I wish I could say I still have it, but it was lost in one of my innumerable moves.

John Hayes and I had been scrupulous about keeping our relationship on the set strictly professional, but desperate for help, I asked him to have dinner at our house one night. Norm was fidgety and sullen through the meal, then left the table and disappeared somewhere in the house. I put Mark to bed and sat at the table with John, feeling completely despondent.

"I've missed you," he said, and it took my breath away to hear it.

"I've missed you, too, John."

"Honey," he said, "this situation is sick. I want you and Mark to come back with me."

"And Mark?"

"Yes. And soon. Will you?"

"Yes." I nodded, but it tore my heart in two to think about telling Norman.

When I did tell Norman, he tightly said, "I knew it was only a matter of time. Do what you want, but I'm through. You'll never suck me in again."

I mentioned getting a divorce, but Norman didn't see any reason for that.

"Why bother?" he said. "I'm not going to get married again."

But I wasn't comfortable leaving it like that. I contacted Judge Caldwell again, and because Norman and I had actually gotten married a month before my divorce from Tom was final, he was able to make it an annulment. As Norman carried a box down the stone walk, moving out, John was coming up the walk, on his way in. They exchanged a curt nod.

"Good luck!" Norm muttered bitterly.

Norman made his exit from my life for a while, but you can pick up his story in Tom Wolfe's book *The Electric Kool-Aid Acid Test*. He joined up with Ken Kesey and the chemically adventurous Merry Pranksters. In fact, Norman drew that beautiful, iconic "Can you pass the Acid Test?" poster (though he seldom receives credit for having created it), which is still seen in college dorm rooms, head shops, and tattoo parlors.

"Norman, zonked, sitting on the floor, is half frightened, half ecstatic . . . ," wrote Wolf. "The Prankster band started the strange Chinese cacophony of its own, with Gretch wailing on the new electric organ. Norman got up and danced, it being that time."

Wait a minute . . . *Norman?* Got up and *danced?*

When I next saw Norm, years later, he told me he went on fifty LSD trips—forty-nine delicious and one really horrific, after which he quit. But for him, it was apparently a trip worth taking. He'd become patient and tranquil. And clean. He'd learned to value himself, inside and out.

⌐

"Keep your eyes on the highway!" John shouted. "Just in case we have to make a crash landing!"

He had taken flying lessons at Van Nuys Airport, gotten his license, and bought a little Cessna, but he was not a very confident pilot. The same dynamic held true for our relationship, as it turned out. To him, "back with me" meant Mark and I living a block away in a little unfurnished apartment at the rear of a two-story house. This felt like a double-cross to me. I slept on a mattress in the living room and put Mark in the bedroom in an actual bed, with a phonograph beside it, so he could play his favorite record, *The Wonderful World of the Brothers Grimm,* while falling asleep. I went back to Wil Wright's, shuffling babysitters. The tips were still spare, but I ix-nayed the ice cream and got down to a size ten. Then the people in the front house offered me a waitress job at their coffee shop on Hollywood Boulevard. Whenever I returned from a day off, Fran, the short-order cook, would remark, "Oh, kid, you shoulda been here yesterday. We were busier'n catshit!"

Oh, baby, I was prancin' in high cotton!

I kept that job a few months, until Mark came down with chicken pox, and the doctor quarantined us for a week. The couple fired me! Astonished, I scrambled for another job, which was several desperate weeks in materializing. (And would you believe it? Six years later, when I was on Broadway in a play with Dustin Hoffman, this couple came backstage to see me, sweet as pie, and like a dope I was nice to them, but I was thinking, *A pox on thee, you putzes!*)

I found a position setting type for a small newspaper, putting together articles claiming that the rabble-rousing Abraham Lincoln was part Negro and General Grant was a Jew who'd ruined the South. Desperate as I was, I refused to aid and abet these reactionary fools, so I answered an ad from Upjohn Pharmaceuticals looking for a "Private Secretary to the Regional Manager. Must type and take shorthand." Well, I'd never studied shorthand, but I convinced the boss I could write longhand really fast. And boy, did I learn to write fast. I kept that job eleven months, earning $95 a week but barely escaping being bored into stupefaction.

The afternoon of November 22, 1963. The boss burst in and announced, "President Kennedy has been assassinated in Dallas!" The entire company gave a joyous cheer. I sat stunned, noticing one dear older woman also sitting there in shock. I went to her desk and we touched hands as the others danced around the room, whistling exuberantly. Having witnessed the civil rights conflict since childhood, I knew that not everyone wanted to believe that all people are created equal. I was aware that not everyone was as inspired and filled with hope as I was when charismatic Kennedy beat out Nixon for the White House, but I would have expected this bigoted response from rednecks, not these Californians with whom I'd had lunch and played cards on breaks. For the first time, I realized what they really were.

A few weeks later, I got cast as the heroine's sidekick in a television drama called *I Make a Circle, You Make a Circle*—a sizable part requiring a week's work. Like most aspiring actors, I'd kept my showbiz ambitions a deep, dark secret from Upjohn, strictly under wraps, certain they would fire me if they knew about it. So I "got the flu" for a week, shot the TV show, then returned to typing out weekly reports and eating lunch with the hatemongers.

I was delighted when John and his cousin, Jay, invited me to share the rent on a big house in Studio City. Mark and I had a large, lovely bedroom, a small bedroom, and a bathroom to ourselves. Jay was very smart, and he and I played word games to our hearts' content. I enrolled Mark in a little preschool, where the cost was figured according to one's income. It wasn't a very good curriculum and he was bored to tears, but for two dollars a day I couldn't do any better.

"Mother," Mark asked me one day later that summer, "do I have a father?"

"Of course, sweetheart, everyone has a father," I replied.

He asked, "Where's mine?"

The question broke my heart. He hadn't seen Tom since that day in Pasadena when he was seventeen months old, so of course he didn't remember. Did I owe it to Mark to try again? Might Tom have softened in the intervening years? I was terribly nervous about calling, but a mother lion will go to any lengths for her cub, and my cub needed me to do this.

"Hello, Tom. How are you?"

"Oh. Hi, babe." Tom replied nonchalantly.

"Mark has been wanting to enroll in a five-day swimming class at the YMCA," I forged ahead. "But the class is at nine, and I have to be at work at eight. I was thinking if you took him and then dropped him off at preschool . . . well, the class is only an hour, and he really wants to learn to swim."

"Okay," he said, to my relief, but then added, "As long as it's only five days."

So for five days I dropped Mark at Tom's apartment before eight, and Tom took him to swim class at nine, then dropped him at the little preschool. Surely, Tom would quickly come to love this remarkable child, I thought. After the week was over, Mark could swim, but there was no follow-up from Tom. Mark never asked about his daddy again. He seemed mollified. Not me. In fact, I was angry.

"Maybe you could just help out with the cost of a better preschool," I suggested.

"Sure, babe," he said. "I'd like to. But I know I won't unless you enforce it legally."

"I could do that through a process server," I said.

"Great," he said. "Do that." Then he deftly avoided the process server all three times required by law, and that was the end of that.

⟶

John had begun going out alone, all but ignoring me, so one night I stopped him at the door and asked, "What's going on?"

"I've been thinking we should loosen the reins," he said.

Keep your eyes on the highway, kids, in case of a crash landing.

John was shooting another picture—without me—and one night Jay offered to watch Mark so I could visit the set, just to be with people for a while. There was a smart, funny fellow from Chicago, Marty Schlar, also visiting the set, and we started chatting. He invited me to his apartment to have a bite to eat, and I accepted. No hanky-panky, we agreed. And we meant it. In his big one-room studio, we were sitting on the daybed enjoying food and conversation when we heard an odd scrambling on the roof. We looked up and saw a large figure spread-eagled on the skylight, spying down on us. John Patrick Hayes had followed me and managed to climb onto the roof. He was shouting something, but his words were garbled through the glass.

"John! Climb down and come in for something to eat," Marty called to him, amused.

Moments later, in charged John, full of righteous Irish wrath.

"Rue! Come home. Now!" he demanded, and I followed him home, laughing all the way.

So let's see . . .

I was rotting at Upjohn. Tom didn't give a fig about Mark. John wanted me to loosen the reins, while keeping me haltered. A change was definitely in order, and like an angel from heaven, Mervyn Nelson came out from New York City to visit Theatre East.

"Rue, you're one of the two or three best actresses in the business," he told me, and I said, "Thank you!" but I was wondering, *Who are the two he considers better?* Maybe Kim Stanley and Geraldine Page, to whom I admittedly took a backseat—but not too far back.

"I'm directing an Off Broadway musical in October, and I want you to audition for the producers and conductor in September," he said. "New York's the place for you, Rue. You're New York material."

Well, hell, Mervyn, tell me something I don't know.

"Do you think you could be happy in New York?" I asked Mark the next day. "With no yard to play in?"

"Sure, Mother, I'll play inside," he said with his heart-melting, matter-of-fact sweetness.

It didn't take any more hippos to fall on me. The last week of July 1964, I gave Upjohn a week's notice and gave Hollywood the finger.

CHAPTER ELEVEN

"You will see things and say 'why': but I dream things
that never were and say 'why not'?"
— GEORGE BERNARD SHAW

I left everything in Los Angeles. My grandmother McClanahan's quilts, my diaries, most of my clothes, my old car, and
a whole lotta baggage, if you know what I mean. I dropped Mark
off with my parents at the Dallas airport—almost more than I could
bear—and met Melinda's new baby, Mimi, who was even then a special
sort of critter. My family, Lord bless them, didn't raise an eyebrow over
my move to New York. I guess they had gotten used to my behavior.

So New York City, *hyar ah come*!

With two hundred dollars saved from my job at Upjohn, plus two
hundred my parents gave me, I had enough to make ends meet for six
weeks. (That was 1964, remember. These days, you can hardly buy
lunch for that kind of dough.) Mervyn offered me an army cot in the
tiny office of his Manhattan apartment for a few weeks. No closet, so I
lived out of my suitcases, sharing the apartment with Mervyn's various
male friends, who came and went at all hours, and a French Canadian
traveling salesman, who occasionally bunked on the sofa. He asked me
out, but *Mas, non!* I didn't lay a hand on him. But *sacré bleu!* Was I lonesome. With a Capital Lone.

I knew only one or two people in New York, so I called the delightful Marian Hailey, who'd starred in that TV show I did while I was at Upjohn. She was busy, busy, busy with offers and agents and opportunities to which I had no access, subletting a gorgeous Central Park West apartment that belonged to the brilliant, aging movie actress Gladys Cooper.

"I'll let you know if one of the other actresses staying here leaves," Marian promised.

Meanwhile, I was stuck on the Army cot without even a Canadian to keep me warm.

And where was Mervyn? At the Paper Mill Playhouse in Bucks County, Pennsylvania, doing the delicious *Bus Stop,* starring Johnny Ray, pop music's heartthrob *du jour,* as Bo. Johnny Ray's huge hit "Cry" was all the rage, so it was a big deal when Mervyn arranged for me to audition for the role of Cherie—a role I'd played, loved, and was dead right for—in Johnny Ray's enormous living room. (Don't conjure any visions of the so-called casting couch. Mervyn was present.) It was a fabulous apartment, with an electric movie screen that rolled down across the windows in the huge living room. I was wide-eyed and intimidated—until I read a few scenes with Mr. Ray. I knew Cherie inside and out and played her to the hilt, but dear Johnny didn't cast me in the role. Mervyn later said it was probably because Johnny thought I would steal the show. (That's my story, and I'm stickin' to it.)

When *Bus Stop* opened, I went to see it. Johnny Ray was bone skinny, wore a hearing aid, and had a speech impediment. To compensate, he spoke very loud and threw himself about the stage like a windmill. The actress playing Cherie was lost in the melee. Heck, the *furniture* was in peril! So while it had seemed at first like a grand opportunity, that job would've been a dead end. Not to mention hazardous. One of those major disappointments that faded into quiet little islands of "Oh, well . . ."

After all, nobody's perfect for every role.

Except me, dammit! *I want to play every role!*

All right, not *every* role. Not the woman in *Misery*. Or *Medea*. And not Lady Macbeth. I don't want to play miserable, rotten—well, now, wait. I loved doing the rotten Miss Hannigan in *Annie* and miserable Madame Morrible in *Wicked*. So I guess I do want almost every role.

But I like the funny oddball characters best. Sort of like in life.

⟿

A room became available in the apartment with Marian Hailey. A bed! A closet! For a week. Then Marian got a job out of town and gave up the sublet, so I and Marian's roommate, Carol—a tall, buxom beauty of about twenty—had to look for our own digs. We sublet a place from another actress, Joan Darling, sharing the pull-out sofa in a tiny ground-floor studio. Enchanting! I was living in Greenwich Village! I walked down the sidewalk feeling like I owned the world. Carol and I peeked into Joan's closet. She'd left behind chic winter outfits and boots she wouldn't need in L.A. Oh, the temptation! She was a tiny thing, apparently, but one really chic black-and-white-checked ensemble fit me. I'm embarrassed to admit that I wore it out on the town a couple of times—with her black boots. Snazzy!

One brisk evening, Carol said, "I have a date tonight with a gorgeous stage manager, and we need a date for his friend. Would you be—"

"*Yes!*" No arm-twisting needed.

These two fellows showed up at our apartment, and wowzie-wow-wow. The stage manager, Oz, brought his funny, handsome actor pal Robert Guillaume, who'd recently done the musical *Kwamina* on Broadway (and later starred in his own TV series, *Benson*). Bob and I hit it off at once. Both men were black and slightly uncomfortable being out in public with us, even then, but we all went merrily off and had a wonderful evening. I was delighted when Bob called me a few days later. Carol and I had been displaced yet again, and Carol was moving in with Oz.

"I'm going to be out of town for a month," Bob said. "You can stay at my place. Come on over and I'll show it to you."

Perfect! His apartment was attractively put together. So was he. We listened to the album of *Kwamina,* and I developed an instant crush on his beautiful tenor. Playing "Goldilocks," we tried out the kitchen chairs. They were too small. We tried out the living room chairs. They were too large. Then we tried out the bed, and it was *juuust* right. I'd give that bed an A.

Bob departed and I moved in, playing *Kwamina* every night, kvelling over his voice.

Oh, yeah. I had a crush.

My first job in New York was Mervyn's *The Secret Life of Walter Mitty*. I had to audition four times, singing, then dancing, then reading, for the writers, for the conductor, for the choreographer, for the producers, for the mice in the corner—and, of course, for Mervyn. At my first audition, I waited in the wings, listening to a gloriously soaring soprano on stage. *Oh, Lord!* I thought. *I have to follow THAT?* As the owner of the golden lungs came off, I told her, "Wow! You sounded absolutely marvelous!"

"Thanks," she said. "I'm Loretta Rehnolds. Everybody calls me Lette."

"I'm Rue McClanahan. Nice to meet you."

"God, your hair is so thick," she said. "I've got this mosquito fuzz, so I'm acutely aware of anyone with good hair."

"Oh, yeah, my coarse Indian mane." I shrugged self-consciously. "Like a horse's tail."

I hadn't yet learned to take a compliment gracefully.

For my singing audition, I'd picked "Shy" from *Once Upon a Mattress,* the show that brought Carol Burnett fame, a song effective for loud if untrained voices. Lette and I made it through all four auditions, were cast in the show, and spent the next fifteen weeks rehearsing, then performing, sharing a dressing room with two other supporting

*Melinda and me
in our blue corduroy
frocks made by
Grandma Fannie,
with Mother.
Melinda hates this
picture of herself.
I think she's precious.*

*My dad, Bill, when he met
Mother. Woof!*

*Four aspiring Pavlovas
(I'm in the front).
Jacob's Pillow, 1953.*

*Doing the
Charleston with
my first fiancé,
Marino Grimaldi.
Oh, you kid!*

*Beauty Queen, University of Tulsa,
1956. Oo-la-la, no?*

Thomas Lloyd Bish,
twenty-three years old.

Tom and me at our wedding reception,
February 2, 1958. Erie, Pennsylvania.

Norman L. Hartweg,
twenty-two years old.

Mark with Norman and me in our backyard
in Aurora, Colorado, 1959.

Lette and I performing "Two Little Pussycats" as Hathel and Ruthie, the night we brought the house down. New York City, October 1964.

My first official publicity shot, New York City, 1964.

Final dress rehearsal of MacBird! *with Stacy Keach, 1966.*

Dylan, *1972 – a minor altercation with Will Hare.*

"The Bunkers Meet the Swingers," 1972, All in the Family.
Carroll O'Connor, Jean Stapleton, and Vincent Gardenia.

Brad Davis as my son in Crystal and Fox, *McAlpine Rooftop Theatre, New York City, 1973. (And Walt Gorney, playing Pedro.)*

The Greek Wedding. The Greek, me, and Norman Lear in a circle dance on the patio. November 6, 1979.

actresses. Lette had been hired for the heavy singing chores and to play the ditzy role of Ruthie. I was playing the equally ditzy Hazel and understudying the starring role of Willa Da Wisp. I got the brainstorm to play Hazel with a lisp, announcing at my entrance, "Hi, my name ith Haythel."

It got a huge laugh, and Mervyn said, "Keep it."

He called me on the Saturday before the Tuesday opening and said they'd decided to rewrite one of the stars' duets and give it to Hazel and Ruthie! It was one of those "The star's twisted her ankle and you two kids have to go on!" kind of opportunities.

"Do you think you can do it in three days?" asked Mervyn.

Did I ever!

"But you have to let me do the choreography," I told him, knowing the somewhat abrupt choreographer would have given us moves that might be troublesome for Lette, who was not a trained dancer. Neither of us liked that butch choreographer. For one thing, she called me "Blondie" in rehearsals, which always gave Lette a laugh but annoyed me no end.

"Hey, Blondie—change places with this one down here." Hmmph! *Blondie.*

Lette and I went into high gear, learning the new song with the conductor, Joe Stecko. It was a tricky piece called "Two Little Pussy-cats." I put together some simple but snappy choreography, we rehearsed till we were blue in the face, and we steeled ourselves to pull it off on opening night. We were nervous but excited—two firecrackers ready to pop. And pop we did! We brought the house down, and all the reviews raved about us the next day.

". . . just about steal the second act . . ."

". . . the most successful tune in the show . . ."

". . . stopped the show with 'Two Little Pussycats.' They do the number so smartly I wonder why Miss McClanahan had to overplay for the major portion of the show."

Hey! Overplay? *Moi?* Well, all right. That last one was less than a rave for me. (But see how honest I am? I didn't have to tell you that.)

This wonderful little musical ran only eleven weeks Off Broadway, but it's still done in community theatres and colleges all over the country, where I'm told the actress doing Hazel always plays her with a lisp. We made a cast album that can be found in "rare record" stores, and the music is marvelous. Lette's soprano can be heard soaring in the obbligati, clear as a buttonhook in the well water, as my father would say. If only the show had run long enough for us to make a real mark for ourselves! But big audiences didn't come soon enough. We were all unknowns. Brilliantly talented unknowns, but unknowns nonetheless. Walter Mitty's song "Confidence" was played before every football game for a few dozen years, however, so at least the composers made some moola, and I came away from the show with a new best pal—and an agent! I waited in line outside the post office in the pouring rain one afternoon and sent letters to seventy-some New York agents inviting them to come see me in *Walter Mitty*. Two actually came. One offered to represent me. And one is all it takes. I had taken a crucial step forward.

⤳

Lette and I became fast friends, and she was in on my adventure with The Italian from the get-go. In 1952, at the tender age of seventeen, he'd been cast in *The Golden Apple*—the youngest chorus dancer on Broadway. Now he was in the chorus of *Walter Mitty,* and Lette and I stood downstage of him during Act Two, our backs to the audience, while he did his specialty dance number.

"Look at those pecs!" Lette would mutter under her breath. "Look at that basket!"

During the first week of rehearsals—when the cast and crew romances almost always flourish—Lette started dating Joe, the conductor, and I started feeling some powerful chemistry with The Italian. As he and I were walking back from lunch one day, he said, "I'm waiting to hear if I got cast in *Galileo* at the Pittsburgh Playhouse. I'll take it if they offer it to me. If not, I'll stay in *Walter Mitty*."

"Well. Good luck," I said, but I was thinking, *Oh, dear God, please let him get* Galileo. *If he stays in our show, I'm sunk.*

The Italian didn't get *Galileo*. He got me.

The first night we spent together, I discovered something lovely: He smelled wonderful. A delicious, natural fragrance. No deodorant! I thought, *Nobody who smells this sweet can be* all *bad.* And I was right. He wasn't *all* bad. Early in our relationship, I had my first orgasm *ever,* and they continued from then on. He was damned good in bed: slow, patient, and sweet. Not at all the way he turned out to be while vertical. For FQ, he gets an A. (Husband Quotient would later turn out to be a Z—for zero.) In November, he asked me to move in with him in Little Italy, and like a little idiot, I did—with the understanding that options were still open.

John Hayes wrote that he'd been hired by a Long Island company to make industrial films and was flying his Cessna to New York. It was audacious of him, a rather inexperienced pilot flying cross-country, and I worried until he arrived safe and sound after a week aloft.

"I haven't stopped caring about you, Rue," he told me. "Let's try it again."

I said, "I'm seeing someone, John. I can go out with you during the week, but I have to reserve weekends for him."

It had always been my policy never to be sexually involved with two men at the same time, but that policy went out the window. As I compared them, each had qualities I did and didn't cotton to. I was leaning toward gentle Irish John, but he hated New York, which tipped the scales toward the volatile Italian, who once angrily threw an ashtray at me across the kitchen, which tipped the balance back toward John, who took me for a walk one afternoon and said he'd now decided he could happily live in New York, since I was there. The most important factor was my firm resolve to bring Mark back to live with me.

John hadn't been a friend to Mark or a good father to his own daughters. What would The Italian be like with Mark? Would John drift away from me again? He'd drifted before, and The Italian was the type to stick like wet cement. I needed time to explore both possibilities, but I was given an ultimatum by The Italian as I was leaving to meet John for dinner.

"You're behaving like a harlot! You should be ashamed!" he bellowed, blocking the door. "You're not leaving this apartment until you promise to break it off. *Tonight.*"

Backed against the wall, I felt guilty and scared, like a scarlet woman. I tried to get past him. "Promise! *Promise!*"

"I . . . I promise," I said meekly. "I'll tell John I can't see him anymore."

Remember, on *The Golden Girls,* how Sophia always said, "Picture this!" and then launched off into some bizarre tale? Well . . . picture this:

A restaurant. A cold rainy night. John and I at a table for two. John tells me he didn't have a job offer at all. He flew to New York to propose marriage to me. The man had flown for a week cross-country to propose to me.

Well. Would someone please help me off the floor? You'll need a shovel.

I had waited four years to hear those words! He wanted to marry me! *And* he wanted to help raise Mark! I stared at him in horror. One hour before, I had sworn to break it off with him. I had *promised.* And I had been brought up never to break a promise. I remember repeating, "I promised, John. I promised."

"You're making a terrible mistake, Rue. You're settling for second best."

I stammered, "But my word is my bond!" Or some such horseshit.

I actually felt honor-bound to uphold my promise; it was not just an excuse for all those other doubts. I was miserable because I knew John was right. The Italian was not the best man for me. And yet I kept thinking how standoffish John was with his two little girls and the whole rein-loosening thing and that double-cross last time . . . good God. What *should* I have said? Come on, now. You knew there would be a quiz on this. What are those all important words?

Let me think it over!

But did I say that? Are you kidding?

"I can't see you anymore," I told John miserably. Boggles the mind, no?

I'll never forget that vision of him. All six-four of him, standing under a yellow streetlight in the rain, tears streaming down his face—big six-foot-four tears—as I left him for a relationship I later wouldn't wish on my worst enemy. Oh, dumb, dumb, dumb. *Dammit!*

Shortly thereafter, I got a letter from Melinda saying she and Sheridan were going to start adoption proceedings unless I got Mark away from Mother, who was spoiling him rotten. She thought he'd be better off with her family. And I actually thought they could do it! Melinda told me later that she'd written that fateful letter merely to startle me into bringing Mark to New York. There in her little Texas house with her husband and children, she had no idea how hard I was struggling to get a foothold, how achingly I missed Mark, and how unprepared I was to support him. But at the time, that terrible letter threw me into a three-alarm swivet. I thought I had to bring Mark to New York. *Now*. Come hell or high water.

So when The Italian proposed (actually, he said, "Do you, um . . . maybe . . . want to get married . . . someday?"), all I could think of was that letter.

"How about next week?" I piped up.

He was somewhat taken aback, but I was desperate to have Mark with me. Maybe it would be possible with a husband, I thought. Round out the old family life, that sort of thing.

Not a good reason to get married. Neither is having regular orgasms.

Something I hadn't paid much attention to along the way—distracted as I was by the orgasms and all—was that The Italian had a chronic postnasal drip that caused him to make this . . . *snort*.

Well, I paid attention to it now. Criminy, did I pay.

One day, we were in a Greenwich Village restaurant and he was doing the snorting thing. Right there in front of people. I looked at the clock on the wall and timed the snorts. One every forty seconds. And I thought, *How am I going to stand this?*

That's 2,110 snorts a day . . . 14,770 snorts a week . . . 770,150 snorts a year.

For as long as we both shall live.

Yee-ikes. Would somebody please pass the Valium?

CHAPTER TWELVE

"Blessed be the ties that bind."

—Fontayne Jackson, at his lynching

Every now and then, as I lounge in bed eating a lovely breakfast—mango, muffin, black tea—I think of the thousands of breakfasts I have cooked. How, when, and for whom. And that breaks open one particular crystal-clear memory: Making Breakfast for The Italian.

I learned quickly how to crack two eggs without breaking the yellows; splash them lightly with bacon grease till they were beautifully white but still quivery; gingerly turn them with my New Homemaker spatula without disturbing their lovely shape; remove them at precisely the right moment, sliding them oh-so-carefully onto the spanking-clean plate; add two strips of flawlessly sizzled bacon, and—*voilà!*—the final touch: half a tomato hot from the broiler, decorated with a sprig of fresh parsley. And, of course, toast. Tawny brown. The pot of coffee. The pitcher of juice. Every morning.

Except when I made pancakes.

Or waffles.

Or French toast.

Also perfectly done.

On the Egg and Bacon Mornings, if I accidentally broke a yellow, the infraction was never overlooked by my meticulous spouse. To this day, I can hear his quiet pronouncement:

"You broke. The egg."

This implied that breakfast was now ruined, and I had been irredeemably careless and would probably go to hell. So nowadays, as I nibble at my mini-muffin, I fantasize about slowly upending the plate over his head, and as the broken yellows slide sinuously through his thinning waves and the tomato seeds drip into his ears, I chirp cheerfully, *"Bon appétit,* y'all!"

Each marriage—and each affair—holds particular culinary memories for me. The Italian Episode (and I use "Episode" here much as a doctor treating epilepsy: "Has he had any Episodes lately?") was noted for its highly regimented breakfasts and for two dishes concocted by His Nibs: Fettuccini Alfredo and kidneys in cream, each of which he prepared twice a year. These infrequent respites from my wifely duties were not given as time off for good behavior, as is the case in any decent penitentiary, but rather came up unexpectedly when he felt the urge to cook. He'd worked as a waiter at a popular Italian restaurant and apparently picked up these two tricks there. (As much as it pains me, I shall exercise restraint and not make a cheap joke here.)

Or maybe he learned them from his mother, one of the most gifted kitchen wizards ever born. She made heavenly pasta from scratch, delectable meats, cakes as sweet as that sweet lady herself, so light they had to be weighted down with rocks. I'd sit at her table and weep with gratitude for the extraordinary taste marvels she set before us. Her husband, The Italian's dad and role model, would take a bite and sourly remark, "You ruined the meatballs, stupid."

This while actual tears of bliss ran into my spaghetti!

I am what's known as an "extreme taster," meaning I experience a heightened reaction from my taste buds. (We did a taster test in a college zoology class; one of my parents came out "taster," one tested "extreme taster," and my sister's litmus paper tested "cuter than a bug.") Exquisite tastes move me to tears of rapture the way great art does. In Florence I stood before Michelangelo's *David* and wept help-lessly. It was the only time I'd ever witnessed man-made perfection (not counting Raquel Welch). Of course, this tendency for waterworks gets a little embarrassing, but it's not a big problem, since truly heav-enly tastes come along so rarely. I never worried about disgracing myself over the cuisine at glitzy showbiz banquets. The food at those swanky Hollywood affairs generally falls short of what you'd expect, given both the amount spent and the overblown importance of such events. (In other words, *it sucks*.)

But back to the fettuccini and the kidneys.

The Italian's fettuccini was superb. Full of cream and butter. As for the kidneys, this was my virgin encounter with that concoction. Never had it before, ate it many times during our marriage, and haven't tasted it since. Not that it wasn't good. The man slaved over those smelly kid-neys for half an hour, patiently trimming away the stringy white gris-tle, making them fit to be immersed in the cream and . . . my God, that must have been fattening! But we were young. It was the sixties. We gobbled bacon and eggs, kidneys in cream sauce, Fettuccini Alfredo. I baked chocolate-chip cookies, peanut butter cookies, sugar cookies, and Mark's favorite, orange poppyseed cake. We had ice cream for dessert—*Lordy!* How did we stay so svelte? Now I look cross-eyed at 2 percent milk and can't zip my Levi's. And cream? Please! I don't even buy eggs anymore unless I have houseguests, or if I need them for the odd recipe.

Bea Arthur contends that all my recipes are odd. Bea is a super cook, and so was Estelle. As for Betty White and me—our talents lie . . . *ahem* . . . elsewhere. (We can tap-dance.)

My father still wanted his fried eggs for breakfast when he was ninety.

"Bill, they're not good for you," I said.

He just smiled rakishly and smacked his lips.

⟿

The Italian and I were married in a brief civil ceremony on a cold spring afternoon in April 1965. We drove up the coast of Maine for a three-day honeymoon. The first evening, we stopped at a little restaurant out at the end of a peninsula. I had fish. What kind of fish, I don't remember. But definitely fish. Back at the motel, I threw up most of the night. Frankly, I don't think it was the fish. I think my subconscious was saying, "Kid, there's something fishy here."

He insisted we have sex every night. Because he wanted it. For the most part, that was okay, because he was a different person during sex, warm and sweet, not at all like he was while vertical. During our interminable heated arguments, he was utterly *alien*—harsh as barbwire, unyielding as a toothache. He insisted we *not* go to sleep until I agreed with him, whatever the difference of opinion. And not in a "let's not go to sleep angry" way—it was more like Stockholm syndrome, where a captive is eventually conditioned to admit that black is white, up is down, in is out. This lasted seven years, the longest of my first five marriages. But only because I dug in my heels and doggedly refused to give up. I'd had two divorces and was darned if I'd have another one—ever. *Ever, ever, EVER!*

While Mark was finishing out first grade in Ardmore, I played the wife, Linda, opposite Vincent Gardenia's Willie Loman in *Death of a Salesman* at Moorestown Theater in New Jersey. I was really too young for Linda, but the plum role was too good to resist. With only one week to prepare that complex play, we worked on blocking and our characters' motivations during rehearsal, then gathered in the lobby afterward, running lines for hours. I came to admire Mr. Gardenia as an actor and a fine person. Vincent was also impressed with me.

"You'd be ideal for summer at the Hampton Playhouse," he told me, and put in a good word with the owners, Al Christi and John Vari, who hired me for three months, to begin in June. The Italian was hired at a playhouse in Minnesota and was upset that we'd be spending the summer apart.

"That's showbiz," I pointed out. "I'm just happy we're both employed."

And I was! Happy as a clam. He was as happy as a—oh, how about a piranha?

I loved the Hampton Playhouse! The whole cast lived in a three-story house run by a delightful lady named Maddie. We had one week to prepare each play, which ran for a week while we rehearsed the next one. Demanding, to say the least. One week, *Mary, Mary,* the next, *Ladies' Night in a Turkish Bath,* then *Tobacco Road*—with real dirt covering the stage, which set off my hay fever something fierce.

The first week, Al and John threw a get-acquainted party for the cast and crew at Maddie's and, to my utter surprise, The Italian suddenly showed up. He hadn't liked the Midwestern summer stock company. Disgruntled, he took his suitcase up to my room, I following.

"I'm sorry it didn't work out for you. Why don't you come down and meet everyone?" I cajoled. "Come on. The party's in full swing. It'll be fun."

I introduced him around and got him some food, and everyone welcomed him heartily, full of high spirits, laughing. I was having a swell time kibitzing with my castmates, full of *joie de vivre,* when Husband came over and instructed me to say goodnight.

"Come up to the room with me now."

"I need to get to know the company," I said. "Let's stay a little longer."

"We're newly married. You should be with me. *Right now!*"

Crestfallen, I said goodnight to everyone and slunk upstairs. He remained miserable and hard to get along with the rest of the summer. I learned and performed some challenging roles, doing my best not to be distracted by Little Caesar's dampening presence.

"Come Take a Bite of My Apple" in Burlesque,
The Hampton Playhouse, 1965.

"We'd like you to come back next summer," John and Al told me at
the end of the season. "We'll find some parts for your spouse, if that
makes your decision easier."

Boy, did it! Maybe if he were acting, he'd be less of a horse's patootie. We returned to New York and Mother brought Mark up to start second grade. I had located a good school on East Eighty-second Street, only two blocks from our rent-controlled fifth-floor walk-up on East Eightieth. Mark made a friend right away: Phillip Arndt, a tall, handsome boy who was half Chilean Indian. We moved uptown, and oh, was I glad to get out of The Italian's gloomy apartment with its black velvet drapes and bathtub in the kitchen! I hoped maybe our married relationship would improve.

Oh, ha ha, and *ha*. Sure.

The apartment on East Eightieth had a mouse-size bathroom, no room for a kitchen table, bedrooms barely big enough for a bed and chest of drawers. I asked Husband if he could build a small kitchen table on hinges to lower and raise from the kitchen wall and a similar piece for Mark's bedroom on which to attach his Marklin train track, which I'd bought at FAO Schwarz the previous Christmas. To my surprise, Husband built those two tables quite well. I'd had no idea he could do carpentry. We scrounged old furniture from friends and from the street: a sofa, chair, two kitchen chairs, some lamps, two beds, and other sundries.

I found two big trunks on the curb and painted one green and one blue. The blue one functioned as Mark's toy box. We used the green one as a table in the living room, and in it I kept Mark's drawings. Unearthly creatures in violent combat. Dinosaurs fighting to the death. I still have his meticulously made flip pads of stories—the kind you flip through to make a "movie" appear—most of which ended violently. Those drawings worried me. They were so full of turmoil. On our little black-and-white TV, Mark watched *Popeye, Mighty Mouse, Bullwinkle*. Heroes fighting evil. Does that tell you something? It told me something.

A clothing budget was out of the question, but one day I ran across an ancient cast-iron Singer sewing machine, which I bought for forty dollars on layaway. Those were the days of minidresses *way* above the knee; simple designs that could be made from two yards of material. I stood outside store windows sketching dresses I liked, then cut patterns from newspaper. I scouted out some fabric for a dollar a yard—linings fifty-nine cents, thread and finishing tape for pennies—and *voilà!* Three new summer dresses for less than four bucks each! All the same design, but various fabrics for a different look. People stopped me on the street to remark on my little white eyelet frock with yellow flowers. That eyelet number was the winner. I wonder if I still have it. My Shirley Temple doll might fit into it, or I could use it for a sleeve. I couldn't make men's shirts or pants, but I did whip up a short Japanese kimono for The Italian. He didn't like it, but I thought it was snazzy and wore it a lot. I kept that thing into the late seventies, which was a lot longer than I kept him!

Husband worked off and on in telephone sales and as a bartender in various places, and I had a few kit-and-caboodle acting jobs. In mid-October I was offered two plays in Moorestown, both to be directed by Arthur Allen Seidleman: *Cat on a Hot Tin Roof,* playing Sister Woman, and *Romeo and Juliet,* playing the Nurse.

"Are there any roles open for my husband?" I asked, and they agreed to cast him as Brother Man in *Cat,* so Mother came up to stay with Mark while we went off to New Jersey for three weeks.

"I hate this role," groused The Italian. "I hate Seidleman."

Good grannies! He hated life in general, I guess. I stayed on for *Romeo and Juliet,* but The Italian went back to New York. Mother returned to Ardmore and Husband laid down the law, "I refuse to be a baby-sitter." So I took a small apartment near the Moorestown school and enrolled Mark in their second grade. They were teaching arithmetic by a new method that totally confused Mark—as did everything else about the new school, which was drastically different from the New York school he'd just been getting used to.

I was equally befuddled by the Nurse role. Arthur Allen Seidleman had cut that juicy part to shreds, eliminating most of the Nurse's lines.

"We need to throw the attention onto Romeo," he said. "This actor has been called the Romeo of the decade."

I had to stifle a laugh. The Romeo of the *decade*? He wasn't the Romeo of the *week*. This turkey was not a top-notch rendition of Shakespeare's masterpiece. To make matters worse, poor Mark got the mumps. I didn't want to leave him but had to ask our landlady to watch him while I performed. One night after I got home, he was still awake, having feverish hallucinations of toy soldiers marching over the bottom of the quilt toward him.

"Here they come, Mother! Look! There they are!"

"It's the fever, honey. It's just your imagination," I tried to explain, but it took a good half hour to calm him down enough to get to sleep. Poor little guy.

The summer of 1966, both Husband and I had jobs at the Hampton Playhouse. Mother came up and roomed with Mark at Maddie's house. Husband was not pleased. He was also not pleased with the roles he was given to play. In fact, he wasn't pleased with much of anything.

I, however, was delighted with my terrific roles that summer. I played Maggie, the tortured Marilyn Monroe character in *After the Fall,* and the wild cat dancer in *A Funny Thing Happened on the Way to the Forum.* The costume department was swamped, so I sewed my own little leopard-print ears, bra, and bikini bottom with a curled tail. I also did a specialty ballroom duo with the show's choreographer for *The Sound of Music,* in which I played the vain and silly Baroness. In the final flourish of the dance, my partner lifted me overhead at center stage under a huge chandelier. One night, as we exited, the chandelier fell, smashing into a jillion pieces. Shaken, I looked at the mess onstage, thinking, *I was under that five seconds ago!*

I wasn't that lucky with The Italian. One late-summer night in our bedroom, I objected to something he said, and he slapped me hard across the face and warned, "You are never to display disagreement or anger toward me again. Or you can expect much worse than a slap."

Playing the Baroness in The Sound of Music,
just before the chandelier fell.

Shocked to my roots, I stood trembling, not a doubt in my mind that he meant it.

The season ended, and we loaded the car to go home to New York. Mother had given Mark a kitten a few weeks before, but Husband snapped, "We're not taking that thing with us."

Mark looked up at me, blinking back tears, breaking my heart. Mother was silently furious. But I was afraid to argue. We drove back to Manhattan in silence. Without the kitten.

One should always take note of how a prospective husband's father treats his wife, but alas, I was married to The Italian before I caught his father's act, the sadistic, humiliating way he treated his darling wife, Olga. It explained a lot—a little too late. During one of his many attempts to whip me into shape, The Italian brayed at me, "It's the wife's duty to wait on her husband, keep his house clean, and bring him his pipe and slippers!"

Staring at this dinosaur, I asked, "And what, pray, is the *husband's* duty?"

Stumped, he stomped off, but after a few seconds returned triumphantly and said, "To mop the kitchen and take out the pail!"

In his father's house, that was the husband's job. No man in my family or, indeed, my acquaintance back home would be caught dead mopping the kitchen. But all his life, The Italian had watched his dad do it, so he did it, docile as a lamb. Family tradition.

More effective than hypnosis.

⌒

In September 1966, Mark entered third grade at his Eighty-second Street school, happy to see his good buddy Phillip again. I was gainfully employed as a lady of questionable repute in the musical *Take Me Along,* starring Tommy Sands and Tom Bosley, at a theatre within commuting distance of home. My agent submitted my picture and résumé to the producers of *MacBird!,* a new play to be done at The Village Gate. This was heavy stuff, a political satire speculating about LBJ orchestrating the Kennedy assassination, just as Macbeth murdered King Duncan with Lady Macbeth hectoring him to do it. My photo was submitted for Lady MacBird, a send-up of Lady Bird Johnson, but she was a brunette, so the producers didn't want to see me.

"Call them back," I said. "Tell them I do an authentic Texas drawl. And I'm a brunette."

I restyled the dark wig I'd worn in *The Secret Life of Walter Mitty,* knocked them on their—*ears*—and was hired as Lady MacBird.

What a show! All the actors were as yet unknown: Stacy Keach, only twenty-five then, did magnificently well as MacBird, the Scottish-Texan despot, in a leather kilt and cowboy boots. Cleavon Little was brilliant as one of the three witches. William Devane was terrific as Robert Ken O'Dunk (and I see he's been busy lately playing Secretary of Defense Heller on 24). The rehearsals were thrilling, the sword-fighting energetic and exciting, the roles complex. The script was dark and riotously funny, enlarged from a treatise by Barbara Garson, a Berkeley student. My role as Lady MacBird was almost impossible to decipher. It didn't really follow the chronology of the Shakespeare text.

"Why did you scramble her part?" I asked the writer, hoping for some insight on how to play it.

She replied, "Oh, I just stuck the role in because it was necessary to include Lady MacBird. I didn't give it any thought. You figure it out."

So I was on my own, with what help I could get from the hot-tempered young director, who didn't offer much, but I got laughs and had a helluva good time in my chiffon dresses and Texas drawl. The play got stupendous reviews and was sold out for months. We had several bomb threats and had to vacate the premises while crews searched the theatre, but nobody ever blew us up. Lots of important personages came to see it at the Village Gate, and later, in the summer of '67, we moved uptown to Circle in the Square.

There was plenty of drama backstage, too. Every actor was considered for dismissal during rehearsals, since whenever a new play is in trouble, the producing entities always think a cast replacement will solve the problem—though that is rarely the case. Meanwhile, the director, a tightly wired, twenty-five-year-old New Yorker, was embroiled in a riotous, hateful love affair with the producer, an English blonde of thirty . . . something. She visited his closet one night and slashed all his clothes to shreds. Someone was always angry. The Vietnam conflict was being actively protested in public meetings and marches, and Bill Devane was obsessed with the cause, cursing a blue streak. Every other word he uttered was "fuck."

"Those fucking empty-fucking-headed shmucks! We've got to fucking get out there and stop this fucking stupidity!" And the like.

During the run of *MacBird!,* both Husband and I auditioned for several playhouses, including the Hartford Stage Company. I was offered a job, September through May of '68, for $175 a week. They said they would also hire my husband. For $125 a week.

"Couldn't you make each of our salaries an equal $150?" I asked. "And please, don't tell my husband I requested it."

They agreed and, of course, we accepted. When I gave two weeks' notice, I had been in *MacBird!,* earning the Off Broadway minimum of fifty-five dollars a week, for nine months.

Just before we left for Hartford, I came home from the theatre one night and saw, crouching under the stairwell, a small frightened black cat. I took him upstairs and, surprisingly, Husband agreed we could keep him. He was sometimes whimsical that way. Mark named the cat Tyrone, and we all moved to Hartford for the fall and winter season of 1967, settling into a cozy two-bedroom within walking distance of Mark's school and fifteen minutes from the playhouse.

Rehearsing one play all day, then playing another play at night, my time with Mark was even more limited than it had been in New York, but The Italian's mother was happy to ride the bus across town to stay with him, and I was relieved beyond words to have her there. I came home from afternoon rehearsal every day to make dinner and be with Mark for a couple of hours. Olga made dinner for her monster husband (who refused to let her learn to drive and told her if she ever tried to leave him, he would kill her), then took the bus to our place for the evening.

I was given leading roles in *Skinflint Out West, The Threepenny Opera,* and several other shows and played the frumpy maid in Noël Coward's *Hayfever,* a play I loved—though, of course, I wanted to play the lead! The Italian was displeased with every part he was given, even the large role of the roué in *Hayfever*. He was actually very funny, playing the stiff, stuffy role with humor and skill. Whattaya know? He was hilarious. But he wasn't happy with it.

And if The Massah ain't happy, ain't nobody happy.

⁓

That fall, a letter from J. Martene Pettypool brought news that hit me like an avalanche.

Rue, did you know Norman was in a terrible car accident? He's paraplegic now.

I called the Hartweg home in Ann Arbor, and there he was on the phone: cheerful, working on his master's degree at the University of Michigan, living at home for the time being. And he said yes, he had been in a car wreck in April of 1966, on his way to New York for an interview as drama critic for *The New Republic*. He'd been traveling with two friends, Evan Engber and a woman called "Marge the Barge," to share the driving. Norm drove from L.A. to Reno, where, exhausted at three in the morning, he turned the wheel over to Marge. Evan was sleeping in the back. Norm fell asleep in the passenger seat. None of them was wearing a seat belt. Just out of Reno, he was jarred awake by a thunderous cacophony of crashing sounds. He was thrown forcibly from the car, skidding over forty feet on the pavement. The next thing he knew, he was on his back, staring up at a beautiful black Nevada sky full of stars.

But he couldn't move his legs.

Evan and Marge, only minimally injured, knelt over him. Medics appeared on the scene and he was taken to a Reno hospital, a chunk gouged from his forehead, another chunk from his right arm, his spinal column broken just above the waist. For the next eleven months, he was rotated from his back to his stomach until he could be moved to his parents' house in Ann Arbor. He never asked the driver what caused the crash, but he was told they'd run through a roadblock of sawhorses and warning signs. I've always figured she fell asleep at the wheel.

He was the same old ebullient Norm. No emotions. Just the facts, ma'am, and funny anecdotes about the other patients at the Reno hospital. I decided to visit him in Ann Arbor over our short holiday break. Husband objected vociferously, but I went anyway. Norm's brother, Jerry, met my plane in Detroit and drove me to Ann Arbor. Norman was in a wheelchair but quite hearty. His sister, Joyce, was also there, and we had a wonderful Christmas. The Hartwegs were still funny, smart, and very devoted to one another. God, they were great.

I had to get back to Hartford to open a play on New Year's Eve, but Norm and I resumed our voluminous correspondence. He wrote to me about his job as counselor in a boys' dormitory, and I wrote back about Mark's fascination with Jean-Claude Killy and the Winter Olympics. Norm wrote to me about the work he was doing toward his Ph.D. in philosophy, and I wrote back that Tyrone (oops, *he* was a *she*) had delivered three kittens, but one was dead, so Mark did a drawing of Tyrone and her kittens, with a gravestone representing the dead one. (I still have it.)

The kitten incident had been the latest in a string of people, places, and things that rankled The Italian. When the final play closed, I told him, "Mark and I are going to visit Norman."

"That's the last straw!" ranted Husband. "If you go, we're through! I'm leaving you!"

As you wish, love-cheeks, I thought, but out loud I just said, "Fine."

After all, I wasn't allowed to argue.

Norman wheeled out of the Ann Arbor house, and he and Mark had instant rapport, as always. We spent a marvelous time together. Kibe, Norm's dad, was curator of the Herpetology Department (fish and reptiles) at the university, and we went to visit his pal, who had built a rain forest room onto his house with all sorts of tropical animals. Mark had read a lot about tropical animals but had never seen them in the flesh. He still talks about that exciting afternoon. Mark and his friend Phillip flew to Oklahoma for the summer, and I flew home to New York. The Italian had made good on his threat to leave me, so I happily moved in with another actress from Hartford who shared her posh Upper East Side flat with me while I looked for a place. I was stunned to learn that she earned money by climbing into bed with an elderly man, who paid her to simply lie next to him since he couldn't perform sexually. First time I'd ever heard of that!

I found a tiny place on East Eighty-third and Madison, two blocks from the best public school in Manhattan, where Mark would enter fifth grade in September. He could walk to Central Park and the Metropolitan Museum of Art. Since there was no kitchen, I got a secondhand hot plate and a roaster oven and washed dishes in the bathroom. A friend had furniture he needed to store, so his sofa bed, chairs, and lamps became our furniture for the next year. Bill, Mother, and Melinda came to visit that September, and Bill built a dandy loft bed for Mark, completing it in jig time despite his cussing indictment of the limited facilities offered by New York lumber stores.

Mark did better at the new school than he had anywhere else. He was cast as the Prince in the school play, and he was marvelous. That is the only time I ever saw him act on the stage. He was very good, but he didn't want to be an actor. Who could blame him? Besides, he was interested in paleontology and art just then.

Meanwhile, this Little Miss Nobody was clawing her way up a very roughly graveled mountain, with hundreds—no, *thousands*—of other Little Miss Nobodies right beside her. And some of them had good connections! Dear reader, it was monumentally difficult. And for any aspiring actress who may be reading this, best she should know what it can really be like. Murderous! Full of dumb jobs only laughingly associated with acting—all paying the hot Equity minimum of fifty-five clams a week. Or whatever it is these days.

"Come back to Ardmore and open a dancing school. Live a normal life!" Mother begged about ten jillion times over the years, but for me it simply wasn't an alternative. This was do or die. I had the talent, I had the drive, and I knew it was only a matter of time and luck.

Unless Life intended to play some monstrous joke on me, that is.

That black possibility haunted me every day.

CHAPTER THIRTEEN

～

"England and America are two countries
separated by a common language."

—GEORGE BERNARD SHAW

*T*he next couple of years were a trip to the carnival, complete
with roller coaster (hold on to your cookies!), fun-house mirrors (boo!), and merry-go-round (grab that brass ring!).

Enough time had passed since my last waitressing gig that I was
finally eligible for unemployment as an actor. Standing in the M line
one day, I looked over to the B line and saw Tom Bish. I wasn't even
positive it was him, but I ran and hid in the ladies' room anyway. When
I returned to the end of my line, he was gone. I'd heard he was a salesman at Brooks Brothers, so I knew he was in New York, but I certainly
didn't want to run into him.

In August 1968, I auditioned for a new Broadway comedy with
music, *Jimmy Shine* by Murray Schisgal, starring (let's have a big ol'
WOWZIE right here) Dustin Hoffman! The role was a prostitute visited by the virginal seventeen-year-old Jimmy in a cat-and-mouse
scene, culminating in a nose-to-nose confrontation, he down to his
skivvies and shirt, she in black bra and panties. She whips open the
closet, out bursts her boyfriend, and Jimmy leaps out the window. A
memorable, albeit "cameo" scene, with Dustin as the naive kid and me

as the jaded thirtysomething crook. (Dustin was actually thirty-one, and I was thirty-four.)

At the audition, I "read" the scene (I had it memorized) for director Donald Driver and the producers. They called me back to read with Dustin. We clicked. I got it! My first Broadway play! One of the best-written little roles I'd ever done. I would also mix with the crowd in the party scenes, singing and dancing in far-out costumes befitting the liberated, psychedelic sixties. Rehearsals began at the theatre we'd actually be playing in, the Brooks Atkinson on West Forty-seventh, which was a boon to the actors and a testament to the faith the producers had in this production. No bleak rehearsal hall with tape on the floor. The actual stage itself! A luxury!

Dustin was red-hot from his movie *The Graduate,* so his fans were legion—particularly adolescent girls, who wanted to eat him with a spoon. He was creative, energetic, and funny, always acting the clown, not at all stuck on himself. Murray Schisgal was still rewriting the script, and some actors gave Driver trouble over suggested changes, but Dustin took it all in stride. He had his character down pat and was undeniably the star of the show. I loved watching him work, but in performance he kept ad-libbing the scene he had with me. He'd stick to the script for a few performances, then start to ad-lib again, so every two weeks or so, I had to request a cleanup rehearsal, which he always attended without complaint. Throughout the years, I've watched his talent evolve, and I am so proud to have worked with him.

In the fall of 1968, we took the show out of town to try it out, two weeks in Philadelphia, four in Baltimore. Mother came to New York to be with Mark while I was on the road, and Bill tolerated her absence because he knew this was the biggest break I'd ever had. Schisgal was rewriting every day, changing lines, changing scenes. The costume department changed our party garb almost nightly. I started out in an orange mini with a yellow boa, then everyone was put in men's white shirts and dark ties for one night, then the whole party switched back to the original outfits—with the addition of a huge orange wig for me. Spare no expense! Full steam ahead!

Our last week in Baltimore, Schisgal took me aside and gave me directions on how he wanted me to play the scene, quite different from what Driver had directed. I tried to make the two irreconcilable viewpoints work for three performances—oh, how I tried!—but the conflict was making me frighteningly insecure. I asked Driver for help, and he hit the ceiling.

"*What?*" he exploded. "The *writer* is giving you *direction?*"

Schisgal was thereafter forbidden to speak to the actors about the play. It's an unwritten rule of the theatre that writers may not direct actors. Chaos will almost always ensue. I went back to Driver's directions and the scene was funny again. Then the producers fired Driver and brought in another director, then another—but none of them tampered with that scene, thank God. It was money in the bank. When the show returned to New York, we opened to rave reviews and were sold out through the run. Hordes of teenage girls came to see their new idol, who even played a snatch of classical music as he passed by a piano in one scene. Classically trained, dontcha know.

Mother and Bill came to see the play with Mark, bringing me a new Singer sewing machine and a very handsome stand-up thread-and-accoutrements box. (I still use that thread box.) Before the show, I took us all to a Greek restaurant I loved. We ordered all manner of Greek dishes, finishing with American coffee. Bill, who'd been quiet all through dinner, took a sip and commented, "Well, at least the *coffee's* good."

He was an Oklahoma meat-and-'taters man and could do quite well without moussaka and spanakopita, thank you. But he and Mother were proud of me. I was in a great show. Mark was happy at his new school. He and Phillip Arndt were still fast friends, trekking often to the Museum of Natural History and Central Park. Life was going splendidly. *But . . .*

Question: Why does there always have to be that *but*?

Answer: Because it's Life, darlings! Every loaf of bread must have its heel.

The Italian started coming over to visit, and I felt myself being sucked back into my old insecurity and panic. Mother came to New York for Christmas, and to her dismay and mine, The Italian showed up and stayed the whole not-so-jolly evening. Mark delighted in his new Marklin Train cars and other toys and politely accepted the clothes Mother and I gave him. Mr. Italy tried to be cheery, but just having him there dumped a big fat cow patty on our spirits.

Shortly after the holidays, a brutal snowstorm put buses and taxis out of commission for over a week. I had to walk from East Eighty-third and Madison to West Forty-seventh near Eighth, a long haul in snow up past my knees. On matinee days, I slogged home, made Mark's dinner, and high-stepped back through the white stuff for the evening show, happy as a speckled pup to be on Broadway. I'd have snowshoed downtown from Siberia if I had to. All over town, the few cars with snow tires offered rides. In emergencies, New Yorkers really do come forth.

⁓

I kept urging The Italian again and again to go with me to marriage counseling, but he felt a Real Man wouldn't be caught dead in therapy. But about the time of the big snow, a Real Man told The Italian that he and his wife had gone to counseling and it had saved their marriage, so Macho Man reluctantly agreed to try it. We met with our counselor, Mandrake Penobscot, who was impartially insightful—brilliant even—picking up on the esoterics of our relationships with our parents and each other. Manny, as he was called by his patients, asked us to include Mark in a session. Mark sat on a stool, stiff as a stone, answering in monosyllables. I'd never seen him like that.

After fourteen sessions, Manny announced, "In all my years of practice, I've advised only one couple to divorce. Only one. You are definitely the second. I think you should end the marriage. And I strongly advise each of you to seek individual therapy." He suggested that The Italian meet with a female therapist, I with a male, since we both needed help dealing with the opposite sex. Manny already had fourteen weeks of background on me, so he offered to take me as his client at a rate I could afford.

One night, Prince Charming picked me up at Penobscot's office after my session, and by the time we had walked to the corner, we were enmeshed in an argument. He became so angry and irrational, I was frightened when he marched into the subway and onto a northbound train.

"Don't we need to go south?" I asked meekly.

He didn't reply. Simply couldn't admit he was wrong. Stations whizzed past. After a while, we were up in the Bronx, heading for Canada. Finally, when he could no longer ignore it, he wordlessly stomped out the door and we crossed over to the southbound trains.

Getting on the wrong train is no big deal, but his response was insane—as if by force of will alone he could make the whole of New York State rotate like a lazy Susan to prove he hadn't made a mistake. And I realized I was doing much the same thing. Penobscot had advised me to end the marriage. Did I? Hell, no! I was neurotically resisting that divorce, stuck on a damn train to the North Pole.

And folks, I really wasn't interested in trying out an Eskimo.

⁓

My L.A. friend Jered Barclay, the star of *The Crawling Arnold Review,* came to New York to direct *Tonight! In Living Color!* at The Actors' Playhouse, Off Broadway. It was an evening of two one-acts by the then-unknown A. R. Gurney, and Jered wanted me and the terrific Tim O'Connor to play Betty and Bill in *The Golden Fleece.* The second play, *The David Show,* featured a fabulous cast, including the gorgeous

Holland Taylor and F. Murray Abraham, who had started out as a Fruit of the Loom underwear guy and ended up nominated for an Oscar. Not exactly chopped liver. I knew it was a great show, but I had no idea *The Golden Fleece* would prove to be a turning point in my life.

The play is set in a suburban meeting hall, where locals have been invited to hear Betty and Bill's famous friends, Jason and Medea, tell the inside story of their turbulent marriage, which culminates (big surprise) with Medea slaying their children. A funny but powerful script, and Tim and I played the boots off it. At the opening-night party, I was seated across the table from our producer's father-in-law.

A guy named Norman Lear.

"Your performance was amazing," he said. "I hope I'll be able to hire you someday."

"Oh, thank you. What are you working on?" I asked, bedazzled.

"A movie called *Cold Turkey*. Then I'm going to Hollywood to get into TV production."

Cold Turkey was hilarious, and two years later, in 1971, Lear's *All in the Family* made its shatteringly successful debut and changed sitcoms forever with its edgy writing, daring subject matter, and fall-down-funny characters.

And bless his heart, Mr. Lear did not forget me.

~

The Golden Fleece got great reviews, but the second play didn't fare so well, and we closed after a few weeks. I was called to audition for *Who's Happy Now?,* a new play by Oliver Hailey. They wanted me for the role of the wife, Mary, but when I read the play, I knew I was made to play the marvelous mistress, Faye Precious. Through my agent, I wangled an audition for both roles. As Mary, I wore a proper little dress and modest hairdo. Then I dashed to the ladies' room, got into an off-the-shoulder peasant blouse, dangly earrings, and blond floozy wig, and came out to read for Faye. Perplexed, Oliver Hailey and the director, Stanley Prager, now wanted me for both roles. After a few anxious days . . . cue The Phone Call.

"They got Teresa Wright for Mary," said my agent. "They want you for Faye Precious."

Bells and whistles! Blow them horns! Bang them drums!

The play is set in the godforsaken town of Sunray, Texas, where a boisterous, irascible butcher, Horse, is carrying on an affair with Faye, a dumb but good-hearted waitress. Mary puts up with this because, besides being in love with him, she is raising their son. It's poignant and hilarious, with raucous action and cornball country songs. The son was beautifully played by Ken Kercheval (who later gained fame on the soapy blockbuster *Dallas*). Our Horse was Robert Darnell, and the local bartender, Pop, was Stewart Germain. All three were wonderful. Stanley Prager gave insightful, meticulous notes after every rehearsal and performance. For my money, that Stanley Prager knew his onions. What a director!

We opened on November 17 at the Village South Theatre. The audience adored the play, on their feet for the curtain calls. Reviews? Well . . . "mixed." Many papers gave us high praise, but the God-Almighty *New York Times* review was lukewarm—the kiss of death for an Off Broadway play with limited publicity funds. We had a running budget for only four weeks. Oliver funded a fifth week out of his own pocket, though he knew it was futile, and we closed a few days before Christmas. Damned show business. I love the "show," but the "business"—*feh!*

But several good things did result from the play. I became fast friends with both Oliver Hailey and screen star Teresa Wright. And I was one of six actors featured in "Faces Made for the Stage," a large page in—cue the drumroll, please—the Sunday *New York Times*! The critic had been especially impressed with me in *Who's Happy Now?*

How d'ya like that?

The Italian and I decided to try the marriage again.

I know what you're thinking. *Just jump in quicksand next time, Rue. It's faster!*

Yes, he was a horse's ass, but he could also be—what?—sexy? Masculine? Or was it that old "gotta have a man" panic? Oh, hell. Why am I even trying to rationalize it? Trying to put some kind of logic to it now just leaves me feeling angry at that damn dumb dame with her head up her wazoo, sitting there in 1969, watching the first moon landing and thinking, "See what miraculous things mankind can do? Maybe he'll change."

Change? He was more likely to fly to the moon. Sans spaceship.

Nevertheless, Mr. Funsies and I—with Mark in tow—moved to a two-story frame house in Fort Lee, New Jersey. Feeling the urge to nest, I made slipcovers and matching curtains, painted the dining room bright red, found a dozen prints of old masters for a dollar each, and hung them all over the house. We acquired a 1967 VW Beetle for $1,200. I put $600 down, and we agreed to take turns paying it off each month. His Majesty coveted a decrepit old silver Porsche at the same used-car lot and paid $300 for it.

"What names shall I put on the titles?" asked the salesman.

"Both cars in my name," answered His Lordship.

I was stunned but remained tightly silent. The Porsche ran one week, died forever, and sat parked beside the garage for the next three years. The VW ran like the 1967 model it was.

"That was VW's best year," everyone told me.

We went to an animal shelter and adopted a little half-grown tan-and-white puppy who barked, "Take me! Take me!" Mark named her Sandy and spent many happy hours pedaling his new bike all over our quiet neighborhood with Sandy running merrily along. Mother had a trampoline in her backyard in Ardmore, but I couldn't swing that expense quite yet, so my innovative son and his buddies jumped from the garage roof onto mattresses piled on top of the defunct Porsche, turning somersaults as they landed. Mark enjoyed sixth grade in his new school and made a good friend, Danny Driscoll, who came over often to play.

The Italian drove into New York most every day—in *his* VW, of course. There was no discord while he was away. We were happy. But when he was home, Mark and I had a lot of rules to follow. We weren't allowed to go barefoot or touch his turntable or enter his sacrosanct den and so on and so forth. We couldn't relax and *live normally*. We began to feel battered and dejected. And eventually, the battering became physical.

⟶

In February of 1970, The Italian and I were cast as husband and wife in an Off Broadway production of *Dark of the Moon,* a play about North Carolina forest witches and their effect on ignorant, superstitious villagers. I played the mother of Barbara Allen, a young virgin who falls in love with Witch Boy one moonlit night. At a village prayer meeting scene in Act Two, everyone becomes religiously obsessed, the mother working herself into a zealous fit. A very meaty role. The play ran eighty-six performances, partly because the beautiful Barbara Allen, gaspingly handsome Witch Boy, and equally gorgeous White and Dark Witches played the forest scenes stark-staring naked, climbing up and down tree trunks in not one blessed stitch.

At first, Barbara was movingly played by Margaret Howell, a graceful, sensitive actress with the body of a sylph. An unfortunately flat-chested sylph. The producers, in their infinite wisdom, fired her after four weeks, breaking her heart (and mine!), and hired the Playmate of the Year, who'd never been onstage in her life—not nowhere, not nohow—but was built like . . . well, what do you think the Playmate of the Year was built like? She twarn't no sylph. *Pa-lump, pa-*

lump! She was stacked. Those were some boobs (or "Hermans," as my friend Lette used to call them), but the girl couldn't act her way out of a damp Kleenex.

Margaret had instinctively given a hundred percent to every scene. Miss Playmate had the theatrical timing of a jellyfish. Astonishingly nerveless. Not one flicker of stage presence. There were rumors she'd been Sinatra's sweetie. Currently, she was hot and heavy with a Hollywood producer on the rise (no pun intended) who hung around our theatre every night like a moonstruck calf. The producers mounted (again no pun intended) an advertising blitz to jack up ticket sales. Lip-smacking newspaper ads and skin-rich posters of her boosted the box office for a week, then leveled off, then petered out (go ahead and take the pun this time). What a travesty.

At the same time, I was also doing a very small film with a *very* small budget, directed by my pal Mervyn Nelson and produced by Marty Richards. This was Marty's first time producing, but years later, after his marriage to Johnson & Johnson heiress Mary Lee Johnson, he created his own production company, skyrocketing to win dozens of awards for his films and Broadway musicals, including *La Cage aux Folles.* This little film, *Some of My Best Friends Are . . . ,* was about the habitués of a Manhattan gay bar. In the cast were fabled singer Mabel Mercer, new comedienne Fanny Flagg, and about thirty other well-known New York actors. Everyone, cast and crew alike, worked on "deferred" salaries, which means you'll probably never see a penny—and I certainly never have. But it was great fun. I played Lita, a sarcastic, highfalutin "fag hag" who sweeps into the bar in a low-cut evening gown, dragging her long mink. Imagine Tallulah Bankhead at her most flamboyant. Lita makes Blanche Devereaux look like Donna Reed.

My few scenes were all in the bar, requiring only a week's work. Driving home to Fort Lee to make dinner, then back to the Mercer Theatre for *Dark of the Moon,* took well over two hours, so I asked The

Italian to make dinner for Mark and himself one day when we were running late on set. This simple request resulted in a contentious exchange that had me weeping on the basement stairs the third day. Andy Greenhut, the set and costume designer, found me there and juggled scenes and logistics so I could go home and take care of Mark. I'm happy to say Andy is still my fast friend thirty-five years later, which is more than I can say for The Italian.

⁓

In May, I was selected by the Village Voice OBIE Awards to receive a Best Actress Obie for my performance in *The Golden Fleece*.

Wow! The Obie is a coveted honor for actors, and I was thrilled to the gills.

Right about then, Jenny Egan of the Four Winds Theatre in New York offered me a play to be done in England; rehearsals in New York were to begin immediately, followed by a couple of days in London, then sightseeing in the English countryside on our long drive up to Cheshire for our first appearance. The script for *The Raree Show,* a musical documentary on the American Revolution, was inspired by letters, diaries, and other papers of soldiers, wives, and mothers on both sides. We four actors would be playing about sixty roles. I told Jenny, "I'll do it!"

The Obie Awards show took place in a Greenwich Village club during the brief (all too brief!) rehearsal period for *The Raree Show*. The Italian and I drove into town together, and by the time we left the awards presentation for the celebration party afterward, Mr. Fun and Games was in a state of—I don't know what. Jealous fury? Frustration? Biliousness? I don't remember if we went to the party. I don't remember a party. I just remember weeping in the VW while he ripped into me about his lousy role in *Dark of the Moon,* the idiots who give out Obies, my impending job in England. But thank God for that England trip. I needed to get away for a while.

Mark flew to Oklahoma for the summer, and I left for London with *The Raree Show* cast and crew. We landed at Heathrow just in time for a proper English tea right there in the airport. The next day, we lunched at Boodle's, Winston Churchill's club, eating Boodle's Orange Fool, Sir Winston's favorite, for dessert. We had orchestra seats for *The Merchant of Venice,* starring Sir Laurence Olivier, as brilliant a Shylock as ever trod the boards. In his final electrifying scene, he demands the pound of flesh he's won from Antonio, and Antonio bares his chest for carving. But "Tarry a little!" says Portia, acting as his barrister. And she points out that the agreement said nothing of Antonio's giving Shylock any blood. Shylock leaves the court, defeated and destitute. The stage direction simply says: "Exit Shylock." It's up to the actor to fill in the rest. Olivier chose to slink off stage right, broken and silent, like most Shylocks.

Ah, but then!

From offstage there came a great bellowing howl of fury and misery, sending shivers through the audience. An unforgettable moment.

Years down the pike, Sir Laurence and I had the same agent at ICM, and the agent offered to arrange for me to meet my idol, who was actually a fan of *The Golden Girls.* I had to decline. I knew I would burst into tears. I couldn't bear the idea. The sheer magnitude! I know he would have been friendly and charming, but how does one make small talk with a God?

"Hiya, Larry, what's shakin'?"

We set off for Cheshire with all our costumes and sets, sightseeing all the way up. Charming villages with names like Chipping Norton and Stow-on-the-Wold. Breathtaking Stonehenge, where I hugged a monolith. Ancient stone walls, herds of sheep. I was in heaven. We arrived at the manor house with the private hundred-seat theatre, and before our second performance, the Queen of Holland's Rolls Royce could be seen approaching from a distance, followed by her entourage. We had a day to rehearse, and that night we were feted in the family's private dining room. The table was resplendent with crystal, silver, and china. But no napkins. I checked both sides of my plate. No linen heirlooms, not even dinky paper. I sneaked looks at my tablemates to see where they wiped their fingers, but nobody seemed to be doing so. I didn't see any finger bowls, either.

Do they use the end of the tablecloth? I wondered.

All the men were in the House of Lords, ribbons blazing across their chests. I sat between two robust personages with huge walrus mustaches, who chatted cheerily with me all during dinner, but not a word could I decipher.

"S'tellmeh, hev y'sinquin Meri's Tauyit?"

I said, "I beg your pardon?"

"Ahnau, I reck'n y've beeeen t'bizeh, eh?" followed by hearty laughter and great harrumphing mustache-twitchings. "Hev y'gontuh th'Leks?"

"Well . . . it's certainly beautiful country you have up here," I ventured, feeling around for the bottom of the tablecloth.

"Y'sh'd hie y's'f dontuh th'Leks!" He leaned around me to his companion. "Behtie! Iw's sehing she mahst ge'dontuh th'Leks! Eh?"

"Oh, yisyisyisyis, yisindeed!" agreed Behtie, who then confided to me, "Wi'mohs tek y'theah!" And there was more hearty laughter and harrumphing.

"That sounds lovely," I replied, hoping my mouth wasn't shiny with chicken fat.

After playing at Capesthorne Hall, we played two shows at the American Museum in Bath, then drove back to London.

What a glorious month!

I was thirtysomething. It was June. I was in England, all expenses paid, with enough cash saved up at the end to pay a modest hotel bill for a week in London, where I saw nine plays in six days, sitting so high up I had to crawl up the stairs on my hands and feet, then go down the stairs backward, holding on to the seats, after the performances.

Life is a lot different in the rafters.

I came home feeling like I'd gotten some much-needed perspective, especially when I realized that the entire time, while I missed Mark and longed to share all this with him, I had not given one thought to The Italian.

CHAPTER FOURTEEN

I had a Yugoslavian lover once (and once was quite enough) who insisted it was nonsense to put thought into planning a party. His method back in Belgrade was to invite twenty people over and upon their arrival start looking for something to feed them. Whatever was at hand—canned beans, hunks of bread, apples. He said everyone always had a terrific time. Maybe so. I never got drunk enough to try that. It sounded too much like soldiers at the front.

Now I have my parties catered, so I'm fresh as a daisy, sampling hors d'oeuvres, mixing and mingling, a firefly flitting from table to table, secure in the knowledge that my caterer knows what she's doing and, if she doesn't, she'd better not ask me. I get overly concerned about my guests' comfort and pleasure. My attention to detail tends to be exhausting. That's why I give so few parties. And look so young.

Back when I had no money, it was easier. Pigs in the blanket, chips, and BYOB. My favorite dessert from the seventies—that spectacular trifle from Boodle's—was a fattening but surefire success at every party I threw in New York—and in Los Angeles, until that day in the eighties when I could no longer look whipped cream in the face without blushing. The chef said it had been Churchill's favorite, and looking at Churchill's ample girth, I believe it. The chef graciously gave me the recipe. Of course, I still have it. And now, so have you. Gird your loins for:

BOODLE'S ORANGE FOOL FOR FORTY FOLKS

Pile four large sponge cakes into a great big punch bowl. Saturate them with the juice of sixteen oranges and eight lemons. Whip five pints of thick cream, adding nine grated orange rinds and four grated lemon rinds. Spread this mixture over the drenched sponge cakes. Sift sixteen tablespoons of confectioners' sugar over all and sprinkle a bit more orange rind for show.

Then stand back to avoid the stampede.

The first time I made Boodle's Orange Fool, my irreverent, outrageous, courageous, and hilarious best friend, Lette Rehnolds—she of "Two Little Pussycats" fame—helped me. It was New Year's Eve in Fort Lee, New Jersey, a few months after I returned from England. The Italian was out of town. He did a pretty good Bogart impersonation, so he was regularly cast as Bogie in Woody Allen's *Play It Again, Sam,* playing theatres hither and yon for weeks at a time. It was the only time Mark and I could relax and be happy. So I decided to throw a New Year's Eve party and asked Lette to come early and help, since she was not only an excellent cook but a big kick in the butt. We made dinner and the Boodle's, thirty-odd (some *very* odd) people arrived from Manhattan, and we had a blast. Mark couldn't sleep that night for the noise, so he got up and sat on the stairs, watching the show. Snapshots show everyone in awful seventies garb and haircuts, looking very happy, consuming Boodle's Orange Fool, and drinking like fish.

This is how Mark and I lived those last few years with The Italian. When Husband was home, we tiptoed around and did our best to not incur his wrath. When he was not home, life resumed. It was party time! We laughed, played, and pretended life was normal. Rather than think about it too much, I immersed myself in work.

⟁

All my professional life, I'd wanted to be a member of the Actors' Studio, an exclusive workshop for actors. Membership is by audition only, so I worked with a partner on a scene from Tennessee Williams's *Twenty-seven Wagonloads of Cotton* (the play that became the film *Baby Doll*). I played Baby Doll. The actor who played Vacarro, the overseer who taunts and stalks Baby Doll, was talented but neurotic. We worked up the scene and presented it at The Studio on the allotted night. Everything started as rehearsed, but this nutty guy suddenly started pelting me with raw green peas that stung like sharp little rocks, and then, out of nowhere, he slapped my face—*hard!*—which threw our audition into a cocked hat, and neither of us was accepted. We were told to work up new scenes with different partners and come back the following spring. Poop! That unprofessional twerp was worse than the Three Little Kittens.

In a dry spell workwise, I did some presentations for backers of an Irish play about Sinn Fein. Playing a seductress, I straddled a young man seated in a chair, wrapped my legs tightly around him, kissed him passionately, and bit off his tongue. I dreaded every performance, but it was $40 a pop. In cash. And not nude. Another challenge was a two-character one-act done in a church basement. I played a housewife, innocently dusting the living room. *Ding dong.* The doorbell rings. It's a blind piano tuner with dark glasses and cane. As he tunes, she gets excited and begins removing her clothes, until she's down to bra and panties, in a frenzy on the carpet, having one heck of an orgasm. The upshot is that it's her husband in disguise. I don't know what it meant, but it took all my courage to do it realistically. I'm glad it was a play, not a film, because I wouldn't want anyone—including myself—to see it now.

I got cast in three films (fully clothed in all of them!), including *The People Next Door,* in which I played the tough secretary—and

With Eli Wallach in The People Next Door.
("Don't think you can just throw me away like an old Kleenex!")

mistress—of Eli Wallach's character. In our major scene, he abruptly announces he's breaking off the affair and the mistress/secretary barks furiously, "Don't think you can just throw me away like an old Kleenex!"

Some line, huh? What dramatic power! What content!

It hurt my toenails. *Like an old Kleenex?* Yep. And say it like you mean it, honey.

I also did the wonderful movie *They Might Be Giants,* playing Daisy Playfair, the innocent, wide-eyed sister-in-law of George C. Scott, who thinks he's Sherlock Holmes. His psychiatrist, played by Joanne Woodward, begins to believe her patient actually *is* Sherlock Holmes and joins his crusade to hunt down the villainous Dr. Moriarty, along with a gaggle of eccentric street people and Daisy in her heels and mink coat. We shot during the winter in snow-covered Manhattan, we actors standing on big sheets of cardboard, our feet frozen into ice sculptures. In my fur coat, I was luckier than the others in their cotton and wool.

I worked six weeks and had several good little scenes, some of which were filmed on location in the Victorian dining room of the Players Club in Gramercy Park. I became a member of the Players in 1997 and had attended many fetes in that room before I learned, at a 2004 screening of *They Might Be Giants* honoring Anthony Harvey and me, that this very room was Holmes's laboratory! Things like that amaze me. The circles and intersections.

Life just loves to fiddle around with us.

In February of 1971, Oliver Hailey offered me the job of standby for the two thirtysomething leading ladies—Marian Seldes and Brenda Vaccaro—in his new play, *Father's Day*. Oliver sent me the script, and I called him immediately after reading it.

"I have a real handle on the role to be done by Vaccaro," I told him.

He said, "I'm sure you do, Rue. But we want a *name* in every role."

And I was definitely not a "name." I couldn't argue that.

They went into rehearsal, and I learned both roles in the unlikely case I'd get to play one. It was excruciating, because Miss Vaccaro wasn't comfortable in the role. Lines were changed to try to help her, but she just never clicked into the character. The play opened March 16, 1971, and closed March 16, 1971. It was like driving through one of those tiny towns in North Texas. Blink and you'll miss it. But even with only one performance, Marian Seldes was nominated for a Best Actress Tony. (Now, *that's* an actress!) But Oliver was once again denied a hit show in New York, and I felt terrible for him. The next day, Ken Kercheval, who was also in the cast, arrived at the theatre, as did I, to clean out our dressing rooms. He had brought liquor and proceeded, as did I, to get sloshed. We tried to console each other but were too smashed for romance. He fell asleep, and I went home and poured myself into bed.

That spring, I made another try for the Actors' Studio. A few months earlier, I'd workshopped some scenes from *Dylan,* in which I played Dylan Thomas's volatile wife, Caitlin, opposite the wonderful Will Hare—who was a pro, a gentleman, and a member of the Actors' Studio. We presented the opening scene from *Dylan,* and I was accepted as a lifetime member of the Actors' Studio. One of the sweetest accomplishments of my career. (So much for you, Mr. Slap-happy Pea-shooter.)

I began the summer at the Hampton Playhouse, but just a few days into rehearsals was called to return to New York to appear in the soap opera *Another World.* I'd all but forgotten the audition I'd done for producers at NBC a couple months earlier. The Playhouse brought in Katherine Helmond to replace me (gotta love Katherine as the dizzy wife in *Soap* and the sexy mom on *Who's the Boss?*), and I began a new phase in my career—soap opera actress. The best thing about it: Mother and her customers at the beauty parlor tuned in religiously. Finally, she figured her little girl had really made it! I never heard another word about a dance school in Ardmore.

My *Another World* character was Caroline Johnson, cook and nanny to Pat and John's infant twins. The best nanny in all Christendom, and one hell of a great cook, to boot. The infants love her, Pat and John love her, the audience loved her. The character was so popular, the producers upped my appearances from three shows a week to five a week at $150 per show! Going to the mailbox and taking out those blessed paychecks was like Christmas every week.

Caroline's one teeny flaw: She was crazier than a bedbug. Many episodes ended with her sprinkling a mysterious white powder in Pat's soup, which resulted in dramatic hospital scenes for Pat and cleared the way for Caroline to be alone with John. She fancied him, you see, and her nefarious plot was to slowly poison Pat, marry John, and live happily ever after with "their" children. This went on for over a year's shooting time, during which the newborn twins turned two years old. Even worse, in a previous story line, before she became pregnant with twins, Pat had had a hysterectomy. Ah, the magical world of soap opera!

Poor Pat kept getting dangerously sick but always recovered. One day, I got a letter from a fan saying, *While I admire your tenacity, you're obviously using the wrong poison.* And then she named the poison to get at the pharmacy, promising it would work, adding, *Just use a pharmacist who owes you a favor, like I did, and soon you'll be happily married to John. It worked for me! Sincerely, Mrs. X.*

I turned it over to the show's producers, toot sweet. We were always getting letters from fans warning us to look out for another character or giving us advice. Soaps are a strange world with a strange audience. It's also the most stultifyingly boring work I've ever done. After fourteen months of this nonsensical plot, which moved forward like a glacier on a mudflat, Caroline was finally hauled off to jail or the funny farm or somewhere, mercifully rescuing me from impending stupor. It was even more mind-numbing than Upjohn Pharmaceutical.

But as fate would have it, Caroline departed *Another World* on Friday and I replaced a lead actress on the CBS soap *Where the Heart Is* on Monday. This character was also a killer, but at least she was a successful one! Barbara Baxley, the actress who was leaving, had been playing her role at the usual soap pace, a combination of treacle and molasses, often reading cue cards. I had my lines down so pat I could fire them off like a horse race announcer. So the viewers got treacle on Friday and popcorn on Monday from the same character—who, after five more months of trying to kill her nine-year-old nephew by various means, chases him across a frozen lake and breaks through the thin ice to her well-deserved fate.

Now I'd done soaps on NBC and CBS. Just to cover all bases, ABC hired me for four episodes as the beer-guzzling mother of a rebellious teenage girl on one of their long-running daytime dramas. That was a bit more interesting but still not really my cup of Palmolive. Soaps aren't funny. They're soggy cereal. Personally, I like snap, crackle, and wit, fast-paced top-rate writing, brilliant costars, bravado challenges. And, kids, there ain't much of that in soaps. Or any-where else on TV, for the most part. Top-of-the-line writing is extremely rare.

I supplemented my sudsy roles with commercials. A wife rubbing Absorbine, Jr. on my husband's shoulder. A zany shopper trying on girdles in a posh shop for I Can't Believe It's a Girdle. A leggy cocktail waitress exchanging wisecracks with beefy guys for . . . gosh, what was that? Something for the beefy guy target market. Hey, it's a living. I was glad to get these gigs after sixty—yes, I counted them—*sixty* fruit-less auditions over four years. Commercial producers had always told me, "We just can't pin down your type."

My type? Maybe I'm the type who can be *any* type.

I think that type is called *an actress*.

⟶

Two dear friends, Henry Murphy and his main squeeze Brent Hicks, bought an old house upstate in the Hudson River Valley, and Mark and I sometimes went up for weekends. The house was—to put it kindly—a fixer-upper. There was an open void at the center of the second-story floor, so we had to edge very carefully around the perime-ter to get to our rooms, or we'd fall smack through into the living room. It was a wonderful place, full of adventures. Brent taught me to do a time step in the kitchen. Another regular guest, a lovely actress named Louisa Flaningam, made whole-wheat-crust apple pies with apples from the ancient trees outside. That ramshackle old house is now the upscale Inn at Green River, one of the best B&Bs in the United

States, but back then it was our beloved wreck, a welcome respite from our city lives.

Mark turned thirteen in the fall of 1971, his voice changing from soprano to baritone. He was my height, hormones running rampant, his conversation more adult and funnier than ever, his demeanor more assertive. As he changed, I had to change with him, learning to deal with this emerging critter. I wanted him to have a place to grow, so Murph, Brent, Lette, Mark, and I drove around upstate looking at land for sale. Four miles from Murph's place was a gorgeous forty-five-acre lot, ablaze with fall colors. Lette and I threw ourselves down in the maple leaves and rolled like horses. I was salivating to buy the place, but it was $32,000 and the owner wanted half down. Not gonna happen.

On Halloween night, our hosts always organized a ghost hunt. About eight of us would line up in single file and follow Murph out to the meadow and across the brook. Every now and then, Murph would call, "Anybody see the ghost?"

"No . . ." And on we trekked, the new kid always last in line.

Suddenly, Murph would stop and whisper, "*Look!* Over there! What is that?"

About forty yards away, a huge billowy white form sailed against the black sky, clearly free of the earth, traveling parallel with us, puffing in and out like a beautiful giant jellyfish.

Murph would shout, "RUN FOR THE HOUSE!" and we'd all turn tail and gallop back over the creek. But on Mark's first Halloween, he walked over to get a better look at the apparition. Turns out the ghost was Brent dressed in black, running along beneath a parachute they'd found at a surplus store. We all hooted about it over hot chocolate and s'mores—graham crackers covered with melted marshmallows and Hershey's bits.

It had been a year or so since I started those weekly sessions with Mandrake Penobscot, learning a lot about myself, the dusk panics, recurring nightmares, my compulsive need for a man. But I still couldn't bring myself to end the disastrous marriage. The Italian and I had settled into an uneasy, always-about-to-blow relationship, made bearable only by the fact that one or the other of us was often out of town.

"I think you should begin group therapy," said Manny, taking a sip of water. (He always sipped water constantly during the sessions.) So I found myself in a circle of eight troubled souls, some with destructive parents, others with abusive mates. Every week, people told the same miserable stories, blind to the obvious solution: *Get away from that person! NOW!* I thought, *Hmm, I fit right in with these nuts.*

One night, Mark said something flip and Mr. Congeniality set off up the stairs after him, catching him in the bathroom. I heard slapping and shouting, but I was terrified to intervene. I heard something metal break and fall. Then, in the quiet, I heard Mark say, "You know, this really isn't the way to communicate with me."

"No? Then what is?"

"You could just talk to me. You don't have to yell or hit me."

"How do I know you'd listen? My dad always hit me!"

"Well, you might try it. I'd listen."

"Yeah? Well, then. Just . . . go on, I guess . . . go on to bed."

And Mark went to bed, leaving me astounded at the foot of the stairs.

The next day, I asked Lette if Mark and I could stay a few nights in her place in the Ansonia Hotel until I could think what to do. She didn't like kids or dogs, so she wasn't happy to have us, and I wasn't happy to move in on her. To make things worse, Mark's dog made a dump on the carpet under the grand piano. The next day, The Italian called and nicely said he had to talk to me. I told him to come over that night at eight and sent Mark out with a friend.

"I need you to call every twenty minutes to see if I'm still alive," I told Lette and, always ready for drama, she agreed, staking us out from her neighbor's apartment next door.

The Italian arrived promptly at eight and began apologizing, asking me in a calm voice to come back home, saying we could work it out, but I kept refusing.

The phone rang.

"Lette Rehnolds's residence."

"Hey, Baby Rue, are you okay?"

"She's not home right now. May I take a message?"

"For Christ's sake, I want to know if you're okay!"

"Okay, fine. Just fine. She'll be back any minute."

"I'm calling again in fifteen minutes! Good-bye!"

More entreating from Cuddles for me to come home, all in his sweetest, most rational and reasonable demeanor. More standing my ground.

The phone rang.

"Lette Rehnolds's residence."

"This is the FBI. Are you okay?"

"That's right, but she's due home soon."

"I'll call again in ten minutes. What on earth is going on over there?"

"Okay, thank you. I'll tell her."

Another onslaught of apologies, entreaties, promises to never fly off the handle again. My resolve was breaking down. What could I do? I really had nowhere to go.

The phone rang.

"Hello?"

"Look, Baby Rue, are you okay or what? I'm getting drunk."

"Lette? Is that you? When are you coming home?"

"Right now! I've had the ass of this!"

"Okay! See you in a few minutes."

With nowhere else to go, Mark and I returned to Fort Lee the next day, but Mark told me, "Mother, I can't live with you anymore unless you leave The Hulk."

In Manny's familiar circle that week, I told them about the incident with Mark, the threats that kept me silent, and a terrible moment in the kitchen some months earlier when I thought he just might kill me.

"He laced into me about something or other," I said. "And I slammed the refrigerator. Suddenly, I was pinned against the fridge, his thumbs pressing hard against my larynx. I couldn't breathe. Just as I felt like I was going to pass out, he released me and I fell forward, struggling for breath. He said it was all my fault, since he'd warned me never to display anger toward him. I was shooting a movie—*They Might Be Giants*. On the set, I pretended to have laryngitis."

When I finished, the craziest guy in the group asked me, "What do you like about him?"

I thought for a few seconds, then said, "I can't think of anything."

"So why the hell don't you divorce him?" the crazy guy challenged.

Something clicked into place. *Plunk!* Like a ball rolling into a socket. I was ready to do it. Just like that. I drove back to Fort Lee and told Mr. Hyde, "I'm divorcing you. There's no need to discuss it. You have to move out."

He replied, "Oh, no way. I'm not moving. You and Mark can move."

"You should really be in New York. In the theatrical environment," I pointed out quietly. "And you can rent a New York apartment for less than we're paying for the house. Besides, you won't need a car in Manhattan. I'll buy the VW from you."

He thought that over, then said, "Okay. I'll move to Manhattan. When I'm good and ready. Not before six weeks. And yeah, I guess I could sell you my Volkswagen."

His Volkswagen! *Ooooh!* Bite my tongue, bite my tongue . . .

But who cares? He moved out. Forever! Forever! Forever! Oh, God, *forever*! Mark and I literally danced for joy. I started divorce proceedings the very next day. He said he'd pay half the legal fee but never did. And as for the VW—for which I had paid $900 and he had paid $300—well, he let me buy it from him for only $100.

Quite the gentleman, *n'est-ce pas*?

CHAPTER FIFTEEN

$\backsim$

"Pull, and let go."
—THOMAS CRAPPER, INVENTOR OF THE FLUSH TOILET

The blazingly beautiful acreage where Lette and I had rolled in the leaves the previous autumn was covered with snow when Murph and Brent took me there in January. I was still in love with it. It called to me in all its glory, even in winter. Oh, how I wanted it! A corner lot on two good country roads, it was heaven in all seasons, wild blueberries and apple trees between tall cedars, maples, and white spruce. Two creeks flowed down to a small waterfall, where you could lie on your stomach to drink the pure, cold water. Ancient stone fences traversed the hillsides. On a clear day, you could see Vermont.

For thirty-two grand.

Half down.

I'd saved $11,000 while I was doing the soaps, and I asked the owner, "Will you mortgage the remaining twenty-one?"

"Nah, I decided not to sell it." His square, short body shifted onto one leg, and he lit another cigarette. "My kids like to snowmobile over there, and I go deer huntin' on it."

He kills deer? I thought. *On* my *property?* But I kept my sweetest smile in place.

"Well, that's too bad. 'Cause I'd really like to buy it. And you could probably use some ready cash. And I could probably get a loan and come up with the full sixteen in a couple of weeks."

"I'll give you till January thirty-first. Half down. In cash. Or no deal."

"January thirty-first is less than a week from now." My smile may have strained a little. "At least make it a full week. February second."

"Okay, but you don't get your deposit back if you're late."

I gave him a thousand-dollar deposit and headed back to New York, gears turning. How to get the other five thou? Mother and Bill lent me two thousand each. Lette said she'd help me out, but couldn't come up with the cash. Forty-eight hours from losing my deposit, I desperately racked my brains. Who in my acquaintance had that kind of dough on hand? Only one person came to mind: Mandrake Penobscot. Anyone in his profession must have money, I figured. My asking my former therapist might seem a little outside the box, but I'd come to know and trust him, and he seemed to care about me, even though I was no longer in his therapy group.

"It wouldn't be appropriate for me to lend a patient money," Manny said.

"Well, I haven't been your patient for a while," I said. "So what about a friend?"

"For a friend . . . I suppose I could invest a thousand. For one-thirty-second ownership."

I'd made it! That heartbreakingly beautiful forty-five acres was *mine*. Well, 31/32 was mine—with a fifteen-year mortgage. And four thousand to pay back to my folks. (Which I did.)

Murph and Brent and Mark and Sandy and I tramped all over that land, taking dozens of photographs, daydreaming about where I'd build my house one day. I was deeply grateful to dear, generous Manny. Skilled, soft-spoken, intelligent Manny, who was not classically handsome but had soulful eyes and a compact body and knew all my deepest secrets.

"Oh, no, Rue," he said when I asked him if he'd be interested in seeing me socially. "I never date patients. Or former patients. You probably wouldn't even like me outside the office. I behave very differently."

Did that little caveat deter this Choctaw? *Please!* One day, I saw him on the sidewalk and called out, "Hey, sailor, want a ride?" Amused, he got in my Beetle and I drove him home. No hanky-panky. But, lo and behold, a couple weeks later, he called and asked me out. Well, *okaaaaay*! Unfortunately, I didn't have the good sense to ask Mark how he felt about it, and I realize now how insensitive that was. Mark was thirteen, we were freshly released from our seven-year stint in the Italian prison camp, and already I was starting an affair? In hindsight, it makes me cringe. At the time, however, I was, as usual, plunging full steam ahead.

Mark and I rented a second-floor apartment from an Italian lady (c'mon, you can't blame all of Tuscany for one bad apple) whose furniture and rugs downstairs were covered in plastic. Pictures of Jesus and the saints populated the walls. Every saint you can think of. Even my personal favorite, Saint Dymphna, patroness of mental and emotional illness. Our landlady didn't allow pets, but I pleaded for Mark's very quiet little dog and our extremely well-behaved cat, paid two months in advance, and promised not to have any parties. Apparently, the saints came marching in and spoke up for us, but they were dozing the day we moved in. Murph and Brent helped us haul our stuff, and on the way, we stopped at a gas station. Murph let Sandy out to pee while I checked my tires. A male dog trotted by, found her irresistible, and by the time the filling station attendant turned a water hose on them, we were expecting puppies.

Ah, how those saints guffawed! And they fairly burst their frames in hysterics as they saw the Mandrake Penobscot circus play out. Saint Dymphna had to have a Klonopin.

The day Manny warned me he "behaved differently" outside his office, he was not just whistling Dixie, darlings. We started spending a few nights a week together. He always brought a fifth of vodka, which he drank to the bottom. Oopsy-daisy.

"I'm into threesomes," he said.

I said I was not.

"My ex-wife and I were into threesomes," he said.

I said I was *not*.

Sitting in the middle of the bed until three or four A.M., crying buckets, relating his woeful life story, he confessed, "I was in therapy for seven years and I won't go back. I'm incurable."

I invited him to a play opening with my friends, and he behaved in a most peculiar way, running around like an undisciplined child, saying inappropriate, embarrassing things to people. *"What on Earth?"* my astonished friends asked, but I was more astounded than they were. I went to one cocktail party with him, even though he cautioned me, "All the other guests will be psychiatrists, psychologists, or social workers. You'll be the only outsider."

"That should be interesting," I said. Which turned out to be the understatement of the century.

The party was full of well-dressed people, solemnly conversing but not laughing. No chuckles. Not a titter. I settled onto a sofa next to one of the psychiatrists and, looking out the floor-to-ceiling windows, commented brightly, "Oh, look! It's going to rain. I just love rainstorms."

This fellow turns to me with a small frown and says, "Oh, *really*. And why do you think that is?"

"Oh . . . who knows? Maybe because I was born during a rainstorm."

"Hmm. . . *interesting*," he said, and stroked his chin.

Manny really was quite sweet. And he rated high on the FQ scale. Maybe an A. But he was nuttier than a Snickers bar! I started looking for a way to end it gracefully.

One astounding night, he brought some pot to my house

"I've only smoked pot twice before," I told him. "A long time ago. And I didn't like it."

"Oh, you'll like this," he assured me, and after some resistance, I took a drag or two.

I don't know if it was laced with something or what, but I turned into a snake, slithering down from the bed and onto the floor headfirst, wriggling along the carpet on my back. I have no idea what happened after that. I just know that I broke it off with Manny.

Gracefully, I hope.

⌐

In April, I accepted the female lead in a somewhat interesting play about a gal who, having been deeply hurt, swears off men and decides she's a lesbian, until a sweet young guy starts wooing her, prompting her to reexamine her true sexual orientation.

Interesting, as my sofa pal would say.

I enjoyed smoking a cigar and stomping around in my overalls, but the actor playing the love interest seemed a little . . . oh, how shall we say it? Saucy in the sneakers? Mincy in the moccasins? Fluffy in the Florsheims? This was the stud who was supposed to ignite my character's libido and swing her interest back to men? But the young director didn't agree that we needed an actor with a bit more testosterone. On opening night, my leading man was sporting heavy mascara. He hadn't worn mascara in dress rehearsal, and now he had on more than I did! His long curly lashes were fairly gleaming. I was mesmerized.

After the show, the director's sister, who was producing the play, threw an opening-night party and, as it ran rather late, invited me to stay in her spare bedroom instead of driving home to New Jersey. How hospitable! I called Mark and told him I'd be home the next morning, but as I climbed into bed, there came a knock at my door. It was our producer—about three sheets to the wind—wanting to climb right in with me. Good grief, Gwendolyn! I explained that I'd only been *playing* a lesbian. Apparently, rather convincingly.

A pretty darn eventful production, but I was glad when it closed after one week. At the last performance, a wonderful Broadway actor named Bill Macy came backstage to introduce himself and congratulate me. As we chatted, he told me, "I've been hired to play the husband in a new Norman Lear series. A spin-off of *All in the Family* called *Maude*."

"What a break!" I marveled. "And you deserve it, Bill. I'm envious, but happy for you!"

Meanwhile, back at the ranch, Sandy had four puppies. Mark and I went through a few nervous weeks trying to keep them quiet, but the landlady dropped by and saw the menagerie crawling happily around, and even the saints couldn't save us. Mark took Sandy to Oklahoma for the summer and I found homes for the puppies, taking the names and numbers of the adoptive parents. Then I focused on forging ahead with my career. (Remember that old thing?)

I'd salivated to get into the Joseph Papp circle for years and finally got an audition with the legendary producer. At an outdoor café in SoHo, I read some scenes for Mr. Papp and he hired me to understudy the leading lady in *Sticks and Bones,* David Rabe's Pulitzer Prize–winning play on Broadway. After two weeks, Mr. Papp said, "I actually hired you to take over the role. The actress has already given notice. I want you to start playing it as soon as you're ready."

Ready? Honey child, I was born ready!

My character, Harriet, spent most of her time serving fudge and cookies to her mundane middle-American family—husband Ozzie and sons David and Ricky. (Subtle, huh?) I made twenty-eight different entrances from the kitchen during the show, uttering platitudes, carrying plates of goodies. I taped up a list in the wings, detailing when I entered and what I carried. I had nothing to latch on to except one good fight with Ozzie. The play was thick with murky symbolism. There was a Vietnamese girl living in David's bedroom. Or was she a hallucination? If she was a hallucination, why did we all see her? The audience was equally puzzled. After every performance, audience members gathered outside the stage door, waiting to ask, "What does it mean?" But who knew?

I guess it means if you write a play in which a disturbed young man slashes his wrists center stage, leaking his lifeblood into basins brought by his mother, who then sits down to knit while she and the rest of the family wait cheerfully for him to die (or does he *almost* die?) as the curtain goes down—well, you just might win yourself a Pulitzer, because *surely* that is some powerfully meaningful stuff!

On the other hand . . . wait a minute.

Now that I think about it without all the fudge . . . the play does have meaningful implications. And it certainly packed a wallop— great gouts of blood spurting like a fountain from that boy's wrists, gushing into the basin. It never failed to get a big gasp from the house.

But Saint Dymphna was up to her usual mischief. While I was still rehearsing *Sticks and Bones,* I got a call from Joyce Selznick in Hollywood.

"Rue!" she said. "You remember me—I saw you in *Dylan* a couple years ago."

Sure, I remembered. She'd approached me after the performance and said she'd like to manage me. But I couldn't afford a manager. I was already paying an agent, so I decided against signing with her.

She said, "I put your picture in a casting directory with my name and number—"

"You what?"

"Rue! I have a job for you! Norman Lear wants you for *All in the Family*! He wants you to audition for the director, John Rich."

Okay. Well. That's an audition, Joyce, not a job, but still—the heart goes *bam! bam!* An audition for *All in the Family*! Straight to the moon! Not even tempted to look this gorgeous gift horse in the mouth.

Broadway plays are dark on Mondays, so I flew out Monday morning, knowing full well Joe Papp wouldn't let me out of the play for a week—and that I'd have to be up front about that. Both Norman and John were tickled pink with my audition.

"Don't worry," said Norman. "I'll find another role just as good, as soon as you can get out of the play for a week."

After toting fudge for another couple of weeks, I was offered a juicy part in a PBS production of *The Rimers of Eldritch*: a lonely woman in a repressed town, in which everyone thinks she's an ungodly tart. *Yummy!* Ungodly is my favorite flavor for tarts! But Mr. Papp laid down the law. "I never let anyone out of a play to do another job. It sets a bad precedent."

I cajoled. He relented. Those saints were back on my side. Almost. The night before I departed for the PBS job, during the fight scene between Ozzie and Harriett, I banged my wrist on the back of the sofa and the next morning it was swollen up like a boxing glove. I put ice on it, but it kept swelling. While *Rimers* was shooting, I took painkillers and devised ways to keep it covered. A dishtowel in one scene, a sweater in another. In the bed scene, I managed to hide it beneath the sheet while being smolderingly sultry. I ended the scene crying, which was easy, because my wrist throbbed like blue blazes.

The Rimers of Eldritch is a beautiful play by Lanford Wilson, and PBS did an excellent job translating it to the small screen. A murder in a tiny town sets off the dangerously religion-soaked provincials, leading to the hysterical trial of the wrong person. I played the owner of the hilltop restaurant who befriends a young biker. Her only other friend is an addlepated old bum whom she allows to live in the shack behind the restaurant—a ragged fellow played touchingly by Will Hare. Also in the cast were Frances Sternhagen, K Callen, and Susan Sarandon, and the young biker was played by Ernest Thompson. This was long before he wrote *On Golden Pond*. Goodness, I think Ernest was all of twenty-two. We had some piping-hot scenes, culminating with the one in bed when he tells me he's moving on, leaving me in anguished despair. (With a throbbing wrist, to boot.)

This was the first film for respected stage director Davy Marlin Jones, who was hampered by the assistant director and others, who took advantage of his inexperience, constantly objecting, "You can't do that, Davy. That's not how it's done, Davy." But most of his fresh, exciting ideas did make it to the screen. He gave K Callen a marvelous piece of business during a scene where she's working a jigsaw puzzle on a glass table. Davy shot from beneath the table, the camera on her face. The pieces fill the space, and in the last scene, she places the final piece in the center as she says her last line, obliterating her face. Neat, Davy!

All the subplots were good. Sarandon played a frivolous high school senior who gets knocked up just before graduation and, to her teeth-clinching chagrin, is bullied by her parents to marry the boy. In the final scene, she is successfully seducing the biker. Go, Susan! My swollen wrist was killing me, but it helped me play the role of a painfully unhappy woman. Actors have to use infirmities to advantage. Playing a bristly, short-tempered person, put a few sharp pebbles in your shoe—that sort of thing.

Just as I was finishing the shoot in Maryland, Norman Lear called.

"I've got a perfect role for you on *All in the Family*. Can you be here next week?"

Damn! And *hot* damn! That darn Saint Dymphna was having a ball.

I nervously called Papp and requested two more weeks. He was not a happy camper. But because my wrist was still hurt, he agreed, God bless him, and I flew to L.A. to start work on "The Bunkers Meet the Swingers"—a superb script in which Edith Bunker sees a personal ad in a throwaway paper and invites a couple over to dinner, thinking they want to be pen pals. What they want is to be bed pals. Appalled, Archie orders them out. In a moving final monologue, I apologized quietly for the misunderstanding, explaining that this wife-swapping experiment was saving my marriage. Vinnie Gardenia, always such a dear Uncle Earth to work with, played my husband with his customary ebullience.

The cast and director were divine. I'd been warned that Carroll O'Connor could be of fierce temperament, known to tear up scripts and generally have conniption fits. Not the Carroll O'Connor I saw. From day one, he was happy, funny, and full of great ideas. Jean Stapleton was a warm hearth. Rob Reiner and Sally Struthers were professional and cooperative. Not a prima donna in the bunch. We had a beautiful rehearsal week, and the episode won an Emmy.

Norman took me aside the third day of rehearsal and asked if I could stay a bit longer. His new show, *Maude,* was in rehearsals on the adjoining stage, and the actress playing Vivian, Maude's best friend, wasn't working out. I'd have to rehearse both shows simultaneously, running from stage to stage, tape *Family* Friday night and *Maude* the following Tuesday night. Just my meat! But holy cats. Mr. Papp was not going to be jumping with joy.

After hearing my request, there was a long pause on the phone line.

"Rue," he finally said, "I *never* let anyone out of a show to do another job! I let you out for *Rimers,* I let you out for *Family*—now you're asking for a *third* out?"

"Mr. Papp, if you'll do this, I'll let my understudy continue to play Harriet. When I get back, I'll understudy *her.*"

"You want it that bad?"

"*Yes.*"

"Okay, Rue. But don't ask for any more outs!"

I didn't have to. The play closed a month later, leaving a trail of fudge behind it.

⌐

No one but Bea Arthur could have played the title character in the groundbreaking series *Maude,* the first (and only) sitcom to successfully portray the emerging feminist sensibilities of the "Women's Lib" movement in a way people were willing to embrace. (Well, *some* people, anyway.) Like *All in the Family,* it presented prickly issues to the mass audience with whip-crack comedy writing and a super-talented cast.

Catapulted into my first episode, I found Bea wonderful to work with—and watch. She was powerful, smart, statuesque, with surgically precise comedic timing, and she wore her star quality like a cherry on top. The moment I walked onto the *Maude* set, she came striding over to welcome me and immediately launched into catching me up on the scenes between Maude and Vivian, since I was a day behind.

Bea and I clicked from the start. She appreciated my talent, and I learned from her daring choices. I was never intimidated, but Bea threw the fear of God into a lot of other people. She abode by a strict work ethic and brooked no fools, but she genuinely appreciated the talents of her coworkers, particularly her director and writers. She had a sharp wit, which did definitely slice and dice someone every once in a while, so not everyone saw the Bea Arthur I came to know over the years. Bea could be dissolved to tears by a careless remark, but she was nevertheless prone to harsh comments of her own—usually muttered *sotto voce,* under her breath, more for her own benefit than to intentionally hurt anyone. Something as innocuous as a backward baseball cap brought down a swift indictment in that famously deep voice: "Scum." Anything she disagreed with elicited an abrupt "Oh, hump!"

When I got back to New York, everyone said, "Ooooh! You worked with Bea Arthur! Weren't you scared?"

Scared? I had a ball! She was a kick in the pants! In fact, all the actors were great fun to work with, as was Hal Cooper, our cheerful director. The writers were still figuring out the Vivian character. She was Maude's best friend, two weeks older. That's all we knew. So I just played her off the top of my head. That first segment I did is the only one with that particular Vivian, levelheaded and low-voiced with gray hair. By Vivian's second segment, months later, she'd been rewritten giddier and younger, and by the time she became a regular weekly character, Vivian emerged as the ditsy, sexy air-brain I came to love.

I couldn't have had a better introduction to prime-time television. Two happy Norman Lear sets, two fabulous scripts, two great characters—I should have sent Saint Dymphna a dozen roses!

Back in the Italian lady's apartment—and now understudying my understudy—I was brushing up my tap skills, taking lessons nearby. One day after class, I encountered a dirty, exhausted dog in the parking lot—a brindle about the size of a German shepherd, tits down to the ground, obviously homeless, thin from hunger, but with an eager, intelligent face. She'd had a litter and been abandoned, I surmised, and was waiting patiently for her owners to return.

Could I turn my back on that? Ignore a lost animal? Not quite hardly.

"You want to go home with me?" I asked, opening the car door for her. "Come on, Gretl. They're not coming back. Let's go home. It's the best offer you're going to get."

She hesitated, hopped up with a small yelp, and trotted over to climb into the backseat like a smart, well-adjusted pooch. We had sized each other up very well. Fortunately, an acquaintance, Trish Tucker, the new house manager at the Brooklyn Academy of Music, was looking for a dog. She came to see Gretl and said, "Oh! She's a Rhodesian Ridgeback! See that tuft of hair on her back? I've always wanted a Rhodesian Ridgeback!"

They immediately liked each other. I hated to let Gretl go, but I was still in an apartment with a landlady who didn't want dogs, and I knew Trish would give her a good home.

A week or so later, a *Times* ad caught my eye: *Mini-estate on one acre in Closter, New Jersey. Three-story house with four bedrooms, two baths, and artist studio. $60,000.* I drove out to see it, and—*zowie!* Proudly surrounded with trees and greenery, it stretched from Closter Dock Road to the city woods. I bought it, intending to move in before Mark returned from Ardmore for the school year.

Oh, I know what you're thinking.

"Hey, didn't Rue just buy land up by Brent and Murph a few pages ago?"

Well, yes. I did. Some people follow baseball, some play the horses or the stock market, some engage in esoteric hobbies they share with weirdos of the same persuasion, some join cults, some become politicians. Me? I like acres. *Lots* of acres. And finally, I had a steady income, so I was in a position to do more than dream.

Of course, I had no furniture, but Trish, who'd had a monumental fight with her roommate and wanted to move, had a lot of furniture. We decided to pool our resources, and she and her stuff—and Gretl!—moved into the Closter house. Mark returned from Oklahoma with Sandy and our cat Panther, and—*voilà!*—we were a family. After about a week, Trish brought in another cat, a dear old gray-and-white tabby with big round eyes and a very gentle nature who'd been bullied in his former home. I named him Grover, and we all gave him a lot of love, which he slowly learned to accept. (Later on, Lette coined the term "Grovering," which applied to anyone needing a little extra love.)

Mark and Trish soon had seven large fish tanks lining the dining room—six for freshwater fish and one that held Mark's saltwater beauties. Held them until they jumped out onto the carpet, that is. Mother came up and bought him a forty-dollar triggerfish that committed hari-kari within hours, somehow finding a small opening near the filter system to leap through. The tanks looked beautiful against the big dining room windows looking out on the front yard. Gurgling and burbling, they provided an ongoing show. Mark was quite knowledgeable about all the varieties: which ones were compatible, which ones weren't, their peculiar qualities.

Beyond the dining room windows was his large new trampoline. Yes, finally I could afford one! He learned a lot of daring trampoline stunts, and I shot videos of him and Phillip flying through the air. I could do a few leaps, but I never tried anything too Flying Wallenda. I'm athletic but no damn fool. For his fourteenth birthday, I bought him a spiffy new Honda SL minicycle like the one he had in Oklahoma, and we took it up to Murph and Brent's, where there was room to ride it.

⁓

Michael Cacoyannis, considered a top-rate director, was casting a production of *Lysistrata* to star his friend, Melina Mercouri, a Greek movie star famous in the States for the film *Never on Sunday*. He granted me an audition for the role of Kalonike, Lysistrata's best friend, and for four blessed hours, I sat at his kitchen table, reading for him, discussing the play, and generally wooing him into casting me. When I left, I had a whale of a headache, but by gollyannis, I had the part.

Rehearsals began in early October. *Sticks and Bones* was posted to close September 30. A convenient segue. This production was to be a hip new American version of the play by Aristophanes, in which warweary Lysistrata calls the women together, convincing them to withhold all sex from their husbands—drive them crazy, no matter how long it takes, no matter how horny the women get—until the men stop this war foofaraw and there is peace and tranquillity. The Cacoyannis rewrite had original music, written and performed by the leader of the pop group The Lovin' Spoonful. Some of New York's funniest actors were cast, and everyone began rehearsals with high hopes.

First day of rehearsal, we started at the top of the play. It's dawn. Lysistrata appears center stage, looking out, wondering aloud where her lazy girlfriends are. Kalonike—that was me—enters from the back of the house and runs down the aisle toward the stage, calling, "Lysistrata! Lysistrata! Why have you summoned me?"

Cacoyannis called from the audience: "No! No! Eet's '*LEE-seestrata! LEE-seestrata!* WHY 'ave you summoned me?' Go back! Take eet again!"

Returning to the back of the house, I ran in again, doing it exactly the way he did.

"*LEEseestrata! LEEseestrata!* WHY 'ave you summoned me?"

"No! No! No! Eet's 'Why 'ave you summoned ME?' Try eet again."
Back to the starting point, run in.

"*LEEseestrata! LEEseestrata!* Why—"

"No! No! Don't use an accent! Do eet like I do eet! No accent! Again!"

Like he does it . . . but no accent. Hmmm.

Me, with American accent: "LEEsistrata! LEEsistrata! Why have you summoned ME?"

"Oh, no! Not 'summoned ME!' 'SUMMONED me'! We don't 'ave time, just move on!"

Every sentence I uttered after that, he stopped me and corrected the syllables he wanted stressed, changing it every time. He gave me no time to get acquainted with the character. Do eet like he does eet! But no accent! And I wasn't the only one. He gave syllable readings to everyone but Mercouri, with whom he conversed in Greek. The morning was interminable. That afternoon, we were turned over to the musician to learn some of the songs, which were confusing and disorganized. How does the music fit into the story? Who's supposed to sing what? And when are they supposed to sing it?

Next morning, we started at the top again, and again there was no way to do it "right." Two of the actors quit. The third day, the oldest character actor, a man of some reputation, quit. That day, an actor who had one of the larger roles invited me to have lunch with him and his friend, Peter O'Toole, who was somewhere between filming *Goodbye, Mr. Chips* and *Under Milkwood*. When I related the week's goings-on, the stunning Mr. O'Toole said, "Oh, darling, just do what we British do. Tell the director to sit there like a good boy and keep quiet, then jolly well do it your way."

That made me laugh, but there was no way Cacoyannis was going to keep quiet. And a good director shouldn't! He is supposed to help the actors find their way. But that was clearly not going to happen here. The fourth day, I gave the stage manager notice that I was quitting.

"Oh, no you're not!" he told me. "You signed a run-of-the-play contract."

"What?" I was horrified. "No! I never signed for run of the play!"

I called my agent, who confirmed that I was right. But when I ran over to the Equity office, they showed me that my contract was indeed filed under "Run of the Play." My heart sank. I was trapped. Held prisoner by that control freak! I cried all the way home to Closter.

Friday morning, I reported for work and the assistant stage manager handed me a pink slip.

"What's this?" I asked.

"You're fired."

"Wait a minute! I couldn't quit, but they can fire me?"

"You actually did sign a regular contract. Equity filed it under 'Run of the Play' by mistake. What's the problem? You wanted out, didn't you?"

Well, yes . . . but I felt oddly demeaned. I'd never been fired before. Still, bottom line, I was out of that turkey. Free at last! Then I realized I was out of both Broadway jobs. It had been a long time since I'd been unemployed, and I immediately began to worry I'd never work again. So, for the first and only time since beginning to earn my way strictly as an actress, I took on a job that popped up out of nowhere. Well, out of Trish's mouth, actually. She wanted to have new outfits made for the Brooklyn Academy of Music ushers. Forty-two peacock blue polyester Cossack shirts.

"Forty-two peacock blue polyester Cossack shirts?"

"Forty-two peacock blue polyester Cossack shirts."

(Say it aloud. Has a nice ring to it.)

"And I need them in four weeks. Can you do it?" asked Trish.

"I can do it."

We settled on a price, and I drove all over New Jersey looking for enough peacock blue polyester material to make forty-two Cossack shirts in an array of sizes. Surprising how much blue polyester I found that wasn't *precisely* the peacock blue Trish had in mind. Finally, I found the right weight, the right number of bolts, the right price, and Lord help us, the precisely right shade of peacock blue. With only three weeks left, I farmed out a third of the shirts to a seamstress at the Metropolitan Opera and a third to a friend, and we worked feverishly, using a pattern I'd bought. I set up shop in my dining room. The fish watched, their tanks burbling and gurgling, as I cut and sewed day and night, swimming in peacock blue polyester.

About halfway through the task—hallelujah!—I got an acting job. Another appearance on *Maude*. But it didn't start until January, so the Cossack shirts got delivered on time.

And I bet you four Cossacks and a peacock I never make another one.

Lysistrata opened in November, with Murph, Brent, and me perched expectantly in the balcony. I'm not a drama critic, so let's just say that show should have been arrested. Those talented, funny actors were not funny, and their talent was lost in the mishmash. Even the stunning Melina Mercouri couldn't inflate that lead balloon. It closed after eight performances.

There's a story about a New York play starring an actor named Guido Natso. Some clever drama critic is said to have remarked, "Guido Natso was notso guido." I can't come up with anything that clever. But from that day to this, I have referred to the director as Michael Kakapoopoo. Maybe I just had an unusually bad time with him. But I don't *THEENK* so.

That October was lovely. Mark and I spent another wonderful Halloween with Murph and Brent, wandering our spectacular Berkshire acreage, scaring the willies out of Mark's friend Danny with the old ghost hunt, sipping cocoa, devouring gooey s'mores and Louisa's apple pie, parting with hugs and promises to see one another soon.

On December 15, Murph and Brent were driving from the upstate house back to New York, Brent at the wheel, the highway slick with sleet. When they hit the black ice, Murph was thrown out onto the right shoulder of the highway, grievously injured but alive. Brent was thrown into traffic, where he was run over and killed instantly.

Oh, my God. Brent. Mark and I were in shock—and heartsick for Murph.

Brent's parents came up from Texas and tried to take all his possessions—things he and Murph had shared for years—as well as half the house, which was in Murph's name. Murph, still on crutches and desolate at the loss of his partner, had to battle them with his lawyer, who managed to beat them back to Texas with only the belongings of Brent's that Murph was willing to part with. Murph sold the house and eventually moved to Florida, where I'm happy to say he found love and friendship with another good man.

As for the house, I rejoice that the new owners made it into a getaway that guests adore. I think our love must linger there, in the walls, in the air, in the yard, and certainly across the creek and in the sky, where Brent runs invisibly under a great ghostly white parachute every Halloween.

⌒

Poor Mark was miserable at the Closter school and reached a low point in January. For a week, he didn't get out of bed, incommunicado.

"I can't go back to that school," he finally told me. "I do want to be with you, Mother, but I think I need to go to Ardmore."

Not knowing what else to do, I called Bill and Mother.

"Send that boy down here," said Bill. "I'll put him to work and make a man out of him."

I agreed but first took him with me to L.A. when I did my second appearance on *Maude*. Mark's motorcycle idol, Evel Knievel, was doing his daredevil thing, and although the show was sold out, we hung around outside the gate, watching from afar. When we returned to New York, Evel was appearing at the Nassau Coliseum on Long Island, and I did get tickets. (Oh, joy—Evel Knievel twice in two weeks!) But Mark still wanted to move to Ardmore, so I sent him. I thought a man's influence might be good for him, and there certainly wasn't another one in sight. Mark finished ninth grade at the same school I had attended and even had the same world history teacher, Mr. Todd, who ended every class by saying, "And that's all they are to it!" And that summer, Bill did put him to work, along with Melinda's son, Brendan.

Living alone—well, alone with Trish, Sandy, Panther, Grover, and seven tanks of suicidal fish—I invited an actor friend over for dinner one night. He stayed late, and we thought it best he spend the night in Mark's room and have breakfast with me and Trish, after which I would drive him to the city. On our way over the George Washington Bridge next morning, he asked, "Why are you living with a lesbian?"

Taken aback, I said, "Huh?"

"You can't tell me you don't know." He made a face. "My God, Rue, it's obvious."

Hmm. Trish did play poker one night a week "with the guys." And she had switched jobs to become a bartender. But a lesbian? It had never even occurred to me. Then, on my birthday, Trish invited me to the bar where she worked. Wall-to-wall women. I felt like such a dumb bunny. But around me, she was always a perfect gentleman!

The ides of March rolled around and found me playing Will Hare's wife in Brian Friel's play *Crystal and Fox*. In the role of my son was a spectacular young actor named Brad Davis, who was twenty-three playing a seventeen-year-old IRA escapee being sought by the police. Crystal and Fox, itinerant Irish gypsies, harbor the runaway son in their wagon. Opening night, I found a bouquet of flowers on my dressing table and a note from Brad, giving me the clear impression that the young lad had a crush on me. Although I was flattered, I was not about to open that can of peas. But Brad was equipped with a very effective can opener.

The play closed a couple weeks later, and Brad got a job with Handy Andy, a yard service. By June, my large yard was begging for pruning and clearing, and he needed work, so I hired him to come out a few times a week. He worked like a Trojan (oh, dear, those puns), doing a bang-up job (yikes, there's another one!) on the yard. I found him very funny and terribly sweet—but still off-limits.

The sparring continued.

"Brad! You're only nine years older than my son, for heaven's sake!"

"What does that have to do with anything—for heaven's sake?"

Late one afternoon after he'd cleared the last of the overgrowth and carried it out to the street, we took a tour of the yard to check it out. He was joking and acting the fool, and we were laughing, heading down the hill toward the artist's studio. The houses on either side of the property were a hundred feet away. All was still. Nobody in sight. In fact, in all the months I'd lived there, I had never seen either of my neighbors.

Brad stopped and said, "This farce has got to end. You know it's inevitable."

And he kissed me. And right then and there, on the grassy hillside under the June sky, we both dropped our Levi's. A little while later, Brad was on his knees, zipping his pants up (and he gets an A, with a capital *A*!), when we heard a cheerful voice across the yard.

"Hello, Miss McClanahan! Isn't it a lovely day?"

About forty feet away, my neighbor lady to the west could be seen striding down her yard, waving. I hunkered down in the grass and wiggled back into my jeans, zipping them as unobtrusively as possible, calling, "Yes, isn't it? So nice to see you!"

Brad burst into laughter, helping me up, dancing around, singing, "Isn't it a lovely day? So nice to see you!"

I grabbed his hand and pulled him up the hill to the house.

That Brad Davis was a caution. Of course, we both knew the affair wasn't going anywhere, but he turned out to be one of my three best friends, along with Norman Hartweg and Lette Rehnolds, and the only best friend I shared with Mark, which I found a charming coincidence.

CHAPTER SIXTEEN

⌁

"When all is done, it won't be Broadway."

—ABIGAIL ADAMS

In the 1790s, to serve the newly founded America, John and Abigail Adams had to move from New York City to Philadelphia, the capital at the time, prompting the above statement from Abigail. In the 1970s, to serve my newly burgeoning career, I had to move from New York City to the film capital, Los Angeles, and let me tell you, Abigail had it right—it sure as all heck wasn't Broadway.

In the United States, the acting profession is divided between New York and Los Angeles, some 3,000 miles apart. As everyone knows, the best stage acting is found in New York. You've heard it a thousand times: "If you can make it there, you'll make it anywhere!" On the other hand, films and television are concentrated in L.A., so which coast one lives on determines the "kind" of actor one is thought to be by many producers. All too many.

It's even more finely segregated in L.A., where TV actors are shrugged off by the film industry. If you make your name in television, most movie producers won't even see you for an audition, judging you incapable of big-screen roles, an inferior talent who can't cut it in films. Of course, if you get your start in films, you can move into TV. And

Broadway producers are happy to have a big Hollywood name they can post on the marquee, but most of them assume that television and film stars really can't handle stage work. Too often, they're right.

New York stage acting being the acid test for serious talent, most film and TV stars just don't measure up on or off Broadway. And, to be fair, some New York stage actors can't handle sitcoms, because sitcoms require not only a gift for comedy but a lightning-quick memory and instant invention of characters in four days. Accustomed to having weeks to learn roles before having to perform at top level, stage actors aren't trained to deliver so quickly. For film stardom, you need one major attribute: gorgeousness. This is a generalization, of course. Some actors are transcendently talented enough to make it big as movie stars, regardless of their not-quite-classic looks. (Witness Dustin Hoffman, Barbra Streisand, Woody Allen, Gene Hackman—not that y'all aren't good-looking, kids! But you ain't exactly gorgeous.) A few actors who start on TV go on to film stardom—Sally Field, Bruce Willis, George Clooney, Steve McQueen—but since these are talented, highly charismatic actors (as well as damned good-looking) for the most part, the rule holds.

In England, an actor is an actor is an actor, and since most of their work is done in London, actors can do TV in the morning, a film job in the afternoon, and end with a stage role that night, but in the USA, with our most peculiar geography, we're stuck with those built-in prejudices. There are some of us actors who excel in all three arenas, but we must repeatedly break down those prejudiced walls to prove it.

It's maddening, I tell you, my dears, maddening!

During nine difficult years in New York, I did eight Off Broadway plays, five Broadway, one in England, four in New Jersey, three major movies, three soap operas, four commercials, two summers of stock, various voice-overs, and a backers' presentation for an unfunded play. I got every acting job but two that I auditioned for. And eight were simply offered, without auditioning. Do I sound like I'm blowing my own horn?

Good! Because most of the time it was a trumpet solo.

In the spring of 1974, Norman Lear called and asked, "How would you like to move to the West Coast and become a regular on *Maude?*"

"Perfect timing," I said. "I just bought my first house a few months ago, so of course, I'd love to move to California!"

That made him laugh. He wanted me to start the new season in three weeks. I called Mark, and he was all for moving back to L.A. I contacted a realtor and put the Closter house on the market, then advertised a garage sale, selling everything we didn't absolutely need, including the trampoline, the Honda minicycle, my VW, and (alas!) Mark's hypnotically lovely fish. I asked Trish to send Sandy and Panther to me when I got settled. Meanwhile, Trish rented the bedrooms to several lesbian friends of hers until the house sold.

Lette Rehnolds had moved to L.A. to marry one of her conductor loves, Fred Sharp (whom she called "F Sharp"), and divorced him within the year, surprising me not. She and another actress, Linda Palmer, were now sharing a condo in North Hollywood. When I arrived in L.A. with nothing but my matching *It Could Be You!* suitcases, both Lette and Linda were about to leave town to do summer stock for six weeks, so I moved into Lette's room and bought my first brand-new car, a blue Mazda wagon, in which I could trundle back and forth from the condo in the hills to the CBS studios in the heart of Hollywood.

That first morning felt like a giant leap forward. We sat down to read through the script, and I looked around at my illustrious coworkers. Bea Arthur, Bill Macy, Conrad Bain, Esther Rolle—what talent! What comedy expertise! And lest we forget, beautiful Adrienne Barbeau was in there to spice things up. Working for Norman Lear is the best thing that can happen to an actor. He is brilliant, cheerful, funny, handsome, self-effacing, and runs a happy ship, demanding the best writers and applauding top-notch performing. He also has a will of steel. Of course, I had a crush on him. Who wouldn't? (He was married, so I didn't even think of such things. Well, I thought them, but—y'know.)

We had the same director, Hal Cooper, for every show, giving us a cohesiveness you don't get when the directors change each week. After six weeks, we had five shows in the can and would complete a few more before the fall season premiered. I was earning $1,500 a show—hardly a fortune by Hollywood standards, but so what! I was working with the *crème de la crème*! And I hadn't forgotten the good ol' days of biting off tongues for forty bucks a pop. My part was small, not much to do, but as the writers got to know me, sexy Vivian began to take shape.

"How do you come up with this stuff?" I asked, and one of them said, "We watch *you*."

We heard every week: "Let's not forget: The name of the show is *Maude*." Our head producer, Rod Parker, gave many funny lines to Bea Arthur that had been written for Bill, Conrad, or me. But we offered no complaints. The rest of us had our share of zingers, and with Norman there to keep things on an even keel, we were a happy cast. His humane use of time and talent made it the easiest job I've ever had. And I learned that if there is a sane, well-balanced, brilliant person at the top, he'll hire similar people right down the line.

We began our workweek on Wednesday morning at ten, gathering around the big table on the sound stage to read through the new script. We discussed it, trying new lines, then the writers went off to rewrite, tweaking it for time and punching up the laughs. Meanwhile, we got our blocking (which means figuring out who goes where at any given moment), getting new pages from the writers all day long. Thursday morning, we read the new script, blocking it anew, and then the writers came in to see us do it on our feet, and then once again, we all sat around and discussed changes.

In my experience, Norman was unique in that he encouraged actors to contribute ideas. Most producers keep the actors on a shorter leash, but Norman wanted us to contribute. Bill Macy was always spit-balling ideas, most of which were too impossibly far out to use. Undaunted, he kept throwing out ridiculous suggestions that made us either groan in disbelief or break up laughing.

We were whisked to costume fittings during the second and third day, on a packed schedule, which often took at least part of our lunch break. On the weekends, the writers rewrote like mad. On Mondays, with yet another rewritten script, the cameras and sound came in to learn their moves. Three cameras had to learn the blocking as precisely as the actors, and we actors had to be carefully placed for our lines. A fourth camera picked up whatever wild shots Hal Cooper wanted, in case he could use them in editing. Monday afternoons we did a run-through in costumes. Tuesdays at 11:00 A.M., we read the (again) new and improved, freshly revised script and went through the play for cameras and sound. Then off to hair and makeup, costumes, and finally, at five o'clock—a live taped performance on camera for a full audience. In between, I often took naps on the carpet behind the sofa.

We broke for dinner in a big hall, getting new lines while we ate. Back to touch-ups, and—whammo!—we were on for the eight o'clock show, wondering how much of the just-revised script we'd actually remember with no additional rehearsal. We had to hit marks and wait a split second before delivering our lines, to coordinate with the cam-eras instead of using stage timing. You can see why sitcoms were beyond many stage actors. They are hair-raising!

"This is somewhat reminiscent of acting," I used to say. Or maybe it's more like walking a tightrope across Niagara Falls without a net. Bea Arthur always made the sign of the cross before her first entrance. And she's Jewish!

We taped three weeks, then had a week off so the writers could develop ideas for new shows. During the week off, I often appeared on game shows. (The PR firm I hired got me just enough game shows to pay their fee.) By working three weeks on and one week off, we got the entire year's work in the can in eight months, wrapping in late February and resuming the new season in early July. So we taped about twenty-six shows a year, half a year's salary.

Today's sitcoms are not usually done this way. Some don't even have dress rehearsals. If the star of the show is also the producer, you might even find ad-libbing going on, and you'll also be likely to find that the show doesn't have a long run. Although *Maude* was a superb comedy, it wasn't picked up to rerun in syndication until fairly recently. Ahead of its time, you see. A show about a militant feminist is almost as tricky in the twenty-first century as in the twentieth. Many weeks, we were right up to taping time, 8:00 P.M., with a full audience, while Norman Lear and the network locked horns over whether we'd be allowed to put that outrageous script on the air. Norman always won. Except once. A minor loss. The CBS station in Cleveland refused to run an episode that dealt with abortion. Our "warm-up" guy, writer Charlie Hauck, who entertained the audience before we started taping, happened to be from Cleveland. Taking questions from the audience, he planted a member of our crew to ask him, "Do they show *Maude* in Cleveland?"

"Yes, they show it," Charlie would reply, "but they don't get it."

It was also Charlie who came up with a great line for me to say in a last-minute note session. We needed a good punch line for a bit about inventors, and Charlie suggested Vivian say in her big-eyed way, "I had an uncle who invented a universal solvent, but he couldn't find a container to keep it in."

Was that brilliant, or what? To be honest, I had a tiny crush on Charlie, too.

⁓

With Mark coming out in a few weeks to start tenth grade, I needed a permanent place to live, so when Lette and Linda returned to L.A., I suggested the three of us lease a house together. They liked the idea. We figured we'd have fun, not to mention being able to get a much nicer place than any of us could afford separately. I looked. And looked. And looked . . . and finally—found!

Pacific Palisades is an upscale community overlooking the Pacific coast, about a forty-five minute drive to CBS. A university couple going on sabbatical for nine months wanted to lease their large furnished home with a backyard and pool for only $625 a month—a fraction of what that place would lease for today. It was beautiful, laid out to perfectly accommodate three single women and a teenaged boy. I installed Linda in the spacious lower level, a private suite with an upright piano and private opening onto the backyard and pool. Lette, Mark, and I took the three small bedrooms on the main floor. I proposed Linda and I each pay $250 per month and Lette pay $125, since she had only her bedroom and would be sharing a bathroom with Mark and me. In late August, we moved in and Linda went off to New York for two weeks.

Back on the old home front, Trish wrote that she was sending Sandy and Panther out, and when I went to the airport to pick them up, I discovered she'd also sent Grover and Gretl.

What? Gretl was *her* dog!

Oh now, this would really thrill Lette to pieces—two dogs and two cats. Gretl and the cats turned out to be no trouble at all, but Sandy had to be shut in my bedroom when I went to work. If I left her in the yard, she barked, and Lette slept very late every morning, getting up around eleven, feeling like hell warmed over, in no mood for Sandy's serenade.

Mother and Melinda and Melinda's friend, Caroline, arrived soon after, having traveled halfway across the country for three days in a van to bring Mark to L.A.—along with four other kids and Mark's gerbils. All three women looked as if they'd spent those three days in a Cuisinart blender. At one point on the trip, they were pulled over, because one of the children had to pee, so Mother gave him an empty paper cup in which to relieve himself and, when she threw it out the window, it flew smack onto the windshield of a highway patrolman. Mother hadn't noticed him behind them.

"I'll handle this," she said, stepping out of the car, and a minute or two later, she came back and said, "Let's go." What did she say to the officer? Who knows? That mother of ours had a way about her.

Also, during the trip, the gerbils kept escaping their box and scampering all over, exploring the van. After three days of this, Caroline was driving when one of the gerbils ran across her right foot on the accelerator. She didn't even flinch. Just remarked, "Well, there goes another gerbil."

I don't know where we bedded all the folks down. Everyone remembers it differently. Mark recalls sleeping in his bedroom, with most of the others in the downstairs den. Melinda remembers that she and Mimi slept in Linda's big bed until one night she and Mimi both felt a "presence" in the bedroom and took their bedclothes upstairs to the living room. We all remember that the kids spent most of their day in the pool and playing Ping-Pong on the deck. Good old Skipper Edelen came down from San Francisco and we had a dinner party, snapping goofy photos, laughing ourselves silly. Finally, everyone but Mark set out for home—minus the gerbils. Panther had dispatched them all, or they had packed their bags and taken a hike, we never discovered which.

Lette christened our humble abode "The Hen House" and initiated *The Hen House Herald,* a thick notebook to which we all contributed. It contained pages of gripes and laughs over the next nine months. Believe me, we had plenty of each. Lette wrote a lot about The Rooster, her name for Jack Quigley, the conductor she was ga-ga over for the next fifteen years. Even Mark contributed, and *The Hen House Herald* still exists, with copious deletions—primarily about The Rooster— that Lette excised before departing this earthly realm. To this day, I haven't been brave enough to read it. One day, I'll get out four boxes of Kleenex and give it a try, hopefully with Linda.

In October, Mother came back out for Mark's fifteenth birthday, bringing—oh, goodie—more gerbils. She'd visited us only a month before, yet she felt the need to return. This was unusual. Knowing she'd be at The Hen House for only a week, we threw a party to which I invited many friends, including the only movie star I knew—the gorgeous John Saxon, one of those character actors who get a lot of the old "Oh! You're *that* guy!" I thought she'd get a kick out of meeting him, and she did, but the whole time, she was strangely unlike her old ebullient self.

One day, Mother and Mark and I took Sandy and Gretl to the beach, and Mother looked at Gretl and said, "You know, Rue, I think that dog's pregnant."

"So that's why Trish sent her! What a dirty trick!" I cried. "And you know how Lette feels about animals. She'll really love this."

"Why don't I take Gretl with me and find homes for the puppies?" Mother suggested.

This was a huge relief to me, but I felt terrible loading such a task onto Mother when I could tell something was troubling her. The night before she left, she confided to Lette and me, "Some days I feel like wading out into Lake Ardmore and never coming back."

This alarmed me. My dear darling mother, seriously depressed?

"When I was in Europe," she told us, "I saw the Berlin Wall, and I sank into a bad feeling that hasn't let up."

"Mother, you need to drive up to Dallas or Oklahoma City once a week and talk to a therapist," I urged, but she pooh-poohed such an unheard-of notion. Lette and I both told her therapy had made big changes in our lives and could help her understand what was going on. But she left for Ardmore the next day, sure she could handle it herself, which worried me.

One crisp morning in October, a golden retriever trotted into our front yard. He had a collar but no ID. I checked the local paper and saw an ad that fit his description.

"Yup," said the man who answered the phone. "Sounds like my dog."

The fellow showed up within the hour, coming from a canyon several miles west of us. Toole saw Josh. Josh saw Toole and immediately ran and jumped onto his chest, licking him joyously. (You can surmise which was the guy and which the dog.) Josh had been missing for a week, and this happened to be the last day of the ad. How lucky!

And speaking of getting lucky . . . this guy was not bad-looking. Fancy that.

Do you smell another escapade? Are your loins girded? If not, gird up.

Toole and I chatted a bit, and while I was less demonstrative than Josh, I found Toole—oh, what did I find him? Awfully nice. Tall and slender with light brown hair, a country manner, easy to talk to, about ten years my senior. We took to each other, as they say, and exchanged phone numbers. (Just in case Josh should decide to fly the coop again, you see . . . *ahem.*) Soon, he called me. Would I like to see his place in the canyon? *Ooooh,* would I. I'm nuts about canyons! Nuts about goldenrod! Hay fever? Nuts about hay fever!

I drove out the next afternoon, finally locating his secluded acreage. He was living in a trailer near the spot where his hand-built house had recently burned down. Seems he'd bought this acreage and built a house, then gone back to Oregon, where he had an apple orchard, which provided his income, and during his absence the house had caught fire. He suspected arson. It was all very intriguing. I liked Toole, but I was nervous. This was such a different sort of man from any I'd ever met. Very sexy, in a low-key sort of way. Quietly masculine. Quietly unlettered. Of the land.

We climbed down to the creek and up to the hill where his house had been, and after about an hour, he asked if I'd like a cup of tea. Yes, I would. We had it inside his trailer. The tea was nice. Toole was nicer. Definitely an A+. Oh, yes. A+. Definitely. He and his wife were virgins when they got married and had found sex easy and natural. He'd been with no woman but her. I was his *second*? Wow! I looked at him like he was a unicorn. He never inquired about my experiences, being not the least bit curious. I seemed to suit him fine.

Need I say we saw each other rather frequently? Usually at his place out there in the canyon, beautiful in a dry California kind of way, with all that shoulder-high, incessantly waving, godforsaken golden-rod. I sneezed, my nose ran, I sneezed, my nose ran. Luckily, Toole had a lot of handkerchiefs. In fact, he usually wore a checkered one tied around his forehead, like a hippie. A hippie farmer. He looked cute and terribly sexy.

One weekend, Toole took Mark and me up to the Mojave Desert for an overnight camping trip under the stars. The desert was blanketed with tiny flowers of all description, and the light changed every second, coloring the bluffs and buttes with reds and golds and purples. I had no idea the desert could be so breathtaking.

We drove to the top of a mountain to "Burro" Schmidt's Tunnel. According to local legend, this guy Schmidt had been told he would die from tuberculosis unless he moved to the desert, so he did, spending the next thirty years in that forsaken place. He'd hand-laid tracks half a mile long, digging through the mountain with just a burro and a small wagon all summer, tending sheep for ranchers in the winter. It was an inspirational story. Mark and Toole and I explored the tunnel with lanterns, coming out high over the desert. Back in the ramshackle house, I bought four kerosene lanterns from the roughshod woman who ran the place. She was quite fascinating herself, telling us how she dug the water well and once fought a mountain lion on her own. Mark still has those lanterns, and they still work! That night, Mark and Toole and I slept on army cots under the stars, more stars than I'd seen since the 1950s in Oklahoma.

The second season of *Maude* debuted to great reviews. It wasn't as popular as *All in the Family,* but it was solid. I was having a marvelous time in the show. And I was having a pretty marvelous time with

Toole. He was so . . . *bucolic*. So unfailingly, easily, sexy. Meanwhile, Mark was happy at Newbridge, a progressive private school. He was drawing and painting like crazy and learning to play guitar with a teacher who judged him inordinately talented. Mother had bought him a guitar that summer in Ardmore, and I now bought him a better one. He practiced for hours every afternoon after school and all weekend.

We had a party at The Hen House practically every weekend, with Mark and Lette jamming on piano and guitar and Lette and Linda singing well into the night. (I must have heard "Cabaret" 460 times.) Lette had a brief affair with a Greek realtor before she met Jack Quigley, the "rooster" who would become the love of her life. Linda was in a new series, and as I recall, sleeping with the lighting man.

Oh, let me promise you, *The Hen House Herald* was full of news.

For one thing, the new batch of gerbils immediately moved to Timbuktu.

⌐

News from Mother in Ardmore in early October. Gretl had her puppies.

Six days later, on October 15, Mother had a heart attack.

She was ordered by her doctor to stay in bed four weeks and not lift a finger, so her sister Irene, who had helped raise me, came from West Texas to care for her, staying for over three weeks. Melinda drove up from Louisiana and took Gretl and her brood home, finding homes for the pups. (Then she had the good sense to have Gretl spayed, and I'm happy to say that Gretl lived with Melinda to the end of her days, and they got along swimmingly. That Gretl was one of the best dogs I ever knew. You couldn't help but love her.) As soon as Irene left, the second week of November, Mother got up and started doing things and had another heart attack, which put her in the Ardmore hospital.

Maude was on a week's hiatus just then, and I was in the middle of a large role on a TV special about mothers and daughters. Torn whether to complete the week's work or go visit Mother right away with nobody to take over my role, I decided to finish the work, then ask to be let out of *Maude* for a week. On November 16, the day the TV job wrapped, I got home to The Hen House, walked into the living room, and put down my purse.

The phone rang.

My uncle Billy Joe, Mother's brother, said, "Well, Eddi-Rue, we lost her."

The bottom dropped out. I fell into a chair. He said she had had a third heart attack at the hospital and died immediately. In the mail that day was a letter from Mother written November 12, saying she wasn't satisfied with the care in Ardmore and thought she'd go see an Oklahoma City specialist at the end of the week—the very day she died.

I told Mark, who took it well. I didn't take it well at all. I was in shock, glassy-eyed. I booked us a flight to Dallas. Billy Joe drove us to Ardmore for the funeral. Everyone in the family seemed to be taking it in stride. Only I and my father, who'd been out of town when he heard, were clearly devastated. Relatives stayed at the house, sleeping all over the place. Nine-year-old Mimi and I shared the pull-out sofa in the living room. As we lay in bed the night before the funeral, she asked me, "Aunt Rue, what if an elephant falls through the ceiling on us?"

"Mimi," I said gently, "never in the history of the world has an elephant fallen through the ceiling on anyone. So don't worry."

She said, "Aunt Rue, this could be the first time."

The kid had a point. I felt as if one had already fallen on me.

⌒

Funerals are obscene. Looking at Mother in the casket at the funeral home—that strange, unrecognizable face, laid out in an ugly dress she had hated—this wasn't my beautiful Mother! It was some clumsy wax effigy. Watching the casket being lowered into the earth—surreal! Impossible! In the limo on the way back home, I couldn't control my grief. All the kids stared at me, embarrassed.

"Aunt Rue," Mimi said, "there's nothing to be sad about."

Mimi had known Mother nine years. But at thirty-nine, I had lost my dearest friend, my most powerful ally, the woman who'd stood by me selflessly, helped raise Mark for fifteen years, the only person I could always depend on, who could make me laugh in a special way. I was astounded to see Mark so in control. My father was obviously shaken to his roots, remaining distant and silent. If anyone had depended on her more than I did, it was Bill. They had been married forty years. She was only sixty-one, he sixty-five. Way too soon.

In my childhood, when I was afraid, I'd say, "Mother, I don't want you to ever die."

"Oh, don't worry, Eddi-Rue," she'd always assure me. "I promise I'm going to live to be a hundred. My father's aunt—my aunt Belle Haney—why, she lived to be a hundred thirteen!"

And now our little redheaded dynamo was gone.

Unable to stay in that Ardmore house, I drove to Denton, Texas, with Melinda and her kids. We picked up pecans in their yard at dusk, my panic raging, then had supper. Sheridan was out of town, so I crawled into Melinda's bed with her, needing to talk, gripped in a paroxysm of grief. But characteristically in control, she went to sleep. I lay awake, reading one of her science books all night.

Thanksgiving day, I flew back to L.A. and walked into the dark, empty Palisades house at dusk. Lette and Linda were away for the holiday. Mark had stayed in Ardmore a few days. Not a soul in the place. As the desolate darkness swept over me, I picked up the phone and called the only pal I could think of.

"Bea?" I said unsteadily. "I'm back from Mother's funeral, I'm alone, and—"

"You're coming out to my house," she said. "Right now. We're just finishing dinner, and there are plenty of leftovers."

When I arrived, there were maybe ten people around the table, including her mother, who lived with her and her husband and their boys. Bea made me a plate of food, then tucked me into bed in a guest room. Her tender, gentle care finally brought me peace, and I slept soundly.

The theme song played at the start of every episode of *The Golden Girls* was a little ditty called "Thank You for Being a Friend." A bouncy little bit of bubblegum music. Hardly a tearjerker. But those words probably don't get said enough. A friend in a moment of deepest need—that's truly something to be grateful for.

I shall never forget Bea Arthur's loving kindness that night.

CHAPTER SEVENTEEN

*"We've been visited by several flying saucers.
One green creature even came into my son's bedroom."*
—DEBBIE, SPA MASSEUSE

Christmas in Southern California. Rudolph the red-nosed coyote. Deck the Hills with plastic holly. Oh, what fun it is to ride in a Porsche Cabriolet. Baja humbug!

Yes, yes, I know the Christ Child story originated in a desert clime, so it makes sense cinematically, but I never got accustomed to all that damn sunshine. I want the schmaltzy all-American holiday magic with chestnuts roasting on an open fire. I want to go caroling and freeze my nose off, then come home and warm my cockles (whatever those are) with a big old mug of hot cider! I need that. That's *Christmas*. Give me a Winter Wonderland. Brother, you can have all that sand.

Toole and I drove up into the mountains one day in December and happened upon a yucca stalk on the ground. It's illegal in California to dig up yuccas, but this one was long dead. Lette and I made it into our Christmas tree. Somehow, it seemed appropriate. Tall, yellow, dead, leafless. We festooned it with decorations and composed a song: "Hang Your Balls On the Yucca Tree." (After Christmas, I tied it to my car aerial with a big yellow bow, and I never had trouble spotting my Mazda in a parking lot.)

The *Maude* production schedule continued without catching a breath, but my grief took its time becoming bearable. Bill came out the week of Christmas, bringing with him a big, blond lady, who stayed a day or two before departing to visit relatives. She ran the Rod and Reel Motel that Bill owned in Arkansas, and I don't know what else their relationship was. He said women had been coming out of the woodwork, and that Marie, who worked in Mother's beauty parlor, was particularly making a play for him. I tried hard to create a somewhat cheerful Christmas for Mark and Bill, who said he still dialed their home number to talk to Mother, although he knew no one was there. Hearing him say that cut me to the quick.

Lette's brother, Huntzie, had a ranch in the hills, and we drove out on Christmas Eve day to spend the afternoon with him and Lette's parents, Bertha and Dickie. Lette did her best to lift my spirits, but this was not Christmas as I had ever known it. It was alien and wrong in that dusty, hot environment with people I didn't know that well—or particularly like. Lette's family was nothing like her. Dickie was a nebbish, Bertha loud and pushy, and Huntzie was a hotshot ladies' man, always on the make. They spent the day watching football, while Lette and I wandered the scrubby hillside trails.

When I was a child, I had a recurring nightmare in which I slogged through knee-deep sand, watching my mother and father fly away in an airplane. Now, how many Freudians does it take to screw in *that* lightbulb? The meaning of the dream was obvious, and now that nightmare had come true. Wandering that arid, alien desert on that hot Christmas Day, Mother's absence was almost intolerable. The bottom of my world had dropped out, and I fell through the hole into panic. *Grief* doesn't describe it. Grief is painful, but it makes sense. Panic is a pervasive, unreasoning terror, and the dark heart of my panic had always been the fear of losing Mother. Being abandoned.

The reality of it gripped me in razor-sharp jaws.

Bill and I struggled through our first holiday without her, then he went home to Oklahoma and the throngs of widows vying for his attention. Still hale and hearty at sixty-five, he was bidding on jobs and building like crazy. He kept the beauty shop going, getting more and more entwined in Marie's web. Bill loved the house he'd started building in 1946 and was still busily improving, planting, watching things grow. Mark continued to go to Ardmore during the summers, riding minibikes with his pals, comfortable in the house where he'd spent much of his childhood. But I had a hard time being there. The empty rooms screamed at me. If Bill was the soul of that place, Mother was the heart. And now the heart was gone out of it.

Looking back at it, The Hen House was similar to *The Golden Girls*. Lette, Linda, and I were three single women in our late thirties, one with a son living with her. Dorothy, Rose, and Blanche were three single women in their fifties and sixties, one with a mother living with her. However, while both routinely qualified as comedy, one was real life and one was pure fiction. All the women had conflicts, that's true, but in Sitcom World, everything works out in thirty minutes minus commercials. The differences between Lette and Linda and me were harder to resolve.

We three little showbiz cutie-pies had our share of arguments and, after I got my Irish up, a couple of monumental fights. Perhaps our lifestyles were—how shall we say—a mite incompatible? Lette was neat to a fault, demanding that the kitchen be kept pristine, always on time with her rent payments and her part of the utilities. Linda was—how do I say this?—much less disciplined. This meant that I was in the middle—not sloppy, not superneat, but in between—so neither of them liked how I did things, and both kept coming to me with grievances.

One day Linda confronted me, furious because a package of cookies was missing from the pantry. I asked Mark, who said he'd eaten them, not realizing they were Linda's. I replaced them, but she was still pissed off. Obviously, she really loved those cookies. Meanwhile, she was almost always late with her payments. I collected the rent and utilities and mailed them out, since the house was leased in my name. I was always bugging Linda for her tardy portion, but it didn't lessen our friendship. She was just lackadaisical. And we had a lot of fun when things were going well, giving dinner parties galore.

Lette was hot and heavy with Jack, Linda dated various guys, and I kept seeing good old Toole. Mark was in love with his guitar and getting quite good. He and Lette kept playing music together, which helped improve his technique. She'd gotten a job as lounge pianist and singer at the Jolly Roger, a North Hollywood restaurant. Never one to disguise her feelings, Lette called it "the Jolly Cocksucker." Many nights I went down to catch her act, that glorious soprano delivering both torch songs and comedy numbers with equal prowess.

"Never forget, Lette love, that you are singing for all of us who would give our eyeteeth to sound like that," I kept reminding her.

Much of the time, her talent made me blubber. But the girl could not act to save her life. Of course, she wanted desperately to get into television, and I coached her, but she couldn't interpret a script well enough to get a role on TV. Put her in a stage musical and she was fine, but in a nonsinging role she was lost. I drove to a dinner theatre near Disneyland to see her play Mammy Yokum in *Li'l Abner,* Agnes Gooch in *Mame,* and other leading comedy parts. Between these gigs, she played and sang at the Jolly You-Know-What. She and Jack were getting to be quite the ticket, but Jack, who was divorced with four teenagers, had no inclination to get married. She was frustrated—head over heels about him.

I, however, was becoming less and less head over heels about Toole. He was basically a laconic ex–apple farmer, not doing much to restore his burned-down house or improve his land. He was odd, offbeat, but not intellectual or artistic, and although he was sexy as could be in a plaid shirt and dungarees sort of way, I felt the need for more . . . stimulation. So to speak.

The Pacific Northwest was his stomping ground, and he wanted to take me on a car trip up the California coast. All the way to Eureka and back—in a week. Eureka is about seventy miles from the Oregon coast, so this would be one heck of a lot of driving. Everyone knows that a car trip—all that confinement—is a valuable litmus test for learning how two people get along, so when *Maude* shut down for its spring hiatus in March, we set off on our adventure, Toole driving so I could enjoy the gorgeous coastline.

Early on the first day, he started whistling "Tea for Two." Not a classic "pucker up and blow" kind of whistle, but a thin sizzy whistle from between his teeth. And not the whole song, mind you, just the first two bars.

"Tea for two, two for tea, me for you, you for me . . ."

Between his teeth, you see. Over and over and over about nine jillion times.

"Do you know any other songs?" I tactfully inquired, nails digging into my palms.

"Nah, just that one," he said, and smiled.

"Well, I'll teach you another one!"

I whistled a few other short ditties, but he couldn't repeat them. He had no sense of pitch, and by the end of the trip, I had no sense *whatsoever,* having been rendered brain-dead long before we got back to L.A. At that point, he could have whistled Mozart's *Magic Flute* in its entirety, for all I cared. I just wanted to get the hell out of that car and shake loose of Mr. Bucolic.

But he was not so easy to shake loose. He kept calling from time to time but finally got the message, and I never saw him after that.

⟶

In May, the nine-month lease on The Hen House was up. Linda bought a place in the Hollywood Hills—a gorgeous four-story house that Lette dubbed "The Castle." Linda asked Lette to move in as her tenant, but she didn't invite me, Mark, and the menagerie. And we would have politely declined if she had. I loved them both to bits, but—grow up, kids!—*The Golden Girls* is a fantasy. Three grown women and a teenage boy are not likely to make good housemates for more than nine tempestuous months. Mark and I happily moved a few blocks up the street to sublet an adorable two-bedroom cottage. It was perfect for us and our little zoo, and Mark stayed with me for the summer, studying "on the street," as he puts it, with an advanced guitarist friend and jamming with musician pals out in the patio laundry room.

One August day at dusk, I got up from a nap to take the garbage out. The laundry room had a wide sliding glass door that opened onto the patio, and on my way back in, I noticed the light on over the clothes dryer and thought, *Oh, that kid. He left the light on in the laundry room. And what's more, didn't close the door. Good grief!* and headed full steam across the brick patio, stepping down onto the short cement walk, meaning to stride headlong into the laundry room, but instead plunging headlong through the closed glass door in an earsplitting burst of shattering glass, and as I was falling, I thought, *Oh, my God, I've gone and killed myself!*

I landed facedown with one foot impaled on the protruding shards at the bottom of the door and smaller fragments sticking out of me here and there. I felt blood pouring down my face from my forehead. Gingerly feeling around up there, I found a large V-shaped flap of skin hanging down to my eyebrows. I pushed the skin back up to my hairline and held it in place as best I could, carefully pulled my foot upward from the jagged scythe at the bottom of the door, extracted pieces from my hand, elbow, and knee, then limped across the patio, crying out, *"Mark! Mark! Call the paramedics!"*

Trailing blood, I hobbled to the kitchen, grabbed dish towels, and made tourniquets for my right ankle and instep. Blood was pouring from the severed toes on my right foot. Sickened and faint, I pressed a cold wet rag to my forehead and called Norman Lear.

Now, I just heard several of you say, "What? You're sitting there practically bleeding to death, and you called Norman Lear?" Well, hell, yes, I called Norman Lear! More than a boss, the man was a friend and father figure to his cast and crew. And he was the only person I knew with the big-time Hollywood clout to get me the finest arthroscopic surgeon in L.A. Which he did.

Fading fast, I told him, "I'll meet you at Santa Monica Hospital in about half an hour."

I sat down outside on a chaise lounge so as not to mess up the kitchen any worse. The paramedics arrived, took one look at me, and ordered me to lie down.

"I'm afraid I'll faint," I said.

"You *will* faint if you don't lie back! You've already lost a third of your blood."

They hooked me up to a blood transfuser and began treating my wounds. Then I was popped into the ambulance. At Santa Monica hospital, we found the emergency room busy with a little boy who had been badly burned, so I had to wait, but Mark was with me, and soon Norman Lear arrived. I was still receiving blood transfusions, but surprisingly, not in a lot of pain. Everywhere I'd been cut was still mostly numb. The surgeon finally rushed in. First, he stitched up my forehead and hand and elbow and knee—*ouch*—then started on the tendons on my little toes, all of which had been cut clear through and had to be sewn back together. *OUCH!* I was waxing quite nostalgic for that good ol' numbness by the time he put my right leg in a cast.

"You'll need crutches for six weeks," he told me. "And physical therapy for about a year. I'll give you some exercises to do on your own, to get some flexibility back into your toes."

Believe it or not, I was back on the set one week later. The show must go on, kids. Writers explained the leg cast and crutches by saying my husband, Arthur, had backed over my foot with the car. The next four or five shows, I played on crutches, then started the weird experience of shedding the cast, which felt like walking on big plumpy marshmallows. (The hardest part with the crutches was climbing the forty steps up to The Castle for Lette and Linda's dinner parties.)

Turns out, the laundry room door had been installed without a permit, using substandard glass. The kind that shatters and can slash people to ribbons. Lette had a lawyer friend, Tom Cronin, who filed a lawsuit on a contingency basis, and after the best part of three years, the case got to court. The owners' lawyer was a big man with a forceful manner. Tom was a little milquetoast fellow, soft-spoken, stumbling over his presentation. I thought, *Oh, brother* . . . But Tom won hands-down, and I was awarded $30,000 in damages, which didn't seem like a whole lot when I sadly realized I'd never dance *Les Sylphides* again. I applied myself rigorously to getting my foot to work as normally as possible, but that poor little tootsie—the same one that had never quite recovered from the cocktail waitress job at the Largo—requires a half-size larger shoe than my pretty little left foot. As for the forehead scar, the surgeon did a great job; it doesn't even show anymore. Besides, I usually wear those adorable bangs.

By November, I was walking normally again, performing in *Maude* with gusto. It's not easy to get through life without injuries—internal or external—and I've acquired my quota, but they're just battle scars, mostly attributable to my own dumb mistakes. If I hadn't been pissed off at Mark for leaving the dryer light on, I wouldn't have charged hell-bent-for-leather into that glass door with such energy.

Mea culpa, all you saints. Now lay off.

⟶

There was a prop guy on the *Maude* crew—Luis from Rio—with whom I'd exchanged pleasantries from time to time. In his midthirties, tall, lean, and muscular, he had dark, snapping eyes and a teasing smile. He had a nice manner, full of fun. Sometimes he would stop by where I was watching rehearsals and we'd have a laugh together.

One day, Bea observed our exchange, and after Luis walked away, she turned to me, and said, "*Really,* Rue!"

"Oh, *really* yourself, Bea!" I laughed. "I like him. Even if he is just a prop man. He's still fun to flirt with. And he has an interesting story."

Born into a wealthy Rio family, Luis had been sent by his father to Hollywood to learn the film business and had brought with him his fiancée, also from Rio. They shared a nice little two-bedroom apartment, but she was a lot younger than he, and after a few months in Hollywood, she broke off the engagement. This threw her family into an uproar, but Luis pacified everyone by promising to continue to look after her, pay her bills, and be her guardian. They slept in separate bedrooms, and she was dating other people when Luis and I met.

He was quite smart and ambitious, aiming to become a producer. And also quite funny. But nobody I'd want to hook up with, except for fun and games. Luis taught me a little Portuguese and a fabulous Thanksgiving turkey recipe he'd gotten from his family's cook. He was as talented in the kitchen as he was in the bedroom. The first night we slept together, he sat up on his knees in bed, gazed down at me, and pronounced, "Now you are *my voman*!"

I swear to God he did. But I didn't laugh. He was completely serious. This was one macho Brazilian. I wasn't his *voman,* but we kept dating off and on, and I made his turkey recipe for a Thanksgiving party at my house.

Mark went to Oklahoma for Christmas, while I still had one last episode of *Maude* to complete before the holidays. As we gathered around the table for final notes one afternoon, our producer, Rod Parker, remarked casually, "Oh, Rue, I ran into someone who knows your ex-husband, Tom Lloyd. She said he was in a terrible accident and almost burned to death."

That slammed me against the wall. First the name, and then the news.

"Tom Lloyd? Are you sure? What kind of accident?"

"A car fire or something. Would you like his number?"

"Yes . . . yes, I would," I said, thinking, *A car fire. Oh, God.*

I tried to focus on notes, but all I could see when I closed my eyes was that gorgeous face. A face I still loved. After all, I saw it every day on my son. The thought of Tom being burned was heart-sickening. I called him the minute I got home, barely breathing when he answered.

That voice.

"Well, hello," he said. "What a pleasant surprise. After all these years."

He said that, yes, he'd been in a car fire about a year ago. Driving from a lady friend's place in Pasadena to his apartment in Hollywood, disgruntled over the relationship and thinking of ending it, he smelled smoke. The driver's seat suddenly burst into flames that engulfed him. He pulled over and ran out—on fire—trying to climb the fence at the side of the freeway, out of his mind with terror and agony. A passing motorist stopped and wrapped him in a blanket to put the fire out. He regained consciousness in the hospital, both ears burned off, extensive burns on his face and torso, his right arm so damaged it never completely recovered. He'd spent most of the year in the hospital, undergoing treatments and surgeries, with more skin grafts to go.

"I'd like to take you to dinner tomorrow evening," he said, adding, "Don't be surprised at how I look."

The next night, I was shaking as I opened the door. Oh, my God, people. Violins swelled. Mark's father. Still gorgeous. Noticeably older, but still handsome as hell. He'd grown a brown and gray mustache and beard to disguise the scars, but his eyes were the same brooding hazel eyes I'd fallen in love with, minus the long lashes.

"You look wonderful," I said, embracing him carefully. "I wish Mark was here. He's in Ardmore for Christmas."

"Well, I'd like to see him when he gets back," said Tom. "Ready to go?"

We went to dinner, and I disgraced myself, weeping at the table. I couldn't help it. My heart was so full.

"Rue. My God," Tom said in annoyance. "You're ruining our dinner."

God knows—and I knew!—I was behaving like a ninny, and I was excruciatingly embarrassed, but my emotions were simply on cruise control.

"Rue, I'm enrolling in this seminar called EST," he told me. "Maybe you should take it, too. It's like a Zen-influenced workshop that takes you from personal weakness to powerful 'beingness.' They say it can transform your life."

It sounded like something I'd find interesting, so I went with him to the EST seminar the following week. It covered, as I recall, one long weekend for about twelve hours a day. Or maybe it was only ten hours and *seemed* like twelve. In his book *Fear and Loathing in America,* Hunter S. Thompson harshly described it thusly: "Erhard Seminars Training (EST), a pricey, psychobabbling series of long and demeaning behavior-modification sessions that preached the virtue of selfishness."

The leader also put us through exercises I'd done years before in acting classes, such as imagining a huge flower, with me the size of a bee, exploring it. Much of the material had been taken from Eastern philosophies and reworded in contemporary English, so it was new to many in the huge class of maybe two hundred people, who asked incessant questions and argued nonstop with the leader, annoying me no end. Tedious. Boring. We weren't allowed to have a drink of water or go to the bathroom for—oh, God, hours on end.

The first night was over very late, so Tom and I went home with friends of his who lived nearby, since we had to return to the next morning's meeting very early. We shared a small sofa bed. I'd entertained a stray thought or two, but he turned on his side, away from me, and I got the message: no touchy, no feely. The second day, the leader took us through a "Truth Process" to the "Danger Place." Many in the class went flat to pieces. One man threw himself down in the aisle near me in a screaming fit and had to be carried out, and I was half tempted to follow suit.

First toe shoes, 1947. (Mother made the tutu.)

With big John Hayes in the yard of our North Hollywood rental house, 1961. He's trying to look stern.

The Italian, me, Mark, and Sandy, Christmas, 1969. Fort Lee, New Jersey.

With Dustin Hoffman during Jimmy Shine, *Brooks Atkinson Theatre, 1969.*

Lette as Billie Dawn, me as The Blue Fairy, and Linda as Carmen Miranda at Linda's birthday party. I borrowed the Miranda drag from the Maude *costumer!*

*With Dabney Coleman
and Jack Gilford in*
Apple Pie, *1978.*

John Wayne with Conrad Bain and me on Maude, *1977.*

One of our early publicity shots for The Golden Girls, *1985.*
Me, Bea Arthur, Betty White, and Estelle Getty
(Blanche, Dorothy, Rose, and Sophia).

"But you'll be in the book!" Emmy acceptance speech, 1987.

Me with "the fifth golden girl," our marvelous director Terry Hughes.

Betty and I dressed for our roles in CATS *in a* Golden Girls *segment. Wish I still had that costume!*

Bill and Marie, taken above my back forty acres in Encino.

Keel repairing the pool. See what I mean?

With Bob Hope the night I appeared on his show, mid-1990s.

With Buster Big Balls in my Encino living room, 1992. Some cat, huh?

Finally, everyone had to report to a counselor to be asked, "Did you *get it?*"

That was the big EST secret, "Did you *GET* it?"

I said, "Oh, yeah. I *got* it."

There were smaller one-night seminars, and I signed up for two: "Be Here Now," which I actually found very helpful, the idea being that we should live in the here and now, which is all we really have. And "Sex," which included childbirth—with a film. For me, this was excruciating. I could barely sit through it. My childbirth experience had been so painful, both physically and emotionally, and the man who was responsible for it was right there in the same room. It brought it all back. I was shaken. On the way home, he was all smiles, in fine spirits, unable to comprehend my being so undone, and I was ashamed—yes, ashamed—to tell him why. That I still loved him, that I longed for him to love Mark, that his rejection of both of us never stopped aching. I couldn't explain it. I was struggling to understand it myself. Maybe it's like the way a baby duck "imprints" upon hatching, latching onto whomever he sees first. If it's the mama duck, fine, but if the baby duck's first sight is the farmer's wife, he follows her around until he's grown up. But even a baby duck grows up. When would I? (Quack?)

Tom didn't come by to see Mark after the holidays, but I went to the hospital while Tom was having more skin grafts, taking him home-baked goodies. He seemed glad to see me and was an obvious favorite of the nurses, joking and laughing. He was always good company for anyone not in love with him. For my birthday in February, he brought me a big box of twelve wineglasses, and I again burst into tears, which made him impatient. He didn't understand what it meant to me—he'd *given me something*.

"Baby Rue," said Lette, shaking her head over the whole thing. "I want you to see my therapist. She's about to retire, but you can get in twice a week for the next few months. She's phenomenal."

Lette was right. This woman *was* phenomenal, calling a spade a spade, more on-the-mark than any human being I'd ever met. Whereas I could always find an excuse for the people who behaved badly, she would come straight out and call them shits. No ifs, ands, or buts. I stayed with her until she retired, and I did begin to see things more clearly. Oh, there would be a few more hair-raising experiences with men, to be sure, but she planted the seed of good judgment that, over time, would blossom into a healthier and healthier plant.

See how versatile I am? From baby duck to budding flower in just three paragraphs.

As the winter drew to a close, good old Luis and I took a trip to Lake Tahoe to spend three days learning to ski. Actually, we learned how *not* to ski, thanks to Fritz, the bunny hill Nazi. (*Hals und Bein brechen,* Fritz!) Luis went home with a wrenched shoulder, I with a twisted knee. Later that spring, Luis actually proposed marriage, and though I thoroughly enjoyed his company, I was never really serious about the relationship. I broke off with him, although we remained friendly, and I have to give my Latin lover an A. Oh, yeah, a big Brazilian A for Mr. "Now you are my voman!" Which still makes me smile.

Also that spring, I got to re-create the delectable Fay Precious— that role I loved when I did *Who's Happy Now?* Off Broadway years earlier. PBS did a divine film of the play, starring John Ritter, Betty Garrett, and Albert Salmi, along with Alice Ghostly and some other wonderful character actors. We shot it in a forgotten, dusty little town up in the Mojave Desert that was ideal for Sunray, Texas. It was a glorious experience, took about two weeks, done on various locations— not sets, but real houses. You should see it. I'm telling you, it's edible.

At the end of my second season on *Maude,* I was making $2,500 a show. (What is that? $60,000 a year?) A nice step up from the first season. I'd hired Jean Stapleton's agent, because Jean was a big star and one of the nicest people I'd ever met, so I figured she'd have a nice agent. Not that a "nice" agent is necessarily a *good* agent, but apparently this guy had just the right amount of pit bull in him. He negotiated my third-season contract to jump to $4,000 a show, and I knew *Maude* was going to run a few more years, with automatic raises every year. So it finally made sense on paper to drop anchor in California and buy a house.

School let out for the summer, Mark went to Oklahoma, and I started house hunting for something comfy and cozy with a good music studio for Mark. The perfect place popped up on Doheny Drive in Hollywood, just above Sunset Strip. My dad came out, remodeled Mark's studio and bedroom, and built a beautiful wooden fireplace façade—his own design—in the living room. He also started replacing all the plastic water pipes under the house with copper pipes, but we had some planks stacked outside the garage, and some inspector came by, asking, "Can I see your permit?"

Oops.

Bill had no permit, and to make matters worse, that section of town didn't allow copper pipes, only plastic, and we also had to change the garage door back to its original form, even though it had been altered by a previous owner. Mad as all hell at the dumb California laws, Bill finished the work and returned to Oklahoma, where things made sense.

At the garden nursery to buy plants for our swell new house, I saw a workman about to heave a half-grown kitten into the alley and called out, "Stop! I'll take that cat!" A black-and-white longhair with a black Charlie Chaplin mustache, Celestine was pure sweetness. Sadly, dear Grover had recently died during surgery for an old injury. *Dammit.* But he had three good years with us, finally knowing that he was loved, the big round-eyed sweetie.

⟿

Before Lette met Jack, she had had a brief fling with a charming Greek realtor. Early forties, six foot two, big head of thick, dark hair, brown eyes, well-built. A mite weak in the chin, but he camouflaged it with a nicely manicured beard. Some people thought he looked like Dean Martin, but I thought he was more of a poor man's Perry Como. Being in residential real estate, he dressed like a high roller, and I must say, he did look mighty good in suits. The Greek remained on the Castle dinner party guest list, and as you may have guessed, one thing led to another, as one thing is inclined to do. Especially when that one thing is little ol' me.

So buckle up, folks. We're about to go for a rather jolting ride.

The first time The Greek squired me to dinner, late in the summer of 1975, he took charge in a glad-handing sort of way. He knew the place, and they knew him. I was impressed with how he handled himself. It's nice when someone is genuinely proud and happy to have you on his arm. The conversation was not especially scintillating. He wasn't witty, but he was high-spirited, so we laughed a lot. We started going to Lette's soirees together, though he always got sleepy and wanted to leave before I was ready. He also went home from work every afternoon for a nap. For a grown-up, he sure needed a lot of sleep.

One afternoon, he came over to my house and totally missed his nap.

The Greek was masterful in bed—not tender or especially original, but he got the job done, performing with gusto. One afternoon, we had sex five times in a row. *Five!* We were both amazed at ourselves. The man obviously loved sex, which gave us something in common, though he had one move that always reminded me of those mechanical oil drills that seesaw relentlessly on the Oklahoma fields. Nonetheless, I'll give the man a B for bumptious enthusiasm.

We had a good time folk-dancing in downtown L.A. He knew all the Greek dances, and I picked them up quickly. (Folk-dancing can be a blast, although the Greek dances always featured the men, the women confined to waving around decorously while the guys jump and stomp.) He also took me to visit his hometown in West Virginia, an economically deprived place where his relatives lived simply with their big families. He and I got along fine and there was a spark there, but I didn't find him smart or interesting enough to ignite much fire, dammit. But he was the only bull in the pasture at the moment, and I figured, hey—you don't have to go completely gaga over every guy you date, do you? (No, Rue, but you sure as hell don't have to marry them, either!)

As we got to know each other, I began to get intimations that he was much more politically conservative than I, voting not for the common good or the big picture but for the best immediate advantage to his business, which surprised me, because he came from a poor immigrant family who ran a little grocery. He'd gone to college on a basketball scholarship, then joined the Marines, and from there moved to Hollywood with the goal of becoming an actor, but he had no natural talent. Ambition, yes—but the bells, he did not ring.

"My father passed away when I was in high school," he said with tears in his eyes. "My mother didn't speak English, and I remember watching her carry heavy boxes of beer, working in that store until she died."

Relating this story always made him cry. I should have realized then that he was scared of being poor and was determined to have money, because I had the same fear and the same goal. I had started Mark's college fund when he was four and always saved whatever money I could, not wanting ever to be old and poor and dependent. Being young and poor is okay, being old with money is okay, but being old *and* poor? Not okay. The difference between me and the Greek, as it turned out, was that I planned to earn my money, not marry it.

—

In the spring of 1976, while Mark was finishing his senior year and I was spending my *Maude* hiatus in Ohio doing a play, a taxi pulled up in front of the house and a guy called out to Mark, "Is this 1201 Doheny Drive?"

"Yes," Mark shouted back.

The guy crowed, *"FAR OUT!"* and ran to get his bags.

It was my Levi's-dropping pal, Brad "Isn't it a lovely day?" Davis. He'd just finished shooting *Sybil,* in which he played the boyfriend of at least a few of Sally Field's several personalities. Mark put him in the front bedroom, and they stayed fast friends for the next sixteen years.

An amateur theatre group in Hollywood was doing a meticulous six-month rehearsal of Chekhov's *The Cherry Orchard,* which came off very well for a non-union play, and The Greek performed relatively well in it. He played the self-made neighbor of the cherry orchard's financially depleted owners. His character makes repeated offers to buy the property, both to save these dreamers from ruin and to cut down the old orchard for commercial development. The family is finally forced to sell, and the play ends, you may recall, with the sound of heavy axes felling the grief-stricken family's beloved orchard. I could have taken it as an omen. (I know, I said I don't believe in omens, but this one was the exception.)

"We need to get married," The Greek abruptly announced in September. "If we don't get married now, we're going to drift apart."

I stood there with the phone to my ear, feeling cornered. The old panic loomed. *Drift apart?* What's *that* supposed to mean? He was going to dump me? I would be alone? But wait, wait! I thought I was over that "I must have a man or I'll die!" neurosis.

"I'm just . . . I don't think . . . I'm not ready for marriage," I finally said.

"I need a commitment from you, Rue," he said. "Now."

Oh, dear. C'mon, Rue, baby . . . say the words . . . *Let me think it over.* You can do it!

"I need to think it over!" I blurted out, and hung up the phone.

Hurray! Therapy *über alles*! For the moment.

I couldn't think. Frozen with panic, I paced the room. *What to do? What to do? Tom doesn't love me. I am alone. Now this man will drift away, and I'll be even more alone.* I felt myself getting stampeded over the cliff again. Why didn't I call a therapist? Why didn't I call Lette, who would have given me a good swift kick? Nothing entered my mind except ending the unbearable panic, so I called The Greek back.

"Okay. Yes. I'll marry you," I said. And the panic evaporated on the spot.

I wasn't happy, but I was enormously relieved. Anything was better than that quagmire of abandonment and desperation. *Heck, it won't be so bad,* I told myself. *He has a lot of nice qualities, I can make it work,* blah blah blah. Cleopatra, Queen of Denial.

The Greek found a pretty house at the end of a cul-de-sac in Studio City: three bedrooms downstairs, a master suite upstairs, large pool, spacious fenced yard for all our animals, including his Irish setter. There was a large roofed back patio where Mark's groups could get together to jam. Not as suitable as the soundproof studio my dad had built him, of course, and Mark was not pleased to leave Doheny Drive, but once again, had I consulted him? Not that I recall.

Throughout all those years, Mark had no notion of my panic problem. He probably figured I *wanted* to marry The Greek. Mark was funny and intelligent, into music and art, while The Greek was into football games and real estate, so they had zilch in common. For that matter, The Greek and I had about as much in common as a blow-fish and a baby's butt.

I sold my house to make my half of the down payment on the new place while The Greek used his real estate savvy to avoid spending any of his own cash. I arranged for the personal portion of my income from *Maude* to go into our joint account, putting the larger portion into my pension plan in the loan-out corporation I'd formed in 1975, when I was finally starting to pull down some real money. The Greek had acted as witness to the signing of those papers, in fact, just weeks before he called with the ultimatum about getting married!

With only six weeks to plan the wedding, we had a gazebo built in the backyard. I wrote a folk song called "I Gave My Love" for Lette to sing with Jack on keyboard and a beautiful ceremony to be read by Bea, Adrienne, Bill, Conrad, Hermione Baddeley, Norman Lear, Mark, Brad, The Greek, and me. He invited every relative and friend he had in the continental United States, from West Virginia to Chicago—about three hundred people—and I invited another hundred. Andrew Greenhut flew out from New York. Bill drove out from Ardmore, bringing Marie, the black widow from Mother's beauty salon. (Yippee.)

The day of the wedding, his relatives brought over suitcases of Greek food for the reception (though I'd ordered quite enough from the caterers, along with shmancy table settings). I wore a Grecian gown designed by Rita Riggs, the *Maude* costumer—a soft lavender silk confection with a circular headdress and veil. (I still have it, though I've yet to find the right occasion to trot it out again. Maybe some Halloween.) The Greek was in a tux, looking oh so suave. Mark bought his first tux, a light blue one (hey, the seventies, right?), setting off his shoulder-length wavy blond locks. Even Brad was in a tux, with long, tousled hair, and I can still see the two of them, heads together, whispering and laughing.

Yep, this shindig was some kind of spectacular. A gorgeous wedding, in contrast with the marriage to follow. It was like one of those opulent display cakes that are actually just tons of sugar frosting and a plastic bride and groom stuck on top of a stack of empty hat boxes. The Greek had a pal of his video the whole affair, which went on until well after dark. Champagne flowed. Norman Lear joined in the Greek circle dance. Bea Arthur, somewhat looped, regaled everyone with an impromptu solo. The Greek's relatives began smashing the expensive rented plates on the patio until someone stopped them. Some little weekly paper printed a large article, with oodles of pictures, and The Greek, having snagged a minor celebrity, bought forty copies. (And he watched that star-studded wedding video incessantly until, to my secret glee, he accidentally taped over it with an episode of *Starsky and Hutch* or some such thing.)

A week later, the Greek relatives finally went home and we left for our honeymoon in Carmel, a lovely community up the coast, one of the most desirable places in California. I remember our first evening there, walking with him at sunset on the idyllic beach, thinking, *Oh, Lord God in Heaven . . . I don't love this man.*

CHAPTER EIGHTEEN

～

"Turn him loose, Edna, that mule's gonna buck."
— Percy Kilbride

I'm not much of a cook. Sort of hit-and-miss. Without an Italian around to keep me on my toes, it's up for grabs. Once I took a Chinese cooking class with The Greek and Bea Arthur ("The Greek and Bea Arthur"—there's a song title for you) and learned all sorts of complicated and time-consuming dishes, each of which required unending chopping and mincing. Shortly afterward, the Greek and I threw a dinner party for twelve, featuring six of the dishes we'd learned. The day of the party, while he was at the office, I started chopping, mincing, slicing, and generally hacking up the mountain of ingredients. By late afternoon when he came home to help, I was feverish, my fingers were sore, I had cut myself twice, and I had learned to swear in Chinese: "Dam fok hung cheet!" I felt as if I'd been dragged full tilt behind a sampan through rough water. That was the first and last Chinese dinner party I ever gave. Or ever intend to.

Living with The Greek came about as easily as the *chop chop* Chinese cooking.

Deeply enamored of Barbra Streisand, he came home every afternoon and put on one of her albums, lowering the living room lights, stretching out soulfully on the sofa, the house filling and overflowing with her mellifluous rendition of "People"—his top favorite, which he played incessantly. I had liked Streisand up till then. But having her in my house day after day, week after week—darlings, had it been Beethoven or Bach, okay, but even people who need people don't need to hear about it every damn day! I walked around the house with my hair hurting.

Before long, I began to feel that The Greek was using my celebrity to impress people. He insisted I go with him to real estate functions, and I felt like he wanted me there solely as a jewel in his cap. I tried to tell him nicely at first, "Honey, I'm a fish out of water at those things. I'm sorry, but I just don't enjoy it."

But he was adamant, his brown orbs turning into cow's eyes. "Rue, I need you to do this for me."

"I don't like being shown off like a mounted marlin," I told him on the days I had a little more backbone. "It's embarrassing."

I rebelled, demanding my privacy, which of course made him very angry. There was no shouting. He simply receded into stony silence for days at a stretch, refusing to speak to me or even acknowledge my existence.

When *Hollywood Squares* invited several stars and their spouses to Jamaica for eight days after Christmas, all expenses paid, The Greek jumped at the chance. We spent New Year's Eve at the Playboy Club, which I found abhorrent, but I did get a kick out of my fellow celebrities. Paul Lynde in his signature dashikis; Rita Moreno, peppy and friendly; George Gobel, funny and sweet; and most delightful of all, Jonathan Winters, brimming with outrageous fun, so original, so full of nutty ideas, I fell out laughing whenever he was around. The New Year's Eve bash was overflowing with too many people, too much noise, too much gratuitous hilarity. I climbed up on a chair to get above the crowd, feeling trapped and claustrophobic.

I've always hated New Year's Eve parties, with their ridiculous festivities based on some dopey idea that this is a great thing to celebrate. We all know it's just a drummed-up notion of when the "new year" starts—according to Julius Caesar. But we're all supposed to go mad with paper hats and razzy whistles. I always stay at home on New Year's Eve, usually going to bed before midnight, so for me, that night was miserable. The Greek, on the other hand, had a ball in that crowded, noisy room full of famous people. I left moments after midnight and went to bed, spending the next day walking alone on the beach, picking up shells and rocks, while most everyone else was back at the hotel nursing a hangover.

⁀

The Equal Rights Amendment reads, in its entirety: "Equality of rights under the law shall not be denied or abridged by the United States or by any state on account of sex."

I was doing what I could to help get the ERA passed, which, of course, it wasn't. Perhaps we'll have to try again later with less violent language. Anyway, The Greek and I went to a big ERA fund-raiser in Bel-Air at which Jane Fonda and Gloria Steinem spoke. (Oddly, Jane was serious; Gloria was funny.) We arrived at the event and joined a few other people in a limo to be taken a few blocks down the street. Chevy Chase was in the backseat, and he leaned forward, extended his hand to The Greek, and said, "Hello, I'm Fernblock Diddleberg."

The Greek shook his hand and said, "Nice to meet you." Not a clue.

Still, he managed to be a great hit with both Bea Arthur and Hermione Baddeley, who now played Maude's housekeeper. He was always a good man to have at a party: handsome, cheerful, skilled at working the room. He flattered and charmed the britches off Bea and Hermione, and they both ate it up. On his forty-fifth birthday, I had given him an elaborate surprise party at a restaurant he often frequented with his cronies, and he was appropriately surprised and delighted. On my forty-third birthday the following February, The Greek arranged a birthday party for me after the taping of *Maude* in one of the rooms below the soundstage. He'd come to Hollywood full of big dreams, and it thrilled him to be part of that world. But we were all tired after the taping. I remember thinking, *How inappropriate. These people don't want to be here, they want to go home.* But everyone strove valiantly to get their spirits up for the party, which was a blessedly short one.

⟋

That spring, Norman Hartweg arrived in Los Angeles. The icy Michigan winters had become too much for him in the wheelchair, so he headed for the land of sunshine, driving himself cross-country entirely by hand. I was delighted to see my dear old friend.

"You'll stay at our house until you find a place," I insisted. "We have plenty of room, and Mark will be so happy to see you."

To my mind, this was a perfectly natural thing to do, but The Greek didn't see it that way.

"Rue, he's your ex-husband, for Christ's sake!"

"He's one of my dearest friends!" I shot back. "And the man is in a wheelchair. He needs a little help right now, and God knows, he's helped me more than once."

Norm had a tube attached to his bladder that drained into a bag he had to empty several times a day, and sometimes during the night it leaked onto the mattress. He was with us for six weeks, and when he moved, I washed the mattress and put it out to air, which didn't bother me a bit. He'd have done the same for me. But The Greek was furious and spent the next several days treating me like the amazing invisible woman.

I was trying to keep this Edsel on the road, though, so I quickly agreed when he came to me and said, "I'd like to stop working and go to commercial real estate school for eight months. Could you handle the mortgage and the bills by yourself? It would be maybe a year before I could expect to start earning money again."

"Of course," I said. "If that's what you want, you should do it. I'll handle the bills."

But when Mark graduated from high school in June, he said he'd like to take a year off before deciding exactly what he wanted to do, and The Greek thought this was a terrible idea.

"He should be doing something useful with his life," he said. "Something that will help him get ahead."

Like what? I wondered. *Marrying a celebrity?*

It made me heartsick when I thought of what Mother might have thought about the way I'd been sucked in again.

By the end of 1977, I couldn't take any more of The Greek's bloody *don't rain on my people who need misty watercolor memories* Streisand ad infinitum—in short, I could no longer stand *him*. In December, I told him I wanted a separation and, without much argument, he moved into one of the suites at the Magic Castle Motel in Hollywood. Ah, but my dad came out to visit us for Christmas with Marie, with whom he'd become quite tight, and finding his football buddy banished from the house, scolded me repeatedly, "Oh, Eddi-Rue, he's a good man. Get him back home. It's Christmas!"

I could barely stand the thought. But I drove to the Magic Castle Motel and asked The Greek to come home for the holidays. I didn't love The Greek, but I *did* love Bill. There was nothing Bill wouldn't do for me, and this was one of the rare occasions he was asking me to do something for him. We all spent Christmas together, Bill and The Greek happy as clams, watching four jillion football games.

But after Bill and Marie left, The Greek stayed on.

～

There are sea-change moments in a sitcom when cast members move on, writers move on, child actors grow up, or an older actor dies. The little snow-globe world that was so carefully created over the years is suddenly shaken up. The trick is knowing when to persevere through the ensuing blizzard and when to call it quits. In March of 1978, at just that sort of crossroad, Norman Lear proposed moving Maude to

Washington to become a member of Congress, but Bea Arthur chose to decline. You know what they say: A lady knows when to make her exit. As we wrapped the series and said fond good-byes, Norman proposed a new series starring none other than yours truly.

Yes, *me*! In my own series! Yippee! Hooray! (Do you sense that I was a tad excited?)

Set in Kansas City during the Depression, *Apple Pie* was based on a little New York play that Norman was having rewritten. A terrific story. I would be playing Ginger Nell Hollyhock, who finds herself alone in a big old Kansas City house during the Depression and advertises in the newspaper for members of a family. Having found a blind grandfather (played perfectly by Jack Gilford) and two sons and a daughter, the pilot opens with Ginger Nell interviewing men to be the father—her mate. Norman called me in to help audition male leads, and I read scenes with several guys, our two top choices being film veteran Tony Curtis and Dabney Coleman, who'd been hilarious in Norman's offbeat series *Mary Hartman, Mary Hartman*. We debated their relative merits, considering the qualities of the character—Fast Eddie Murdock, a charming con man on the run. After much discussion, we made the tough decision to cast Dabney Coleman, and I listened while Norman called Tony Curtis to tell him, marveling at Norman's finesse.

Before we taped the pilot, I had to do a quick movie shoot in Cuernavaca, Mexico—two days' work in *Balls,* a film about tennis (it was renamed *Players* for release) starring Ali MacGraw, Steve Gutenberg, and Dean Martin's gorgeous blond son, Dino (who was tragically killed in a small plane crash shortly afterward). Ali and I strolled through Cuernavaca, chatting and shopping.

"There's a king-sized hand-embroidered quilt on my bed at the villa," I told her, "and I want to make one just like it."

I bought a passel of handmade embroidered coasters, thinking I could sew them together and fill in the spaces with my own embroidery. I figured it would take me a while, and so far it's been twenty-nine years. Don't ever try to embroider a king-sized quilt if you have anything else to do in your life.

I was in Cuernavaca only two days, but I managed to get the trots from the ice in my drinks, so when I returned to California—*oooooh,* boy, I was sick as a *perro.* The night before we were to begin rehearsing *Apple Pie,* I was in my office going over the script, my stomach raging with Montezuma's Revenge, when The Greek appeared at my door, looking hangdog.

"When are you coming up?" he whined.

"I don't know," I said. "I'm starting the pilot of my series tomorrow morning. I'm feeling sick, and I need to study the script."

"But I miss you! When are you coming up?"

I stared at him, astounded. This series was a huge opportunity for me, and I was consumed with the task before me. My intestines were doing a Mexican hat dance, and he obviously didn't give a rat's *culata* about anything but—

"Soon, soon," I answered, wishing he'd just go away.

That was it, as far as I was concerned. As soon as I got the pilot of *Apple Pie* in the oven, he was gonna be out of here.

⟶

Too bad I'll never know how Tony Curtis would have been to work with.

With Norman Lear there to keep a close eye on us, Dabney Coleman behaved himself and was wonderful in the role of Fast Eddie. Much of the action depended on exquisite timing, and he was right on target. The daughter and I got to do a nifty little tap dance. Jack Gilford managed to just miss knocking down any of the furnishings with his flailing cane. It was an hourlong pilot, with James Cromwell coming in as a nervous burglar. After all hell breaks out, we tie it up in a neat finale, with Fast Eddie Murdock saying he'll stay around another week to try the arrangement—but no promises. At the curtain, the audience was on its feet, screaming unanimous approval.

Now we had to wait to see if ABC would pick it up as a series.

Unfortunately, Norman Lear was leaving television, going off to China for a while. Ahead of his time (as usual), he was deeply concerned about the plethora of extreme right-wing evangelists and propagandists and was launching People for the American Way, his liberal activist organization, which is still thriving. It worried me that he wouldn't be around to shepherd us, but Fred Silverman, the head of ABC, who had set the series in motion for Norman, was still very enthusiastic. In late June, we got the word: Our little hourlong pilot would be shortened to a half hour, one of the sons eliminated, the other recast—but we'd been picked up for seven glorious shows, with Charlie Hauck (that terrific writer from *Maude*) as producer and Peter Bonerz of *The Bob Newhart Show* directing. Boola boola! We began shooting early in July, overjoyed.

Well, sir, that's when the caca hit the fan.

With Norman out of the proverbial picture, it was up to Charlie and Peter to keep order, but they had more than they could handle with Dabney Coleman, who behaved as if the series were his own private Idaho. He monopolized rehearsal time, changed the scripts to suit him, consumed precious time with his demands, and drove the writers bonkers. Maybe I should have locked horns with him, but I'm a team player and the stress of dealing with his shenanigans had me pulling my hair out. The rest of the cast was composed of professional, hardworking actors dedicated to making our new series an ensemble hit. Only one of us was doing *The Dabney Coleman Show*.

Launching another cannonball into our bow, Fred Silverman, who'd supported *Apple Pie* from the get-go, left ABC to become head of NBC, leaving his former subordinate Marcie Carcy of Carcy/Warner in charge of all new ABC series. When the seventh segment was in the can, we limped off, exhausted, to await news of how many—if any— more episodes would be picked up. We didn't have long to wait. Carcy quickly dropped us from the fall lineup after airing only two episodes, with scant publicity, never giving the show a decent chance.

A bitter pill, my darlings, a bitter pill.

I'll bet Norman Lear would have taken the show to Silverman at NBC, but . . . *c'est la guerre*. At least I'd gotten to do a soft-shoe number with one of my dancing idols, Ken Berry. And I no longer had to endure being around Coleman. And I do understand the reasoning behind it all: ABC had premiered two heavily advertised new series, *Mork and Mindy* and *Vegas,* two blockbusters. They felt no need to serve up *Apple Pie* for dessert. But the audience was robbed of a really terrific little offbeat series. And my big chance to have my own show got blown away like corn floss in one fell swoop.

～

I didn't sit still for long. NBC offered me a year's contract to be exclusively theirs for two new pilots and two Movies of the Week—pay or play, for $100,000—and I took it. Let me tell you about those two pilots, dear souls. Fred Silverman had an Asian comic he was pushing. I was to play his mother-in-law, with a Vegas comic . . . I'll think of his name . . . I will . . . I will . . .

I won't. I've blocked it out.

Anyway, Mr. Vegas comic was to play my husband. Neither of these guys had ever done any acting. The Korean comic wasn't funny, and the Vegas comic couldn't speak lines and do business at the same time. In one scene, he was to pour a glass of iced tea while speaking his lines, and he never got the hang of how to stop pouring while still talking, so while the speaking went on, so did the pouring, until the tea ran right over the lip of the glass, down onto the counter, and onto the floor, even while we were taping. Need I say the pilot did not get picked up? Need I say *hallelujah?*

Then Fred Silverman came up with another novice he was grooming for stardom, a pretty little blonde in her twenties who looked like a glass of milk—and acted like a glass of milk. This was supposed to be a *comedy*. It was called *Mom and Me, MD*. You can guess from the title how hilarious it was. I was cast as the head nurse of a big hospital, where she—glass of milk girl—was a doctor. To prepare for the role, I arranged to be shown the ropes by the head nurse at a large hospital.

I arrived at the crack of dawn to scrub up and get into booties, gown, and cap, first to observe an abdominal surgery, then visit the children in the burn unit. The nurse ushered me into the operating room, where a female patient was prepped for exploratory surgery to find the cause of abdominal blockage. I was placed about five feet from her head, just above the anesthesiologist. Two surgeons flanked her, one on either side. The head nurse told me to watch as much of the surgery as I could tolerate, and if I began to feel faint, to calm myself by looking up around the ceiling of the room where various antique operating tools were displayed, and not look back at the procedure until I felt steady. (Antique operating tools, I marveled. Now, there's a sight to calm a woozy person right down. You betcha.)

The operation began with one of the surgeons expertly opening the abdominal cavity with a scalpel. Very neat. So far, so good. Then they reached over and pulled her abdomen apart and began hauling her intestines out, piling them beside her on the operating table. Great handfuls of intestines. As the doctors chatted and dug around, I felt a sudden burning interest in the array of fascinating antique operating tools on the ceiling.

Hmm, I thought, *what's that thing? Looks like a garden trowel. Wonder what that was for?*

Down at the operating table, playing "Gut, gut, who's got the gut?" one surgeon asked the other, "Did you get to the shore over the weekend, Harold?"

"Oh, yeah, great fishing. Almost landed a marlin."

"Wow. Well, I don't see anything unusual in here, do you?"

"Nope, nothing cancerous. Pull out some more of that gut on your side."

And I'm musing, *Gosh, that rusty little hand saw up there must have two dozen teeth . . .*

"Wait a minute, Harold, what's that mass there, under the colon?"

"Oh, yeah, let's see . . . well, my God, Mike, look at this!"

"Bingo! There's our problem!"

I peeked down at the operating table. Harold and Mike were pulling out a length of stiff intestine about three feet long, black as coal. They clamped off both ends, cut it free, and laid it aside. A few more seconds of rummaging revealed no more dead gut.

"Okay, I think we got it all, Harold. Let's get her stitched up."

At that point, the head nurse appeared at the door and asked if I was ready to visit the children's burn ward. And you know, I was. After a very educating morning, I felt ready to play a head nurse. But definitely not ready to *be* a head nurse. It turned out the pilot wasn't ready to be a series, either. It was only slightly funnier than abdominal surgery and did not get picked up.

Now I'd done my two obligatory pilots for NBC and started reading scripts for the two-hour movies of the week they sent me, none of which was worth doodly-squat. The contract was for play or pay, so I didn't have to do any of them, but my agent and I agreed that I should be a good scout and find two I could bear. In *The Day the Bubble Burst,* which had a few pithy scenes, I played a blue-collar wife in the Great Depression. My contract almost over, I agreed to do *The Great American Traffic Jam,* playing an upper-crust wife who, with her husband—Ed McMahon—gets stranded in a limo on the freeway.

Oh, it was about as funny as *Mom and Me, MD*.

⁓

I see you back there. You with the beehive hairdo. Waving your arms from the back of the theatre, calling, "But Rue! What happened with The Greek? Don't leave us dangling!"

Good Lord, Luanne, do we really have to go there? It was a divorce. Connect the dots. He juiced me like a ripe tomato. My lawyer wasn't able to protect Mark's college fund, but he did earn himself a hefty legal fee. Thirty grand, as I recall.

When the worst of the carnage was over and it came down to dividing the last trappings of our so-called marriage, we agreed to divide the wedding gifts equally—with one caveat: The Greek insisted that he keep all the wedding gifts that came from his guests and I keep the gifts from mine—a considerably smaller number, since he'd invited three times as many people.

But I said, "Okeydokey!"

Lette came over, I uncorked a bottle of wine, and we cracked open the wedding gift book—a three-ring loose-leaf binder in which Lette had carefully recorded each gift as it was received so I could, like a well-brought-up Southern girl, write thank-you notes. Since it was in her handwriting and the loose-leaf pages were easily removed and replaced, we went through it page by page, making what I decided were a few well-deserved adjustments.

We were careful not to change the more obvious gifts, since I knew The Greek would remember certain ones, and there were quite a few I didn't need or particularly like from my side of the aisle, which I magnamimously donated to him.

"A garden fountain shaped like the Statue of Liberty," said Lette, raising her wineglass to the huddled masses yearning to breathe free.

"Definitely not from any friend of mine. He can have it."

"Cuisinart food processor?"

"Mine. From Norman Lear."

"Hand-painted five-foot wooden screen of Mohammed's life, huge plastic salad bowl, and a bronze eagle to go over the fireplace?" said Lette. "To the asshole?"

"Oh, yeah!" I raised a toast to her.

I had personally selected all the dinnerware at the wedding shop, but most of it had come from his friends, so I had to let go of the lovely twelve-setting dinnerware ensemble.

"Hey, wait a minute, Baby Rue. He ended up with fourteen plates," tallied Lette.

"Credit the two extras to my aunt Wenonah Sue!" I told her. "Hell, I shopped till I dropped for that pattern."

Lette and I got shnockered on red wine and laughed till we ached.

And I still have those two plates.

CHAPTER NINETEEN

⟨⟩

"Never sneeze into a full ashtray."

—RUE MCCLANAHAN

Once when Lette was out of town, she asked me to guard her little trunk with her birth certificate and other papers. She was hardly out the door before I rushed to check her birth date. I knew she was a Taurus and was tickled to see that we were born the same year.

"I have a confession to make," I told her years later. "I peeked."

Astonished, she said, "Why, Baby Rue, I would *never* have done that!"

But my feeling was "What red-blooded best friend could possibly resist?"

By that time, Lette and I had shared plenty of drama and comedy, onstage and off. But she hadn't told me her age. And she didn't tell me she'd discovered a lump in her breast. Returning to L.A. from a brief trip to New York, I was stunned to learn that she'd had a mastectomy and was still in the hospital.

"Hey, Baby Rue." She waved from her bed, blond and smiling, sitting up, sassy, "Surprise!"

She soon went into remission and kept performing, singing as powerfully as ever. She left The Jolly Cocksucker for a much better gig at

Maldonado's, a popular Pasadena restaurant. I went to hear her perform, and she was invariably hilarious. When she and Jack moved to a
North Hollywood apartment she called "The Piss Pit," she had to sell
her grand piano, which she'd painted fire-engine red, so I bought it
and had it refinished in mahogany. She gave me voice lessons, and I got
her to go to French classes with me. Later, she started chemotherapy
and we girlfriends took turns taking her to the hospital, where she
sometimes stayed for a week or two. I visited, confused. The nurses
behaved as if she would soon be out for good. I never asked Jack or
anyone else what her prognosis was. I assumed she was going to get
over it, and she seemed to think so, too.

I wasn't doing much interesting acting work. Guest shots on one series
and another. *Love Boat, Fantasy Island,* that sort of thing. Then, in 1981,
I was cast in *Mama's Family,* a spin-off of a *Carol Burnett Show* sketch.
Vicki Lawrence played the bossy, brash Mama, with Ken Berry as
her weakling son. I was to be her nemesis, Aunt Fran, a fireball who
matched Mama insult for insult. What fun! I love playing spitfires. But
when the pilot script arrived, Aunt Fran had been rewritten as a
mousy, uptight minor character. The producers had seen an actress
they loved on the soap *All My Children* and decided Mama's nemesis
should be the white-trash floozy wife of Mama's spineless son.

Well, poop. The pilot got picked up, and we made shows throughout the summer. Not the standard sitcom schedule.

That fall, I played Karl Malden's wife in *Word of Honor,* the true
story of a lawyer wrongfully sent to prison. The producers were appreciative of my talent, which was heartening, and the marvelous cast
included Ron Silver and some young Detroit and Chicago actors. John
Malkovich, one of the founders of Chicago's new Steppenwolf Theater,
played my son-in-law and kept me in stitches every day during lunch.
On a day off, Gary Sinise came and drove us to Chicago, where I stayed

with John and his girlfriend, Glenne Headly, and went to an excellently acted and directed Steppenwolf production. It was wonderful to watch John and Gary go on to huge success. And Glenne Headly gave a perfectly crafted performance in the movie *Dirty Rotten Scoundrels*. She's aces. Our *Word of Honor* played on TV the other night and holds up quite well, I'm happy to say. Lord, my butt was trim.

Meanwhile, a tall, handsome émigré from Yugoslavia moved in next door to Norman Hartweg. Drago Zdenko had been an award-winning film actor in Eastern Europe before moving to the United States three years earlier with aspirations to be a director. He married his mother's cousin so he could stay in the States and learned English from watching television. Drago was sexy beyond words, intelligent and amusing, and his apartment was neat and orderly, in contrast to Norm's, which always looked as if hordes of gypsies had pitched camp.

Growing up in post–World War II Belgrade, Drago and his mother and sister had to share a one-bedroom apartment with another family. His mother chose the bedroom and bathroom for their half, leaving the other family the living room and kitchen. She figured cooking in the john was less off-putting than doing daily ablutions in the kitchen. Consequently, her son developed a decidedly cavalier attitude toward home cooking and an even more nonchalant open-door policy toward bathroom privacy. Mercy! (Talk about being caught with your pants down.)

Linda had sold The Castle to our friend, Ronnie Claire Edwards, the parsimonious Corabeth on *The Waltons,* whom Lette called Ron Éclair, and I took Drago to a party there one night. Ronnie never served supper before eleven, following an extended cocktail hour, but around nine-thirty, Drago wandered into the kitchen, loudly inquiring, "VEN DO VE EAT?" with ever-increasing volume until Ronnie Claire suggested I not bring him to her next soiree. Or ever again. He was full of more bravado than a Veterans Day parade. In the two years I knew him, he never paid a traffic ticket; he always went to court and argued, and always got off. His ego was a tad overweening (and by "tad" I mean . . . "boatload"), but he was engrossing, full of original ideas. It had been a while since I'd been with a man, and Drago and I had immediate sexual rapport. At thirty-three, the energy surged.

Rating? I have to credit him with an A. Or a *yat,* in Serbo-Croatian.

"It is best and proper I must to move in vith you," he informed me, but I insisted he keep his own place. I did allow him to install a tooth-brush and other sundries at my house, however, and over time, he pretty much settled in to stay, driving to his place for mail once in a while.

That December, I was invited to join a celebrity group in Colorado for a film premiere and took Drago along as my guest. One lovely con-sequence of the trip was getting to be friends with writer Bob Parnell and his wife, actress Marsha Hunt, who had both been chewed up and spit out by the McCarthy witch-hunt blacklisting scourge, having refused to testify against friends under investigation. I don't recall who else was on the top-heavy plane other than the beautiful and charming Joan Hackett, a popular actress who'd done guest shots from *Dr. Kildare* to *The Love Boat.* That night in Colorado, we all attended the film and ate a late supper, then I went to the room assigned to Drago and me. But he never showed up.

He'd spent the night with Ms. Hackett. Well, hooray for Belgrade.

"I am conzoomed with pazhion for her!" he told me when we got back to L.A.

"Zvell," I said. "Move out!"

But he wouldn't go. For three excruciating days, he continued to hang out at my house, spending the nights at Joan's place in Beverly Hills.

One night, Joan called me and said, "Rue, does this strange creature belong to you?"

"No," I told her. "He does not. In fact, I'm trying to get him to leave."

She said, "I can *feel* him calling to me over the mountains. He has a strange connection with me I can't explain."

"You're welcome to him," I assured her, and a day or so later, he finally left—for good.

This split with Drago had an unexpectedly disastrous effect on me. Once again, I was crippled by panic. I couldn't understand it, because I wasn't in love with him. The rejection felt like a stone thrown at a wasp's nest. The old fears swarmed out and overwhelmed me. Mark had moved out earlier that year and was living with roommates in Van Nuys, so he knew nothing of what I was going through. For several nights, unable to bear the agony, I slept on the floor at Norman's, doubled up on a pallet behind his TV set. I had no pride about it. Dear Norm talked me to sleep. He didn't indulge or patronize me. He simply made small talk, speaking evenly about this and that until I could stand to close my eyes.

Shortly after *Mama's Family* began shooting in July of 1982, the pain in my side, which I'd had since I was pregnant with Mark, grew worse. During rehearsal one day, the stabbing pain was suddenly more acute than ever before.

"Sounds like gallbladder trouble," said my doctor in Studio City. "Go home, eat two pieces of bread covered with butter, and call me if the pain gets noticeably worse."

I ate the buttered bread and within minutes was writhing on the floor. I was rushed to Sherman Oaks Hospital, and after three days of tests went off to surgery. When I woke up—minus my gallbladder and a portion of my liver—I felt relatively okay but couldn't draw a regular breath. The best I could manage were fast little pants.

"It's the psychological trauma," said the doctor. "Do you have a therapist?"

"It's not psycho—logical—trauma," I gasped. *"I—can't—breathe!"*

They finally tumbled to the fact that I had adult respiratory distress syndrome, a condition that sometimes follows major surgery, and my chances for survival were not good. Not good at all. They whisked me to intensive care, trying to intubate me.

"Rue!" said the doctor. "I need you to cough. C'mon, Rue! Cough for me!"

Cough? I thought. Where do you *cough?* I tried to find the muscles, the apparatus for *cough,* but everything felt paralyzed. I finally willed myself to cough, and the doctor said, "You just saved your life." But I wasn't out of the woods. Intubated, I spent the next four days under heavy sedation, only briefly awake enough now and then to scribble in a wobbly hand on a large tablet.

Am I dying?

My doctor answered, "Not if I can help it, Rue."

Is there anything I can do to help?

"Just stay strong." She smiled down at me. "Hang in there."

I scrawled in large letters: *Please keep Drago Zdenko out of here!*

Drago was annoying the hell out of me. He had moved on from Joan Hackett to live with a volatile French woman and, having heard from Norman that I was seriously ill, insisted on visiting, striding into the ICU every day, cheerfully bubbling, "Don't vorry! Everything is juzt vine!" Everything was not *juzt vine*! I was quite possibly dying. Poor Mark was scared out of his mind, and my doctor was frantically consulting the *New England Journal of Medicine* for a clue. It was terrifying. And yet . . . fascinating.

Alone inside my brain, I felt myself enter a single cell, observing all the machinations and chemical reactions, and as I watched its machinery buzzing along like a little robot, I thought, *Well, you little dickens. How primitive. How marvelously organized. Tootling along your appointed rounds, without an ounce of compassion. You don't give a damn if I live or die. But I do! And I'll lay you eight to four I win this contest, you unemotional little dick-head.*

The doctor called my dad and urged him to get to Los Angeles as soon as possible if he hoped to see me alive, but Marie didn't like to fly, so the two of them *drove* to L.A., and by the time they arrived, much to everyone's surprise, my prognosis was much better. I was moved from the ICU back to my room, and there Marie shared the happy news that they'd gotten married without telling any of us. I don't know exactly when. The doctors had been rather hasty during the emergency intubation, so I couldn't speak. I could only croak tepid congratulations.

One day, as my shy little Catholic nurse was bustling about, and Oliver Hailey was visiting with his wife, two little girls, and his mother, a gorgeous young man appeared at the door with a boom box, from which issued sexy, slinky music. He slowly began to strip. Yep. Strip. Vicki Lawrence had sent him as a surprise. And surprised we were! The dear little nurse squatted down in a metal locker and tried to close the door. The rest of us stared, transfixed, until he was down to his G-string. Oliver's mother remained quite composed, the girls giggled, and I just tried to live through it. I do hope I remembered to tip him. He needed encouragement. Turns out he was a sweet young man from Peoria and this was his first strip job. My God, the least we could have done was egg him on a bit, twirling some pillowcases or something. Hollywood can be tough on newcomers.

All told, I stayed in the hospital a little over three weeks. Doctors' orders called for me to stay longer, but I decided the hell with doctors' orders. I weighed 133 when I checked in, and when I got out of intensive care, only 121. They wanted me back up to 133, but I left at 125, and they could jolly well like it. (I did.)

"You're smart to leave," my little nurse told me as I packed. "The entire floor above you has come down with pneumonia."

Drago insisted over my weakly croaked protestations that he drive me home. I thought he was the last person on earth I wanted to see, but even *he* was bumped up a notch when my dad said jovially, "Oh, guess who I invited to come visit you!"

And in walked The Greek. Good Christ and little spanakopita.

Drying my hair with a towel, I ignored him until he left, which was blessedly soon, but not soon enough for me. Back at my house with Bill and Marie, feeling like my insides were going to fall out onto the carpet at any moment, I crawled into the daybed in my office, too sore to climb even one stair. Bill went up to bed, but Marie pulled a chair up to my bedside, opened her Bible, and began badgering me to accept Jesus Christ as my personal savior.

"Marie, I'm extremely tired," I croaked diplomatically. "I don't feel like visiting."

But she droned on and on and on. I don't know who I wanted to strangle most—her, Bill, or myself. The next morning, her proselytizing done, they departed for Ardmore and I began the difficult healing ordeal. Getting around was difficult. I couldn't sit in a chair; I had to perch on the arms. The drugs played hopscotch in my brain. I tried to sign a check and couldn't remember how to spell "and." Was it *a-n-d*, or *a-d-n*? A favorite poster of Koko, the gorilla who'd learned sign language, now terrified me and had to be taken down. Norm talked to me every night on the phone. Once, I fell asleep listening to his voice and woke up to a dial tone.

I croaked for the next two years, my range lower and noticeably impaired. Where were those high notes? Gone, my darlings, *all* gone. No more *Lucia di Lammermoor*. Now I sounded like a muted whiskey baritone. *Mama's Family* was miked, of course, so I was able to croak my lines until the season ended early and we went on hiatus. I'd been cast as the Fortune Teller in Thornton Wilder's *The Skin of Our Teeth* at the Old Globe Theatre in San Diego with Sada Thompson, Blair Brown, and Harold Gould (who later played Rose's beau on *The Golden Girls*), but I couldn't project past the first few rows. Director Jack O'Brien had me use a megaphone, with disappointing results. We also recorded it for PBS. My hoarse six-note range made it impossible to develop that juicy character the way I heard her in my head. I was only middlin' fair in this role I was so right for! Maybe someday I'll get to play it again—on a double bill with "The Three Little Kittens."

I went to some no-frills health spa for weeks of colonics and raw vegetables. Infused with new energy, I was frisky as a young goat, when one day, my old friend from high school, Lynn Pebbles, called.

"Eddi-Rue, you'll never guess who I saw recently. Tom Keel!"

I was suddenly back on the bus with my high school squeeze in his hep leather jacket.

I just want you to know, Eddi-Rue, I'm not a sex fiend.

"He just got divorced, and he looks great," said Lynn. "If you don't go after him, I've half a mind to give him a call myself."

You don't have to worry, Eddi-Rue. I won't take advantage of you.

Wanna hear about Husband #5?

CHAPTER TWENTY

"Did you ever see a dream walking? Well, I have."
—Revel and Gordon song lyric from *Sitting Pretty*
"Did you ever see a dick dancing? Well, I have."
—Me, paraphrasing

*M*y dear reader, whatever else you might take away from this book, please hold fast to this idea: *Be careful, careful, careful whom you marry.*

We've covered four very good reasons not to make that fateful trip down the aisle: pregnancy, pressure, panic, and . . . more panic. Good looks and romantic notions are nice, but not enough. I hate to admit it, but sometimes, love is not enough. There was something to love—or at least like—about each of my first five husbands. There's no such thing as an Ideal Man, but if I could take a few ingredients from each of the men I married and mix them in a big bowl, I might whip up an Almost Ideal Husband Pudding. Take a pint of meltingly great looks, musical talent, and humor from Tom Lloyd Bish. Equal parts kindness, genius IQ, literary talent, courage, and artsy quirkiness from Norman Hartweg. A pinch of smelling sweet and a dash of orgasm from The Italian. A soupçon of high spirits from The Greek. And from my fifth husband, Tom Keel, a generous dollop of vigor and good looks, plus a gallon of gasket-blowing sex appeal.

Yum. My pudding bowl runneth over. Almost.

I called Keel in Dallas, and he was delighted to hear from me. He was planning to visit his mother, who lived in San Juan Capistrano, an ultrachic town down the coast from L.A.

"I'd love to drive up and see you," he said. And I said, "Terrific!"

It would be a blast to see him again. It was so easy talking to him on the phone. After all, I'd known him for thirty-four years, we'd been good friends as kids, dah-dee-dah-dee-da . . . Okay, it was also pretty damned exciting, and when he showed up a week later—well, well, *well*, Miss Pebbles was right. He did indeed look great. These days, it's not unusual to look great at forty-nine, but you never know; in reunion photos of my high school mates, some looked pretty haggard. Tom was vibrant. Same familiar grin, same sturdy body, same broad shoulders. *Vavoom*. This was one sexy dude.

We talked and talked, laughed and laughed. I don't remember what we had for dinner, or if we had anything for dinner, except each other. What can I tell you? Hot and heavy when we were teenagers never went further than my bringing him to climaxes by hand while we were parked out at the lake. I remember standing in my parents' driveway in 1953, saying good-bye to Keel after a visit, aware that this was not the man I wanted for life. At nineteen, however, my life was before me. At forty-nine, the terrain looked quite different.

That night in 1984, with none of the old guilt but all the old chemistry, we finally had an adult sexual experience. And that man had a penis that would stand straight up and dance. No, really. *Dance*. It was a sight to behold. Can other men do that? Certainly none I've ever known. I found Keel to be highly sexed and pleasantly uncomplicated and just as big a sweetheart as he always was. FQ Rating? Oh, definitely A. With extra credit for his amazing dancing *oo-hoo* (as Mother called our private parts).

A lot had happened in Keel's life since we were kids. He had had four children with his ex-wife: three older girls and a son, David, then fourteen. Just before Christmas of 1979, his father (that old bear, Louie) had gotten desperately sick while in Mexico with his wife, Lil, and her twin sister, also named Lil, oddly enough. Tom flew down, put them all on a plane for San Juan Capistrano, then drove Louie's car back, arriving three days later—the day after Louie had died and been immediately cremated. In Louie's will, he left everything to his wife. Nothing to Tom, not a sou. Nada. Not even a memento.

Ah, Lil. And Lil. Therein lies a tale. Lilian and Lilly, both widows. They lived within blocks of each other and looked identical, except Aunt Lil had a sweet face and Mother Lil had hard lines etched by a lifetime of crankiness. They shared an astounding dinner-table dynamic that usually ended with Aunt Lil rushing off in tears. Aunt Lil died not long after I met her. I was sorry I didn't get to know her. And sorry I *did* get to know Mother Lil.

I went to visit Keel at his pleasant Dallas condo with his happy little Scottie named Harrod, and Tom drove us around Dallas in his pickup, drinking beer at the wheel. (You could do that in Texas in those days.) We were residents of two very different worlds. I, an ambitious actress with laserlike focus on my career. He, not particularly happy or unhappy in his job as a computer specialist for the phone company, not looking for advancement, just troubleshooting whatever problems were handed to him. He knew computers like the back of his hand, but I think he was bored.

"I tend to drift downstream. Like flotsam," he told me. "I go along until something reaches out to snag me."

On the one hand, this sounded like a lovely Zen way to be, but on the other hand . . . *Oh, dear,* I thought when he gave me that analogy, *we could get into trouble here*. My style was the opposite of passive. I tended to run for the cliff like a stampeded buffalo—*BAH-RUMPH! BAH-RUMPH!*—and leap over, all feet flying. Maybe not the best setup for a lasting relationship, but have I ever let anything like that stop me? Hell, no. *BAH-RUMPH! BAH-RUMPH!* Stand back, Sally! I'm dangerous! And you can't teach an old buffalo new tricks. At least, not without more therapy than this buffalo had had.

It was easy for me to start rationalizing: "Hey, this Keel thing could work. This *should* work. He's a good man with a lot of qualities I find very attractive. Lovely, masculine, sexy qualities! What's not to love?"

The man could shinny up a tall tree to get me a bird's nest. Up he goes! Like a kid! Where does a man of fifty get that kind of energy? His physical gifts were bewitching. His personality was fun. His Texas accent and colorful way of expressing himself were charming. He made chili from scratch. He mixed well with people. He drove like a pro. He was reliable. Maybe a bit unenlightened, but he was willing to be taught. (Like I knew enough to be teaching anyone. Please! I was a fourth-grader teaching a kindergarten kid. I tell you—I'm dangerous.)

Long story short, we were married April of 1984 in Ardmore at my father's house, with about a dozen old friends. The night before the wedding, we went to The Hamburger Inn, a place we used to frequent in high school, and although I was now a vegetarian, we ordered the same humongous hamburgers we'd had in the good old days. With all the fixin's! Yum, yum! I spent the subsequent hours of that chilly, moonlit night in the front yard, upchucking like crazy, Keel at my side. I kept remembering how I'd thrown up my fish dinner during my honeymoon night in Maine with The Italian. Was this a foreboding, or just my natural reaction to eating a hamburger? Buffalos are vegetarians, after all.

The wedding was very nice. I wore a little white silk suit and he wore a dark one. We looked terrific—trim, young, and very happy. On our way to L.A., we stopped at some little town in New Mexico, where he bought me a lovely pair of silver and amethyst earrings. Of course, I still have them. We found a justice of the peace, then went to a motel, where he started drinking beer, his libation of choice. He downed one after the other and quickly . . . got somewhat *plastered*. Glued to the TV. *Oh, no, here we go again,* I thought. *Everything's fine until the honeymoon, and then*—thud.

In L.A., Keel's son, David, joined us, following his mother's wishes. He did need his father at his age, and it was fun having him around.

Tom Keel and me in high school, Ardmore, Oklahoma, 1950.
Hot 'n' heavy at the time.

Tom Keel and me cutting our wedding cake, 1984.
Hot 'n' heavy again.

He was a cute kid who wanted to be a rock 'n' roll drummer. Mark was still into rock 'n' roll, although it had caused tinnitus in one ear, a condition he's struggled with ever since. David kept the drum set in his bedroom—Mark's old bedroom—and practiced a lot. Hey, drummers gotta drum. Rockers gotta rock. But I was happy when Keel told me, "I play a classical music cassette in the car when I'm driving him to school."

I said, "Oh, that's good. Classical music."

Keel and I were in an L.A. bookstore one day and ran smack into Norman Hartweg wheeling around a corner. I'd neglected to tell Norm I was getting married. Caught off guard, I made awkward introductions.

"Norman Hartweg, meet Tom Keel . . . my husband."

Norm blatantly gave me a look like I had lost my mind. Yes, Norman. I got married—*again*! You don't have to look at me like I've been caught with my hand in the cookie jar.

Norm said, "Rue, I've been thinking we should write a play together. I've done some research on an old play by Plautus about an Athens merchant and his son."

I was intrigued. I bought an IBM home computer, Keel taught me the bare basics of operating it, and Norm and I started writing.

⌒

Keel was very dependent on my company, which soon became a problem, but what else could he be? He'd left his life and everyone he knew in Dallas. I knew he was lonely, and oh Lord, it made me painfully aware of how selfish I was. While he waited for a job to open up at the phone company, he did repair work on my pool. He knew how to do that kind of thing, a talent that's always thrilled me. And how sexy he looked doing it! Watching him repair that pool was a treat for me. As I sat at my computer creating a whole new ancient Greek world on paper, he'd pass by the window pushing a wheelbarrow full of cement, grinning in at me with an expression I can only describe as . . . sweet and full of longing. I was working on my creation, happy as a clam, and he was working on the pool with that lonely-puppy look. I would often go out to visit him while he worked.

Watching Keel when Lil was around was harder to take. She told him when to roll the car windows up or down, how fast to drive, practically told him when to breathe!

"Why don't you tell her to go to hell? Make your own fortune," I urged him.

But he just shrugged. "I don't need the aggravation."

He eventually got hired by the phone company and started to make acquaintances, bringing one or two fellows home for supper. I thought they were *stupnagels,* boring, not in his league. Still, I was grateful he had some new friends. He was really a darling, happy to drive me to rehearsals for a play I was in, happy to come to the performances, happy to meet my showbiz friends, who of course found him an odd choice for me but never said so. (God knows what they said behind my back.) He got along with everyone, and we had some great chili parties.

Having snagged him as he drifted by, I felt responsible for this marriage. I tried to develop more patience and endurance, but there was just no intellectual connection. Within a year, I was around the bend, trying to make the ill-fitting match a success. I felt like I was in a leghold trap. He and David went to Texas for Christmas, and before they left, I bleakly said, "Maybe we should call it quits when you get back."

Perhaps because he was also unhappy—or perhaps because he was drifting downstream—he agreed.

Over the two weeks he and David were gone, I was at peace, then toward the day they were due back, I started to feel lonesome for sweet, sexy Keel. When they drove up, I ran out to welcome him, asking him to stay longer, and he was happy to. But nothing substantially changed.

That April, Lil gave Tom $2,000 for a wedding anniversary trip to the same Kauai resort hotel she had stayed in umpteen years ago. (Of course, $2,000 wasn't nearly enough to cover it, so I kicked in the rest, but it's the thought that counts, right?) The hotel Lil had picked for us was one of the most luxurious on the island, but it was covered in tall palms that dropped coconuts like bombs every few minutes. *Whomp! Whomp! Whomp!* After a day or two, the hotel personnel warned us not to walk on the grounds, since some people had been conked out by the falling coconuts. We moved to a less expensive—and less danger-ous!—place, drove all over Kauai, visited the perpetual rain forest, and saw *Arsenic and Old Lace* at the VHW lodge, played by the townspeo-ple. The postmaster played the Cary Grant role facing upstage to deliver his lines and walking with his left arm moving forward when he stepped with his left foot, his right arm forward when he stepped with his right foot, like a toy soldier that had been engineered wrongly. It was sheer heaven!

We snorkeled, surrounded by bewitching fish of all colors, and took a kayak trip up a river past the ruins of an ancient village. So peaceful. Unforgettable. The island of Hawaii had eucalyptus trees of unimaginable beauty and a bubbling volcano interspersed with green growth. We walked barefoot on black lava, and I picked up a small, long-cooled hunk of volcanic rock to take home, although it was illegal and Tom objected. (Hey, now—I still have that rock!)

We stopped at a diner for lunch one day, and while Tom went to the men's room, I shuddered at the music being piped through the restaurant—various short snippets of classical pieces with a *BOOM-da-da BOOM-da-da* disco rhythm accompaniment underneath. *BOOM-da-da* under Beethoven's Fifth, *BOOM-da-da* under Mozart, *BOOM-da-da* under Tchaikovsky. Tom came back and, as I was about to take a bite of some juicy island morsel, he said, "Oh, that's the classi-cal tape I play every day in the car for David."

If this had been a movie I'd have done a spit-take. Folks, there's only just so long you can pretend you're listening to the same Beethoven. When we arrived home, I said to Keel, "Let's face it. We really don't belong together."

I remembered something told to me by an actor friend who'd married his high school sweetheart and subsequently divorced: "I was hoping she'd grown up, and she was hoping I hadn't." That rang a gong in my head.

Keel and I parted with no animosity, just regret. He wanted to leave Harrod, which was fine with me but not with Harrod, who began to howl and bark after Tom drove off and kept it up for two months. He did eventually settle down and get contented, though, becoming my dog. A year later, Keel came back for him.

I know people were urging Keel to sue me for half the money I'd earned during the marriage, and I was nervous about being tomato-juiced again, but he says he never even considered it. When our tax return of $5,000 came in, he asked if he could borrow it for a while, and I said sure. Hell, the man deserved compensation for putting up with my foolishness. He signed the divorce agreement and our business was settled. And he did some mighty nice things for my father—and for me—over the next many years, including repaying me the $5,000 in 1995, when Lil died, finally leaving him his inheritance of half a million hard-earned bucks, which he quickly and cleverly parlayed into a million.

All this time, Norman and I had been whizzing along with our musical farce, having a great time. Still untitled, it was set in Athens in 457 B.C. We alternated writing every other scene, and I wrote all the music and lyrics. Norm was a terribly talented writer but needed to be ridden herd on, tending sometimes to go too far for my taste. He whipped off the final scene in one long night's session, pulling all the disparate threads of the farce together. Well, it was certainly full of action, but it was a holy mess. He had characters leaving through windows and coming immediately through doors in totally different costumes—things like that. I spent weeks straightening it out, taking what he'd created, and making it flow.

Meanwhile, *Mama's Family* wrote my character out of the show. The fates that ruled Mama's Universe had Aunt Fran choke to death on a chicken bone.

I did not grieve her passing. In fact, that turned out to be the luckiest chicken bone ever choked on. Must've been a wishbone!

In February of 1985, I was languishing in *Love Boat* limbo. By this time, I'd done five stints in Captain Stubing's celebrity purgatory, as well as guest shots on such timeless classics as *Gimme a Break!* and *Charles in Charge*. I was cautiously optimistic when Sylvia Gold, my agent at ICM, gave me the heads-up about a pilot script she was sending by messenger.

"I think you'll like it," she said. "It's called *The Golden Girls*."

CHAPTER TWENTY-ONE

"We can be bought, but we can't be bored."

—LYNN FONTAINE OF LUNT & FONTAINE

When I opened the bright yellow pilot script from NBC, a tingle ran up my spine, giving rise to a strong, immediate feeling:

"This one's a winner."

The *Golden Girls* story line concerned four women of a certain age joining up for financial reasons to share a house but finding in each other the love and support of a family. I started reading. And I started laughing. The zingy, spot-on dialogue crackled like sparklers.

I instantly loved these characters: Sophia, the nursing home escapee with outlandish tales of her Sicilian girlhood. Dorothy, the acerbic divorcée with a wisecrack for every occasion. Rose, the farm-fresh ninny with her sweetly guileless take on life. And—ooh-la-la—Blanche, the Southern miss with her free, joyful sexuality and sassiness.

(BLANCHE ENTERS)

BLANCHE

Oh, Dorothy, can I borrow your mink stole?

DOROTHY

It's Miami in June. Only cats are wearing fur.

ROSE

Are you going out?

DOROTHY

No. She's going to sit here where it's a hundred and twelve degrees and eat enchiladas.

BLANCHE

I just need some cucumbers to put on my eyes.

DOROTHY

You'll have trouble seeing, Blanche.

BLANCHE

It's very good. It reduces puffiness.

ROSE

Does it work on thighs?

BLANCHE

I don't know, honey. I don't need it on my thighs.

(SHE EXITS)

I called my agent at once.

"Sylvia? Rue. This script is definitely for me. I'm perfect for Blanche!"

"Actually, they're thinking of Betty White for Blanche," she said. "They want you to read for Rose."

"Oh, God . . . *Rose?* But I have no connection with Rose. And I know exactly how to play Blanche!"

"Well," she said, "you can either go in tomorrow and read for Rose, or pass."

I read and reread the script, becoming more certain that Blanche and I were made for each other. Oh, dear Saint Dymphna! Don't pull another Aunt Fran on me! I went to NBC and read Rose for the pilot director, Jay Sandrich, and after a scene or two he said, "Rue, I know it's an unorthodox thing to ask, and you're not prepared, but would you mind going down the hall to an empty room and taking a look at the role of Blanche?"

"Why, Jay," I cooed, my heart leaping. "I wouldn't mind one bit!"

Not prepared? Please. I'd all but memorized it. I went down the hall for a few minutes, then came back and gave Jay the full Blanche treatment: "In high school, I had to break up with Carl Dugan, captain of the football team. I was very nervous, but I just spit it out—'Carl, I'm dumping you for Coach Wilkins!'"

Next day, they asked Betty White to come in and read Rose opposite my Blanche. Caught by surprise, Betty gave Rose an absolutely hilarious interpretation, with a childlike charm that was not your run-of-the-mill ninny: "What a great day! It's like life is a great big weenie roast and I'm the biggest weenie!"

Susan Harris, the creator of the series, called me later that day.

"Rue, we offered Bea Arthur the part of Dorothy, but she turned it down," she told me. "Do you think you could help persuade her?"

I hadn't seen Bea in seven years. We didn't really stay in touch after *Maude* closed in 1978, because, for one thing, she'd kept The Greek on her party guest list, while I was summarily removed. Being excluded from my former pal's parties hurt my feelings, but I didn't hold that against Bea. The Greek was great at parties. Hell, I should've kept him on *my* party list instead of marrying him. Over the years, I'd hear news of Bea through the grapevine—a Woody Allen play at Lincoln Center, a couple of pilots that fell on their fannies. But I loved working with Bea, and she was perfect for Dorothy. I was on the phone within minutes.

"Bea? Can you tell me why you're not jumping at the best script to come along in twenty years?"

"Because, Rue," Bea replied in her distinctive baritone, "I don't want to do *Maude and Vivien Meet Sue Ann Nivens*. Boooorrrrrring!"

"No, Bea, I'm doing the sexpot, Blanche. Betty is the dimwit."

A pause, then, "Oh, really? Well, now, *that's* interesting."

Within a day or two, NBC had us three, along with Estelle Getty, who'd already been hired as Sophia, come in to read for the big suits. We read cold—no rehearsal—but the chemistry was plain as a preacher's daughter.

(BLANCHE ENTERS)

BLANCHE

Oh, Rose, I'm borrowing your earrings. Lord, I'd love to get a face-lift by eight o'clock.

DOROTHY

Blanche, who is Harry?

BLANCHE

Oh, girls, he's just wonderful. He's very gallant. He's a perfect gentleman. He's a great dancer and doesn't make noises when he chews.

DOROTHY

Chewing. That's way up there on my list. Comes right after intelligent.

BLANCHE

He doesn't talk loud at the movies, doesn't take his own pulse— and he's still interested!

ROSE

In what?

We had those guys wetting their pants, and—bam—that afternoon, it was settled.

Like Rose says: "Dorothy, you're the smart one, and Blanche, you're the sexy one, and Sophia, you're the old one. And I'm the nice one. Everybody always likes me."

To which Sophia replies, "The old one isn't so crazy about you."

We taped the pilot, which had the audience inebriated with laughter, and were picked up by NBC for thirteen episodes, to begin taping in July.

Heaven on wheels!

⟶

Our set was a happy one. Guest stars always remarked on how congenial it was, how different from most TV shows. This was remarkable, since Betty, Bea, Estelle, and I came from drastically different performance backgrounds. Bea had worked on the stage in New York for years before Norman Lear brought her to L.A. to do *Maude*. Though she was a natural for sitcom, her roots remained in the theatre. Betty, on the other hand, was truly an American television institution, getting her start on one of the first TV broadcasts in 1939 and doing her own daytime talk show in the early 1950s.

"I actually started in silent television," she used to wisecrack.

A graduate of Beverly Hills High School, she was a TV baby, playing not just to, but with, the audience, flirting with them between scenes, hiking her skirt up and calling out, "Hi, sailor. Long in town?" She wasn't fond of stage work, but she loved TV game shows, interviews—I think she even liked the public service announcements we did, staying late after taping. We never had time to learn the copy, seeing it just minutes before we had to perform it. The rest of us read the copy from big cue cards, but Betty, blind as a bat, couldn't read the cards and wouldn't wear her glasses, so she had to memorize her lines after seeing them once. And she never made a mistake. I just figured she was a witch. There's no other explanation.

Estelle Getty, meanwhile, had raised two sons in New York, doing Off Off Broadway plays until she was almost sixty, when she was cast as the Jewish grandmother in Harvey Fierstein's hit play *Torch Song Trilogy*. She toured the country with it for four years, finally playing Los Angeles in 1985, where she was seen by the *Golden Girls* producers, who snatched her up to play Sophia. I'd seen her in *Torch Song* and she was dead-on funny. For me, she saved the play. But not having done sitcom, she was a fish out of water and kept asking, "Can't we make Dorothy and Sophia Jewish?"

Estelle always had me rolling on the floor with anecdotes about her Jewish neighbors in Queens. I kept telling her, "Estelle, you should do stand-up!" and made her repeat one story in particular over and over. She did a priceless imitation of her elderly neighbor. "Oh, Eshtelle, vas terrible! You shudda been dere! I bang over to pick up the hong-yungs and I cou'n garrup!" And Estelle acted it out, bending over to "pick up the onions" and not being able to "get up." (It's impossible to write the thick Jewish dialect with anything approaching the inspired Getty delivery.)

Her little quirks gave Betty and Bea and me a lot of laughs. She never got the point of a funny line; we had to explain every joke, why Sophia was saying a particular line and why it was funny. She also had a way of delivering certain lines with the accent on the wrong syllable. We called it her "marble cake" delivery, because she had once had a line about marble cake but had pronounced it "marble CAKE" instead of "MARBLE cake," leaving us in stitches. It was like saying, "I'll tell you a bed TIME story," or "I used to have a COCKER spaniel." Give me a slice of marble CAKE? As opposed to what—marble popcorn?

I don't know how the rumor got started (possibly Estelle's PR firm), but a lot of people who watched the show thought Estelle was the youngest of us four, and that Sophia was a combination of brilliant acting and clever makeup—which, of course, she was. However, folks, let me set the record straight: I was the spring chicken on that set. Bea, Estelle, and Betty were all born during the Harding administration, and I came along a dozen years later with FDR's "New Deal." By the time that always-on-hand cheesecake appeared in what would become one of the most familiar kitchens in America, I had done a lot of stage work in New York, seven or eight movies, played five years on *Maude*, two seasons of *Mama's Family,* seven episodes of *Apple Pie,* and felt at home in all media. Although I, too, observed the theatrical fourth wall for the first few seasons, I eventually said, "What the hell," and began joking with the audience between scenes with Betty.

My salary was based (as they do in television) on what I was paid for my most recent series, *Mama's Family*—peanuts. Lower than peanuts. What's lower than peanuts? Squeegee sponges? Probably the lowest of us all, certainly tens of thousands below what Betty and Bea were paid, but, hey—all I can say is *tanks Gott* for that chicken bone, or I would have still been stuck in prim little dresses playing Aunt Fran, bored out of my gourd, and not available for *The Golden Girls*. Whew!

In May, the pilot of *The Golden Girls* was taken to New York and Chicago to be played for subsidiary market heads—the bigwigs who decide what programs they'll run on local stations—and we girls were asked to go. Betty and I happily complied, and it was thrilling. Reception in both cities—overwhelming! People were on their feet! They knew they had a surefire hit on their hands.

⌒

Mark was off living his life, playing guitar, traveling the world, studying Stone Age cultures, collecting primitive art. I was so proud of the good man he had become. Over the years, I never stopped encouraging his father to get to know him. I had stayed in touch with Tom after the whole EST adventure, and after Keel and I divorced, Tom and I occasionally went out to dinner and jazz clubs. He was full of gaiety and fun, and when I gave one of my frequent parties, he was right there. Mr. Sociable. I have scores of photos of him looking handsome, laughing and chatting with Mark and Lette and Jack and other guests, carrying on like monkeys. He was full of cheer, friendly, even affectionate at times.

He always left my driveway with a warm hug, saying, "I love you, lady."

And I always said, "I love you, too." Whatever the hell I thought that meant.

The old addiction, the Tom Lloyd fever, still had me by the curlies, and over time I started to believe again that things might somehow work out between us. Early that fall, while *The Golden Girls* was taping, we saw more and more of each other, and eventually we came up with the brilliant idea that he should give up his little apartment in Beverly Hills, move his few pieces of furniture into my house, and make a stab at getting closer. Hey, stranger things have happened . . . right? (Can you name three?)

Tom was working as a composers' agent, and every night he brought home three bottles of champagne, which we drank before, with, and after dinner. The conversation and laughter were as bubbly as the bubbly, but when I asked him to sit and talk, he went dumb. I kept urging him to tell me what in God's name had happened back in 1958. Even after twenty-seven years, I was still trying desperately to make sense of it and thought honest conversations might help.

"I'm not trying to attach blame," I told him. "I'm just trying to understand what happened. What were you going through?"

"I don't know, babe. I can't give you any answers."

"Well, did you ever miss Mark or wonder about him all those years?"

"Lady, I don't have any words to talk about this. What good would it do, anyway?"

"Tom, you must have some memory of how you felt."

"I can't talk about something that's not there. It's impossible!" he said in frustration. "I don't have any words!"

His inability to answer reminded me of my inability to find the place to cough after my gallbladder surgery. There seemed to be no mechanism for it.

"Okay, how about this," I persisted. "You told me a long time ago that you felt like you were thirteen. Do you still feel that way?"

He thought for a moment, then said, "No, I've gotten to eighteen."

Eighteen? At *fifty-two*? At this rate, I wouldn't live long enough to see him grow up.

During the nine months he lived with me, we slept in the same bed but had no sex. Zilch. He never touched me. I kept looking for ways to please him, like when I'd had my hair dyed auburn for our wedding. Only this time, he said he was put off by a woman's hair south of the Mason-Dixon line, if you get my drift, so I got waxed in that tender area, which is less fun than getting your tongue unstuck from a frozen lamppost. He still had the libido of a box turtle.

All through the first season of *The Golden Girls,* Blanche was enjoying a wahoo sex life, but this gal's name was under "celibate" in *Webster's.* I appeared as Cinderella in the Macy's Thanksgiving Day Parade, but I didn't ride in a golden carriage. Appropriately enough, my magical conveyance had turned back into a pumpkin, and I was carted down Broadway in the bitter cold, decked out in a décolletage off-the-shoulder ball gown over my long underwear, mouthing the song "A Good Prince Is Hard to Find." A bit too much irony that early in the morning. I don't do Macy's Thanksgiving Day Parades anymore.

But ho ho ho, the holidays were upon us. For Christmas, Tom gave me an electric vibrator. I assumed it was a joke, but he said it wasn't. Yep, nothing says "Happy Birthday, Jesus!" like a three-speed sex toy, right? This from the man who'd found my gift of Levi's to be in bad taste? *Hello?*

And no, I *don't* still have it.

⟶

People always ask if I'm really like Blanche, and I say, "Well, consider the facts: Blanche was a glamorous, oversexed, self-involved, man-crazy Southern belle from Atlanta—and *I'm* not from Atlanta!"

There's a scene from one of the last shows of our first season that beautifully sums up who Blanche is and what she and I have in common. The episode revolves around an unwanted visit from Blanche's pen pal, Merrill, who's just been released from prison. Sophia dryly observes, "That's going to be rough. I bet after ten years in the jug, he's going to be pretty short on foreplay." But when Merrill shows up, quick-thinking Dorothy tries to save the day, pointedly telling

Blanche, "We were just explaining to *Merrill* that there's no telling when *Blanche* will be back."

Immediately catching on, Blanche says, "Oh, Lord, no. There's no sense waiting around. You wouldn't like Blanche anyway."

"She's not your type," Rose chimes in.

"That's right. She isn't," Blanche agrees emphatically.

"She's very cold," says Rose.

"Frigid! Hardly likes men at all," says Blanche.

"And she's ugly, isn't she?" says Rose.

"Well . . . ugly is a strong word," says Blanche.

"And wrinkled! Isn't she?"

"No, she's not wrinkled!"

"And fat!"

"Stop it! Stop it right now!" Blanche stamps her foot. "She's none of those things, Rose Nylund! She's gorgeous! Gorgeous, gorgeous, gorgeous!"

"Sounds good," says Merrill. "Tell Blanche I'll be back." And he exits.

"And stupid," says Blanche. "Stupid, stupid, stupid!"

Playing the scene, I realized, "Hey, Blanche thinks she's gorgeous, and I look just like her, so . . ."

I learned a lot from Blanche about optimism and *joie de vivre,* feeling confident about what you have to offer the world, and the ability to bounce back from life's momentary failures. Blanche Devereaux is a masterful rebounder, never down for the count, always back up to fight again, to look again on the bright side. I loved that about her. When Blanche's daughter Janet doubts the existence of God, Blanche says, "Oh, honey, of course He exists! Just look at the beautiful sky, the majestic trees. God created man and gave him a heart and a mind . . . and thighs that could crack walnuts."

Of course, it's that last part that gets her into trouble. And me, too. Too often.

Blanche and I both have a lot of love to give, and I don't mean just in bed. She and I do share a genuine enjoyment of men and an adventurous spirit. I loved her matter-of-fact acceptance of that part of herself.

"Is it possible to love two men at one time?" Rose wonders, and without missing a beat, Blanche says, "Set the scene. Have we been drinking?"

She figures, hey, it's natural, it's fun, why make a fuss? Even though this inevitably sets her up for a lot of razzing from her housemates. Dorothy quips that Blanche going without sex is like Raymond Burr saying, "No gravy." And Sophia never hesitates to use the word "slut." Or "slutpuppy." Or "Sheena, Queen of the Slut People."

I decided right away that Blanche would laugh whenever Sophia shot a poisoned arrow her way. One of the best instincts I had in creating Blanche's character was that choice to see Sophia as a darling old thing whose barbs were *endearing,* not hurtful. After all, putting up with that sort of thing was, as Blanche breezily put it, "the curse of every devastatingly beautiful woman."

⟶

The Golden Girls kept me very busy, not just taping the shows but going to unending events. We were the toast of the town. After we completed the first season and went on hiatus, I found an opportunity to drag Tom Lloyd to my therapist, who gave our story serious thought before saying, "Tom, I think you see Rue as your father."

His father? Could I have heard that correctly?

After a moment, Tom said, "Yes, I think you're right."

Me, his father? But—he *hated* his father. The Authority Figure, The Tyrant, who demanded that he behave responsibly. Good grief! What guy can have a romantic relationship with his *father?* Tom became crystal clear to me that instant. And after it really sank in, I was finally cured of that old fever. That long-crippling Tom Bish virus.

Still, I had been planning to take Mark on a trip to Europe that summer and had invited Tom to go with us, because I continued to hope that the two of them might become closer—unless Tom was confusing Mark with his hated aunt Edna, of course. We decided to stick with that plan and flew to Amsterdam, where we bicycled through the impeccable woods that connected the impeccable residential areas to the impeccable business areas. (My Lord, those people are clean!) We flew over the Alps and drove from Milan to Florence to see Michelangelo's *David*. In Venice, we mingled with jazz artists in a villa bordering a canal. We had nice accommodations everywhere we went, but I wished to God that Tom and I had been given separate rooms. He picked a fight with me every night. Mark stopped talking to both of us. So much for the big bonding experience. And to top it all off, not one Italian man pinched my fanny.

When we returned to L.A., Tom moved out of my house, and finally I was glad to see him go.

I didn't need him. Wasn't in love with him. Didn't want him back.

I was free.

⌒

A few years later, when Tom was diagnosed with advanced liver disease, I rushed to see him in intensive care at Cedars-Sinai Hospital. Beside his bed was a blond bombshell in a snow-white gym suit. She looked over and said, "Hi. I'm Tom's lady."

I said, "Hi, I'm his ex-wife."

Tom wasn't expected to make it, throwing up fountains of blood, but he pulled through, and after a few weeks was released, weak and pale. A few days later, he returned to intensive care. More fountains of blood. Once again, he recovered. After that, I didn't see him again for almost fifteen years.

In 2005, Mark decided that he wanted to pay a visit, so we tracked him down in Los Angeles. Tom was seventy, looked eighty, and acted ninety, although seeing us did pick up his spirits. His slurred speech got clearer, and he kidded around and laughed. It depressed me to see the dreadful change in him, but Mark felt good about the visit, and we were both glad we'd gone.

Eleven months later, Tom died quietly in his sleep.

When I heard that no one had stepped forward to claim his body or belongings, I thought about that spring day in 1985 when I had just started *The Golden Girls* and Tom moved in with me. I was on the brink of something really wonderful in my career, and now I had another chance with this man who'd owned my heart for so many years. At the time, a big tomcat had been terrorizing the female cats on our street for several weeks. I'd been putting out food for him in the front yard, but he wouldn't let me get close to him.

The day Tom moved in, he appeared at my front door carrying that cat.

"Hey, babe!" he said. "I got Buster Big Balls here."

Buster moved in, becoming docile and happy, but he did wander off now and then. He wore a collar with my phone number on it, so sooner or later someone would call and I'd go fetch him home. The last time he left, nobody called and I never found him. My father said he'd gone off to die.

Some cats do that.

CHAPTER TWENTY-TWO

⌒

"Listen, Sir Walter, elephant shit or chicken shit,
it's all the same on your shoe."

—QUEEN ELIZABETH I

B ack in 1972, I watched Secretariat win the Belmont Stakes,
finishing a full record-smashing thirty-one lengths ahead
of the rest of the horses.

"Secretariat is all alone!" blared the track announcer. "He's into the
stretch . . . Secretariat leads this field by eighteen lengths . . . Twice a
Prince has taken second . . . My Gallant has moved back to third . . .
Here comes Secretariat to the wire! Unbelievable! An amazing performance!"

That horse was the Isaac Newton of horsedom. A phenomenon.
The rules of horse racing are simple and finite. The fastest pony wins,
and anyone with the sense to stay sober at the track can plainly see which
horse that is. Showbiz awards don't work that way. Occasionally, an
actor wins an Oscar, Emmy, or Tony by rising head-and-shoulders
above all competitors. But that's rare. The Great Winner is usually
among equally excellent competitors. The decision of the judging committee is entirely subjective, their opinions divided by a hairsbreadth.
The Nobel Prize is sometimes divided between two equal winners, but
show business awards insist on one big winner in each category. It's just

plain silly. How can any one performer—or any one show, really—be "The Best"? Maybe one of the five best, or one of the three best, but let's be reasonable here.

I don't cotton to awards shows. Back in the seventies, during my first sojourn in La-La-Land, as Brad Davis called Hollywood, I was invited one year to be on the Emmy Awards judging committee to choose Best Actor in an Hour Comedy Series, and the next year, Best Actress in a Sitcom. What an eye-opener! We were presented with the five best performers picked from hundreds of actors by the Television Academy voters. The best five. So far, so good. For my money, all five were winners, having been voted by the entire Academy as the best of the bunch.

But now a dozen judges were to pick the Best Performer. And who were the venerable twelve? Well, there was a disc jockey, a daughter of a local L.A. radio personality, a few small-name actors like me, and a handful of even dimmer bulbs on the marquee. Might as well have been a dozen hardware store owners. We watched one show each entered by the five competitors, then ranked them #1 to #5. The actor with the most #1s got the Emmy. That's how it's done. And my #1 choice never won, so I maintain the system is a crock!

That first season of *The Golden Girls,* Bea, Betty, and I were all nominated for Emmys and Betty won, along with all the writers and Terry Hughes—seventeen Emmys in all. The second season, we were all nominated and I won. The next season, we were all nominated and Bea and Estelle won. The fourth season, we were all nominated and Candace Bergen won. Oops. Oh, well. Hers was a new show that year. The kid needed a break. She also won for the next several years, but hey—we stayed in the Top Ten, which seemed to amaze Betty, who expected us to get canceled every year, the funny little skink.

Over my career thus far, there are many awards I've won and some biggies that I haven't (yet). It sounds clichéd, but being nominated really does mean as much to me as winning, and I'm most proud of awards I received for service rendered, rather than competition. But I can't deny it—winning that OBIE thrilled me to pieces, and I also loved winning the Emmy, even knowing how it was decided. The audience didn't know! And I had finally been acknowledged.

Sort of.

When the envelope was opened, Emmy presenter Howie "Deal? Or no deal?" Mandel announced, "And the winner of this year's Emmy for Best Comedy Actress is—*Miss Rue McCallahan!*"

Rats. Do your homework, Mr. Mandel.

⟶

The first two years we had a prop department that was as funny as the show, the two prop men, Kenny and Jim, full of mischief. They had a toilet sitting right spang in the middle of the prop room and huge inflatable dinosaurs hanging from the ceiling. Once during rehearsal, Kenny dashed through the set upstage of the action, dressed in a woman's nightie, breaking everyone up. Their most memorable prank was a prop they concocted for an episode in which Blanche gives each of the other girls a "Men of Blanche's Boudoir" calendar for Christmas. In the scene, Rose and Dorothy were supposed to open their calendars and gasp at the pictures.

Well, our creative prop masters had put together a real calendar with eight by ten photos of themselves and a few other young rapscallions who worked on the show, all scantily clad in sado-masochistic garb with all the fixin's—whips, chains, you name it. They posed flogging each other, riding each other as horses, anything they could dream up—which was plenty. By the time Bea and Betty got to March, they had completely fallen apart laughing. We had to stop rehearsal, and everyone crowded around, flipping through to December. It was priceless, and of course, I still have it. Those two goofballs kept us laughing for two years.

As the show grew in popularity, rumors abounded about shark

tales swishing just under the idyllically calm surface of our happy little set. Wanna hear the juicy inside stories?

Go ask someone else.

I'm not going to dish.

Anyone who's ever been near a cheerleading squad or a PTO committee or a sorority house or the kitchen during a family reunion or any roomful of women knows that women can be bitchy sometimes. Women can and often do simultaneously love and hurt each other. For heaven's sake, look no further than *The Golden Girls,* if you want an example. In one scene, big-eyed Rose says, "The doctor explained to me where babies come from. I should never have believed Elsa Kreb's story about the fetus fairy. Call me gullible!" And Dorothy shoots back, "That's way down the list of what I want to call you."

Dorothy's strength and assertiveness might sound mean to someone who didn't know how much she loves Rose. She routinely smacks Rose over the head with a newspaper and verbally chops her off at the knees. On the flip side, Rose's sweetie pie act might strike some as cloying and fake. But somehow, it all works, because underneath they love each other. So it was with us four actresses. Four strong-minded, talented women tossed into the sitcom soup together. Things got pretty spicy once in a while, but what mattered most to each of us individually and all of us as a group: the chemistry worked. We were damn funny. And we did it together. That's what counts at the end of the day.

Betty and I had so much fun together and even got to do some terrific little dance routines together over the years. We used to play word games backstage, including one where we'd go back and forth making lists in alphabetical order. Wild animals, devastatingly handsome actors, movie titles. Every once in a while we'd get all the way to X or Y and have to go and do a scene, and the whole time, we'd be thinking, "Hmmm . . . Xavier? There must be a handsome actor named Xavier!"

As for Bea Arthur, Queen of Timing, there's no one with whom I'd rather play a two-person scene. Betty's shmoozing with the audience seemed to get under Bea's skin, since Bea with her stage-acting background assiduously observed "the fourth wall," that invisible barrier between the performer and the onlookers, while Betty, a TV baby, had always flirted with the crowd. Both schools of thought are professional and each has its own value, but they are diametrically opposed. I think there's something to be said for both. Does that sound wimpy? I usually see both sides of the question, as Pisces are prone to do. (You may have heard the one about the Piscean who was asked, "Is it true that Pisces are wishy-washy?" And he says, "Well, yes and no.") I love both Bea and Betty and got a huge kick out of each of them. Their relationship with each other wasn't all I wished it could be, but it never interfered with their work.

It was awkward to be pitted against one another in the nominations year after year. When Betty won the Emmy that first year, it didn't seem to set well with Bea. Of course, she behaved impeccably in public, a composed pro on the red carpet, but behind closed doors, she seemed hurt and outraged. When I won the second season, I felt that Bea wasn't able to be happy for me, even with the history we shared. She was making a lot more money than the rest of us, which you'd think would be a dandy consolation prize, but—no, scratch that. Money is never a substitute for love. The third season, Bea won for Best Comedy Actress and Estelle won for Best Supporting Comedy Actress, and I was thrilled for both of them. *Tank Gott!* They deserved to win. It obviously meant a lot to them and it made things a little less awkward. After that, we all had to bite the bullet together and put on our happy faces for Candace Bergen.

Despite any rumors of lurking tension, Bea refused to go to lunch without Betty every day. On Fridays, we had dinner in our bathrobes between the afternoon and evening shows, across the lot in a big dining room full of the cast and crew, where we got rewrites for the evening show. Bea would never walk across the lot to dinner until Betty was ready to walk with her, even if Betty made her wait, and they sat next to each other in the dining hall.

One running gag on the show was that whenever Rose said something dumb, Dorothy would say, "Rose, hand me that newspaper." Rose would cheerfully hand it to her, and—*whack!*—Dorothy would hit her over the head. Betty never asked Bea to take it easy. She just made an *Ow!* face and patted her hair back in place.

Meanwhile, Estelle was having a hard time holding herself together enough to do the show. By the end of that season, she had grown terrified of performing, fluffing her lines repeatedly. The first three days of rehearsals she was fine, but by Thursday she was under a black cloud of anxiety, and on Friday—tape day—she was too uptight to think. Finally, she asked for cue cards, which appalled us all, and at first, the producers refused to stoop to such an unprofessional thing. But eventually, she had to be given cue cards for those deliciously funny Sophia stories.

"Picture it. Sicily, 1912. A beautiful young peasant girl with clear, olive skin meets an exciting but penniless Spanish artist. There's an instant attraction. They laugh, they sing, they slam down a few boilermakers. They run naked through the piazza and almost start a war. Shortly afterward, he's arrested for showing her how he can hold his palette without using his hands. But I digress. He paints her portrait and they make passionate love. She spends much of the next day in the shower with a loofah sponge scrubbing his fingerprints off her body. She sees the portrait and is insulted. It looks nothing like her, and she storms out of his life forever." Sophia takes a meaningful beat. "That peasant girl was me. And that painter . . . was Pablo Picasso." And when the others are skeptical, she shrugs and says, "Believe what you want. But while I'm spending my waning days in a tract house in Miami, my picture is hanging in some executive's penthouse in Tokyo!"

The lines were just too delicious. Dear Estelle hated not being able to learn them. Even with cue cards, her panic grew worse each season. We tried everything we could think of, including hypnosis and an assistant to go over her lines with her every day, but nothing helped. I kept telling her, "Estelle, don't try to think of it word by word. Just picture the story, what you want to tell, and it will flow naturally."

She couldn't. She was gripped in panic, and not only was it agonizing to watch, it brought us all down. Often, we stayed after the audience left, to retape her lines. This was a naturally funny woman, and thanks to clever editing the shows look fine on tape, but man alive, it took hell to get there! I'd seen other series being taped, and fluffed lines are not uncommon. But Bea and Betty and I were not of that ilk. One of us might make a fluff once in a while, but very rarely. We took professional pride in our ability to tape an entire show without stumbling.

⟶

Our producers had their hands full and told me on more than one occasion, "Thank God for you, Rue. You hold things together. You're the glue."

Yeah? So how about a big gluey raise already?

Awards are nice, but let's talk turkey. *The Golden Girls* was a massively popular smash hit, and the salary I received for a week's work was a fraction of what the network received for one thirty-second commercial placed in the show. The third season, I hired myself a crackerjack lawyer to joust with the Disney moneyman, and he was able to get me a salary commensurate with Betty's. (Betty, you may be laughing up your sleeve, but they *said* it would be commensurate with yours!)

Bea and Betty were already set for life before we began the show in 1985, both living in Brentwood in truly gorgeous homes. Bea had divorced Gene Saks, the director of *Maude,* after it was over, and Betty had inherited the rights to several game shows from her husband, Allen Ludden. (They'd built a lovely home on the ocean in Carmel, completed just four days before Allen died in 1985. Live for the day, people. Live for the day.) Estelle had been married to, then divorced from, a fellow who made plastic novelty gadgets, and she lived in a large Beverly Hills condo. Living in the little Studio City house I'd bought with The Greek back in 1976 was like living "thirteen telephone poles past the standpipe north of town" all over again.

We gals saw one another constantly at all the celebrity events we had to attend, but we moved in very different social circles. Betty's old friends were Hollywood names: Mel Tormé, Adele Astaire, Carol Channing. Bea had her actor friends from New York and held court for a large following of gay men, some of them well known. Estelle also had a large coterie of young gay guys, many from *Torch Song Trilogy*.

I was mystified at first about the immediately huge popularity of *The Golden Girls* among gay men. Greenwich Village and West Hollywood gay bars began having Golden Girl Night, with patrons in costume and Best Blanche beauty contests. Gay Halloween parades began to feature the famous Miami housemates right alongside the swishy goblins and fairies. Recently, Mark and I were having a cappuccino at a little place in the Village, and a young gay blade came in, spotted me instantly, and squealed. As I signed an autograph for him, I asked, "Why is it that you gay guys are so crazy about Blanche?"

"Why, *honey*," he said. "Isn't is *obvious*? We all want to *be* Blanche!"

I still had the same motley crew of friends I'd made when I moved to L.A. in 1973, some straight, some gay, none famous, except Brad Davis, but all terrific. My Four Wise Men, Larry, Ken, Michael, and David—all of whom were Jewish—gathered at my house every year to decorate the tree, adding a lot of life to every Christmas party, along with Lette and Jack, Norman Hartweg, Brad, and Mark. My three *Golden Girls* castmates didn't appear regularly at my parties, nor I at theirs. We all went to Estelle's big birthday parties every summer, six months after Betty's birthday. But never together.

Bea did attend a dinner party at my place with about forty guests, including a new acquaintance, the wonderfully funny and talented movie actress/singer Martha Raye. Many of my friends were too young to remember her, but plenty of others did, including Bea. During after-dinner drinks, Martha began to sing, accompanied on the piano by her escort. I came into the living room teeming with people, to hear her belting away, the guests enthralled. She still had powerful pipes. Not

*Mark and me at a party at my house in Studio City,
California, 1987. Lookin' good!*

seeing Bea among the group, I asked a friend where she was, and he
said, "Look in the garage."

The garage?

At the end of the hall, I went out and found a small group gathered
in the garage, listening to Bea sing. A cappella. No piano in my garage.
A glass of wine in her hand, she was having a smashing good time. She
sang one more tune, then wended her way homeward.

As the night wound down, Martha and her tipsy fella were backing
their small black car down the driveway, swerved rather drastically,
and straddled the curb with all four wheels, leaving the car perched up
there like a showroom display. No amount of pushing could dislodge
it. They had to get a ride home with another guest and return the following morning with a tow truck. As they dragged the little car away,
I was still laughing. And wishing Bea had stayed long enough to see it.

⟶

For about five years, since 1982, I had been waking up, looking at my bedroom ceiling and walls, thinking, *Something's wrong. I've got to get out of here!* One morning, I was hit with the realization that never before in my life had I lived in any house for over four years, and I'd been in this one for over eleven. *Well,* I thought, *no wonder!* I need a change.

So after work and on weekends, I started looking at all sorts of houses from Studio City to miles out in the boondocks—adorable little renovated places perched on hills, big ridiculous mansions the Middle Easterners were building chock-full of marble and chandeliers, ranch houses with ten acres and outbuildings, funky canyon houses with seasonal creeks, and everything in between. Some I could afford, some I couldn't, but none of them was right. Then one day my Realtor took me to a 3,900-square-foot house on three acres in Encino, and well . . . it had possibilities. An ugly old swimming pool. Three acres of dead or dying trees and weeds going up hills on all three sides. You could barely get through the overgrown brush. A neighbor's pool at the top side of the property had broken and swept trees and brush down into the area at the back. But through the tangled mess I saw potential for an astoundingly beautiful fairyland. The house was badly planned and old-fashioned, but with a lot of work from a talented architect and a good builder . . .

"How much?" I asked.

"A million five."

Gulp. A lovely dream, but the asking price was out of my range, the market still going through the roof. But you just didn't find three acres in a lovely area in Encino! All but unheard of! And I was earning money, I reasoned. *Real* money for the first—and possibly the *only*—time in my life. I'd signed a lucrative contract with Disney for the next three years. I probably wouldn't be able to afford the property for long, but for once in my life, by God I was going to live in a breathtaking place, like a real Movie Star! Besides, the real estate market had done nothing but shoot up, year after year, so I figured I'd be able to sell the place after three years for—oh, three or four million! (And you thought it took a man to get me this excited.)

I got it for $1,350,000, put half a mil down, and took on a hefty mortgage—eight times what I'd been paying for the modest house in Studio City. I found a good builder, met with Carla Champion (the widow of Gower), who had become an interior designer, and we began making plans for the renovation.

Did I say renovation? Rebuilding! Reinvention! Resurrection!

We tore that house down almost to its foundation. You could stand in the front yard and look straight through to the back. After a massive amount of work, the new house would be five thousand square feet. The landscape architect took on the staggering job in the huge back-yard—a new irrigation system, a tiled pool with a waterfall, a private little haven with a hot tub off my bedroom, a patio covered with lattice and tile and plants, pathways winding through the wild lilies, a big gazebo wired for sound. The area adjacent to where the neighbor's pool had swept debris down the hill became a wildflower hillside, where one could sit on a bench with a glass of wine and look down to the house far below. Jungle flowers bordered a path to a kids' swing, high above the fruit trees. The property was so gorgeous, so varied, so wonderfully landscaped, helicopter pilots thought it was a city park. (I only wish the city had been paying the water bills. I kept trying to come up with a scheme to achieve that.)

It was my piece of earth! Big enough to include two vegetable gar-dens and every kind of fruit tree you can think of. Even some you can't—like kumquat. Yes, I had a small kumquat. I also had two tall loquats, even comelier than, though not as low as, the kumquat. (I've been trying to make a joke about those trees for years.) I planted figs, lemons, oranges, apricots, adding peaches and pears later on. One year, my apple trees yielded so much fruit, I ended up baking twenty apple cakes in October and freezing them for Christmas presents. Don't ever try that. In October, they emerged from the oven, piping hot, crusty, and delicious. In December, they emerged from the freezer, soggy, shmushy, and ill-tempered. But I do think food is a terrific holiday gift, both for giving and receiving. Particularly receiving. Charlie Hauck, one of our superb writers on *Maude,* made mustard every year and gave it out in pretty little jars. I rationed mine jealously and made it last into summer. (Charlie, if you're reading this, I want more mustard!)

But I digress, as Sophia would say.

That yard cost a bundle—more than rebuilding the house. Always prone to saving money, I was now spending it, but I was creating something divine. Even if I couldn't afford it for life, for a while I would live in a little bit of heaven.

⟶

During an early season of *The Golden Girls,* Tom and I went to see Lette in a production of *I Do! I Do!,* a two-hander musical, up in Solvang. During dinner afterward, Lette and I left the restaurant, crossing the street arm-in-arm, to go get God knows what. Jack told me later that Tom turned to him and said, "Now, there go two real girl friends."

He said a mouthful.

Lette had been having pains in her left hip, and it was diagnosed as bone cancer. The goddamned breast cancer had metastasized. Eventually, she had a metal rod put in her leg, then more bones replaced with more metal.

"It's incurable," she said with minimal drama. "But it'll progress very slowly."

"Oh . . . Lette . . . oh, dear God . . ."

By 1987, the cancer was in her neck. If this was "moving slowly," it was too fast for me.

"You know, they probably do have a cure," she said. "The bastards are just withholding it to milk people out of money."

In 1988, during the fourth season of *The Golden Girls,* I was busy with work and the Encino heaven-building, but I went over to Lette and Jack's several times a week. Mark was still living in Van Nuys, working in his garden, teaching guitar, playing jazz. He had a steady girlfriend, a pretty little blonde who was a born-again Christian.

"I don't like this uptight little miss very much," I confided in Lette.

"I'm sure she has her own fire-and-brimstone opinion of you, Baby Rue."

Lette was growing weaker, getting thin. She sat curled up on the sofa, still full of the devil. We still made each other laugh. I would take my king-sized Mexican quilt over and work on it, sitting by her bed. I'd been embroidering, embroidering, embroidering on it since 1979. One night, when she'd been bleary on heavy sedation for several weeks, I said, "Oh, Lette, this quilt goes on forever! What am I going to do with it?"

She took a good look and said, "I'd send the damn thing straight to hell."

An acting group I belonged to had chartered a trip to Russia for two weeks that spring to see plays and museums, but two days before we were to fly to Leningrad, I got a call from someone—I can't even remember who—with the news that Lette had died.

I drove over early that evening and there she lay in bed, covered with a spread. Jack was in the room along with one of his daughters, Lette's doctor, and two other close friends. After a few minutes of talk, her despicable doctor, whom I had never liked or trusted, said, "Want to see the mastectomy?" And the idiot whipped off the spread, exposing her left breast, flat and scarred. In front of all of us!

The breath went out of me. *He can't do this to you, Lette!*

Oh, if only I had crossed the room and slapped him to the ground! I've always been sorry I just stood there—in shock. Why didn't I jump to her defense? Why didn't Jack? She would never have shown us this sight herself. She was too proud of her once-perfect breasts. And now, defenseless, at the mercy of that scummy doctor—oh, God, it was immoral.

Ronnie Claire Edwards held a huge memorial service in her backyard, but I couldn't bring myself to go up and speak. My little darling Lette, full of life and hilarity, irrepressible, with that amazing, soaring voice. A major player in my life for twenty-four years—seven with The Italian, three with The Greek, one with Keel, and all the years between and after. What would I have done without her? It was a long time before I could listen to the tapes we made—our French and singing lessons and the cast album of *The Secret Life of Walter Mitty*— but when I do, her spirit springs out at me, as fresh as when those recordings were made.

Once upon a time, back when I was a scrambling New York stage actress, I did a five-week tryout of a new A. R. Gurney play, *Scenes from American Life,* and since the work was still in progress, I asked Gurney to write me a solo scene to be "done in one" (speaking directly to the audience). In two hours, he wrote a wonderful older woman who studies opera but is kept from realizing her dream by her disapproving family. She trains and trains and finally debuts with the aria from *Lucia di Lammermoor,* whose story mirrors her own. She begins confidently, but her voice cracks on a high note and, devastated, she realizes she doesn't have the chops. It is a moving scene that speaks eloquently about the hopes and fears of any aspiring artist, about the difference love can make, and about the power of desire itself.

In life, in love, in song, Lette never stopped reaching for the elusive high notes.

I'll never understand why a voice like hers was stopped so soon.

CHAPTER TWENTY-THREE

~~

"I once sat on a couch beside Rue McClanahan
and let her play with my snake."
—DR. HAROLD C. LAUGHLIN, PH.D.

I used to insist to Lette, "Digging in the earth is every bit as good as sex!"

She never bought it either.

But I'm here to tell you, there's nothing like a vine-ripened, organic, God-given sweet red tomato to give you religion! Hallelujah! Praise the Lord! There's a certain therapy in puttering around the tomato vines in the springtime, pinching back the crotch buds (maybe I should've tried that on The Italian), dosing the yellow flowers with Tru-Grow, watching as the young green fruit appears, turns pink, then orange, and finally harvesting those beautiful red jewels! Of course, I always grow too much of everything and end up giving the surplus away to anyone who'll hold still. But that's true of every backyard tomato nut. You just have to find someone who doesn't grow tomatoes. And can't run very fast. During the *Golden Girls* years, Betty, Estelle, and Bea were happy recipients. I've always loved hunting Easter eggs, and for me, spying ripe tomatoes behind the leafy branches is much the same. Oh, I *like* okra and cucumbers, lettuce, scallions, carrots, beans, cabbage, potatoes—particularly new potatoes, which you have to dig for, like treasure. And because they're good for burying in the dark of a new moon to ensure good luck in romance.

There's just never a good new potato around when you need one.

During the fourth season of *The Golden Girls,* I got a call from an acquaintance who had a girlfriend who had a father whom they wanted me to meet. I wasn't all that eager to be fixed up, but they eventually cajoled me into meeting him for dinner.

I got a good look at Gregory Steinmetz, a Beverly Hills psychiatrist, as he came striding up my front walk. Hmm. Five-eight, skinny, brunet, narrow face wreathed in a big grin, eyes that crinkled, springy and energetic at fifty-two. (Later, when I introduced him to Mark, Mark said, "I expected you to be dating someone who looks like Robert Redford." His gentle way of saying that Gregory was hardly handsome.) But Gregory and I got along very well on our first date. He was intelligent and friendly. I thought the guy was worth dating occasionally. He showed me his house on the beach and his office in Beverly Hills. He was obviously doing quite well with his practice. I brought him to a taping one night and he behaved decorously. He seemed to have no bone to pick with his parents and had good relationships with his daughter and son, as well. He was nice people. Sounds pretty good, huh? We saw each other several times over the next three weeks, always having a fine time. No sex. We agreed to get better acquainted before we moved on—*if* we moved on.

Well, one night we moved on. And lemme tell you, folks, this guy could move.

My upstairs bedroom had a huge mirror next to my queen-sized bed. (Oh, roll up your tongues. It was the only place in the house with a vacant wall that size.) It had never witnessed any goings-on. Well, I became fast friends with that mirror. The sex that took place with Gregory was outside my experience—outside my *imagination*. I was already fifty-four, y'all, and I'd never had a lover remotely like this. When people would ask me about a man, "How was he in bed?" I'd always answer, "Good. It was good. What's not to be good?"

Little did I know. *Oooooh,* little did I know. This wiry little Stein-metz guy was—I don't know—was he simply innately talented? Somehow tuned in to what a woman needs and wants? He was a mas-ter, leading me on with the most subtle, stimulating, maddening fore-play—blatantly in charge, making me crazy for almost too long before he issued the *coup de grâce*. We watched ourselves in that big mirror, which stimulated me further! I was without reserve, throwing myself into this game with abandon, aware that I was being manipulated, helpless, and loving it. I don't have to rate this man. He was off the chart. President Emeritus of The Casanova Club. And he was good company on his feet. We were feeling inklings of being in love. Time, perhaps, for the travel test?

Queen Elizabeth II held a "Command Performance" gala every year, inviting entertainers from around the world to perform. That fall, two acts were invited from the United States, *The Golden Girls* and Jackie Mason. Bea usually turned down about half our invitations, and if she didn't go, nobody got to go, but this was one event that even Bea was eager to attend. We would be in London for about four days, which happened to coincide with our Thanksgiving in the States. The writers began rewriting one of the scenes we had done in a past episode, and our costume designer got to work on outfits. I asked Gre-gory, who had never been to London, to be my guest.

During a hiatus week in November, I was asked to ride an elephant in an animal show in San Diego. I felt a bit conflicted, because I don't believe in making elephants perform, but I was assured that this ele-phant was very well treated, and *oh boy,* did I want to ride an elephant, my favorite critter. I was in San Diego about three days, dressed in an abbreviated tux and high heels. The procedure was for me to step on the elephant's lowered trunk, which she then raised so I could climb over her head and sit on her shoulders, after which she carried me around in a big circle while the TV cameras filmed us. Elephants are so damned sweet. And smart. I'm glad to say this grand lady was indeed treated very nicely by her trainer, or I would have pitched a hissy fit.

Gregory came to the final rehearsal, staying a few hours before returning to L.A. That night, he called and proposed marriage. I was thrown, but he was very persuasive and . . . yep, you got it. I ended up accepting.

A week or so later, he began returning his clients' phone calls from my house in the evenings, talking to patients who called in distress. Since he used the kitchen phone, I couldn't help overhearing and was surprised at how harsh he was with these people. Maybe that was good psychiatry, but to me it sounded cold and impatient. I'd never seen this side of him. I felt bad for the clients, who were obviously in pain, and I began to worry that I might have been too hasty accepting his proposal, so I gathered the nerve to tell him, "Gregory, I want to give this more thought, get to know you better."

I expected him to say, "Of course, take as long as you need. I want you to be sure."

You could've blown me over with a dandelion puff when he replied, "Oh, no. No, no, no. That's not being responsible. You made a decision, now stick to it!"

"Gregory, I'm just not sure," I explained. "I need more time."

"Stop acting like a child, Rue. It's time for you to grow up!"

This really threw me. I felt like a kid being reprimanded. A child? Was that what I was being? Now I was really confused. I went to see my own therapist and related the conversation.

"He said *what*? That's manipulation, Rue!"

"It is? Then that's why it seems so wrong."

"You bet it is."

"Will you see the two of us together?"

"Gladly!"

Oh, boy. A highfalutin Beverly Hills psychiatrist versus my Burbank psychologist in a head-shrinking Battle Royale! This would be interesting. Well, sir, it was more than interesting. It was educational. I felt as if I'd had a nice bath that washed the guilt and shame right off me and I could see things clearly. By God, Gregory *was* a manipulator! It makes perfect sense. Isn't any great lover a great *manipulator* by definition? I broke the engagement, simply saying I'd made a mistake, but it was only a week before we were to leave for London, so I made a second mistake in saying, "I know how much you were looking forward to the trip, Gregory. So even though we're no longer a couple, my invitation to London is still open. If we just go as friends."

And he made the mistake of saying, "Okay."

We were put up in an expensive hotel with a lovely bedroom with a queen-sized bed, which saw no action. On Thanksgiving Day, I went to a pub for Thanksgiving lunch British style—kidney pie and beer— then to see a matinee of the thirtysomething-year run of *The Mousetrap*. The theatre seated me in the Queen's box. (Wow! The royal box!) Sadly, that didn't help the performance. *The Mousetrap* was the most famous play in umpteen years, but it was also the tiredest. But by the good Lord, I've seen it! In contrast, our performance for the royals at the Palladium was a smashing success. After the show, we were all presented to the Queen Mother and Princess Margaret (who was looped!), and we actually curtsied. Even Bea.

Our last afternoon in London, ye gods, Gregory pleaded with me for "one last time," but I couldn't do it, no way, nohow. An uncomfortable, painful experience. He was a decent person and I have never borne him a moment's ill will, and I felt I'd made progress. It was a watershed moment: I'd said the magic words, "Let me think about it." And then—will wonders never cease!—I actually *thought* about it! I'd picked a good man who didn't cheat me. I'd skated free of marriage and felt no panic. Well, whattaya know. I was definitely emotionally healthier . . . right? Go ahead. Say "right." It's getting safer.

⸺

On January 1 of 1989, a year after work began on my Encino dream home . . . work was still going on at my Encino dream home.

I had agreed with the purchasers of the Studio City house that I'd be out by December 31, which the contactor and I had agreed on as the Encino move-in date. But autumn rolled by and he was nowhere near through, so he quickly finished the maid's rooms, and I moved into them while he continued working on the main house, the maid's rooms still smelling of paint. My three cats and small dog, Angie, bunked with me, while the three big dogs had the run of a large fenced area out back. I loved living in the maid's quarters! One room just big enough for my computer, desk, TV, and big bed, plus a little kitchenette and a walk-in closet with a built-in chest of drawers next to the bathroom. Just the right size for me: cozy, comforting, and convenient. What more could one want?

Every morning, seemingly at the crack of dawn, I was roused by the cacophony of building just outside my window. *Buzz, roar, VZZZZ, RRRAUW!* The yard crew at work, the house carpenters at work. But I had the joy of walking through the house and around the yard, watching the progress. Finishing touches went on till June. There were problems, of course. Oh, *boy*, were there problems! But who builds a house without problems? (Words to live by.) The beautiful red oak floors began to warp. The skylights leaked. The alarm system went off whenever a cat or dog walked through the dining room, and I got to meet a lot of cute young security men who rushed out to the house before I could call in and stop them. You know, I never did get the hang of that pesky security system. (Drat!)

Through an agency, I interviewed three possible housekeepers—a Swedish lady, a Cockney Englishman, and a Filipina named Celi. I hired Celi, who moved in that summer, knocking me out of my cozy maid's room into the master bedroom, miles away. The house was gorgeous, but too damned big. Who needs five thousand square feet? There were twelve rooms. And five baths. Sometimes I count thirteen, but I think there were twelve. Celi asked if she could bring her younger sister, Alma, to live with us, and God knows, we had plenty of room. Celi

wanted to be my gardener, with Alma my housekeeper. So I sent Celi
to gardening school, she taught Alma housekeeping and cooking, and
by fall, we were a jolly group. Celi turned out to be a super-industrious
gardener, with her work boots and overalls, wood shredder, and every
other new tool she could weasel out of me. Alma, a sweetheart, made a
passable cook and housekeeper, teaching me to avoid boiled fish heads
and various other unidentifiable Philippine delicacies.

⌒

My lovely Celestine was a born feline model, appearing in two animal
calendars. Most cats won't cooperate with cameramen and the lights
and all the hubbub. Celestine would jump up on the white sheet spread
over the raised hearth and Vogue it like crazy. What a ham. I can't
begin to measure the joy she and Gracie and my many other animal
friends have brought to my life, beginning with that happy little bird
who lifted me from my depression after Bill Bennett had abruptly
turned me loose back in college. (Gee, I wonder what his mother might
have to say about the dangers of being a "dreamer" now?)

I went to scores of fund-raisers for various animal societies, and
Estelle and I did two PETA jobs together. Bea, Betty, Estelle, and I all
attended a fund-raiser for Actors and Others for Animals. At one of
the PETA gigs, two puppies were brought in—a brown German shepherd mix and a black-and-white part-Australian sheep dog, both about
three months old, both adorable—and when I learned they were going
to be returned to the pound, I took them home. Four days later, Betty
said Mary Tyler Moore's brother had thirteen puppies for adoption
after an accidental romance between his black lab and his German
shepherd, so I brought Jackson to join Ginger and Belle.

All the puppies slept together in a pair of old stuffed rockers, chewing them to shreds. I figured what the heck, I could always get them recovered. At another PETA TV job, I worked with a funny-looking
little tan dog with long hair down nearly to her feet. Her bottom teeth

Polly, me, Angie, Ginger, Belle, Winnie, and Jackson, being exclusive, in my yard in Encino, California, 1989.

extended beyond the top ones on one side, giving her a wise-guy expression, and one ear stuck up all the time, and—yep, you guessed it. Home with me. I suppose some people are thinking, "Enough already!" but there's no such thing as too much love. Eventually, with Celi's two shi tzus, we had six dogs and eight rescued cats.

Bea kept two enormous German shepherd guard dogs. Betty had a little dog (a poodle, as I recall) and a cat, and she adopted a retired seeing-eye dog every few years. She wrote a book, *Leading Lady,* about one of them. For the first three years we were on *The Golden Girls,* Estelle had no pets.

"You should get a cat," I said, "so you won't be lonesome when you go home."

After holding out for months, she got one, but it was rambunctious.

"Get another one," I suggested. "If he has a pal all day, he won't be so hyper."

Again, after months of protest, she got a second cat, and from then on, you'd have thought she had invented cats, and her cats were the only two cats in the world. All was well on her home front.

⁓

Season five of *The Golden Girls* sped along too fast for Betty and me. Our beloved director, Terry Hughes, whom I always called the Fifth Golden Girl, had left to direct *The Butcher's Wife,* a film starring Demi Moore. On his last night, I was sobbing too hard to attend his going-away party. The film was excellent but made no box office waves, and Terry returned to television—but alas, not with us. Producers hired him for other shows, including a long run on *Third Rock from the Sun*. We had one director after another during our fifth year, with Bea not liking any of them. They did only one show each, if they got hired at all. One fellow was particularly good, but he wore a baseball cap turned around backward, something Bea couldn't abide, and she vetoed him. Finally, she liked someone who, in my opinion, was not inspired, but pliable, and he became our regular director.

Most of the brilliantly gifted writers on the show went on to form their own production companies, several of the top ones leaving every year, new ones being hired. Writing for a comedy series is one of the most demanding jobs in television, but despite the turnover, we were consistently blessed with the cream of the crop. Sadly, the prop men who'd been irrepressible in their hijinks, giving us laughs every day, had been let go, and we had a normal, well-behaved prop crew from then on. Without them and Terry, the old set just didn't feel the same.

Estelle's loss of memory grew steadily worse. I suspect now that her fluctuating ability to focus was an early sign of the terrible Lewy body dementia that gripped her later in her life. I honestly don't know, but she and I shared a quick-change room, being the two at the bottom of the totem pole, so I endured the largest share of her black panic, trying to change costumes four or five times a show and stay in an upbeat frame of mind under her cloud of doom. My heart went out to her, but it was a real pain in the butt. I'd always thought Sophia was the best role in the show, with those slingshot insults and perfectly written stories. Now she had to read those stories from the dratted cue cards.

Oh, well. I had the next-best role in the show with some real gems.

"I'll never forget that night with Benny . . . or was it Bobby? . . . Or Billy? . . . Oh, well, I know it started with a B!"

"She's a lesbian? What's wrong with that? Danny Thomas is one."

Yeah, I did okay.

⸺

I filmed eight TV movies during hiatuses from *The Golden Girls*. No rest for the wicked (thank God). I did those *Children of the Bride* comedies you watch on Lifetime on a rainy afternoon and a few nice dramas, including *The Dreamer of Oz,* starring my old pal John Ritter as L. Frank Baum. On the stage, I played Bananas, the batty wife in *The House of Blue Leaves,* at the Pasadena Playhouse. Didn't get paid a farthing's damn, but who cares? Getting to play Bananas was an artistic high point for me—a role I'd always wanted to tackle—and I got some of the best reviews of my life.

I also made some commercials for which I was paid $250,000 each. (In the immortal words of Edith and Archie, "Those were the days!") I made a Raisin Bran commercial dressed in a gown and peignoir à la Blanche, a bathroom cleanser commercial dressed in a gown and peignoir à la Blanche, and a cold-remedy commercial in a gown and peignoir à la Blanche.

Are we sensing a trend here?

I didn't mind being perpetually costumed in typical Blanche style. In fact, I loved all those floaty, colorful fabrics, the flattering kimonos over comfy basics, and the silky, sensual nightware that practically rolled a red carpet up to the bed. Everywhere I went, women said, "I want to dress like Blanche!" So with the help of my assistant, Chris Reynolds, and one of my Four Wisemen, Michael Thornton, I started a clothing line, "A Touch of Rue," for QVC. I selected fabrics I loved and designed Blanche-inspired garments with my own practical spin, making the exquisite Blanche creations wearable in real life and available at affordable prices. Every three or four months, I'd do a guest appearance on QVC, modeling the new pieces. From my fan mail, I knew that Blanche's gorgeous gown-peignoir sets would sell like hotcakes. But the QVC buyer, Laverne, in her infinite wisdom, refused to include any nightwear in the QVC line, insisting on nothing but daywear, sportswear, and one or two party dresses.

"I know my audience!" she insisted.

"Yes, dear," says I. "But you don't know *my* audience."

We finally talked her into two gown-peignoir sets in a group of twelve items for the premiere offering, and the day my line went on QVC, all the outfits did well, but of course, the gown-peignoir sets sold out in minutes. The handwriting on the wall was so big even old Laverne couldn't miss it.

"From now on, we want nothing but gown-peignoir sets!" she announced.

"But these ladies who write me also want party dresses, splashy things to wear on cruises, to weddings, to bar mitzvahs, as well as daywear . . ."

For three years, we tore out our hair, power-struggling with control freak Laverne and the QVC suits, which made the whole thing more hassle than it was worth. We gave notice, selling the last remaining items. And let me tell you—*never again*! Women still ask me when I'm going to reinstate my clothing line, and I tell them, "Hey, you want to dress like Blanche? Do what I did back in the good ol' days. Make your own, sweethearts!"

Lord knows, I had plenty to do. During the 1990 hiatus, I shot a funny, charming film called *Modern Love,* written and directed by and starring Robbie Benson, whose real-life adorable wife and child played his adorable wife and child in the movie. I played the wife's mom, with

Burt Reynolds as my estranged husband. I scouted out some fabulous antiques while on location in South Carolina, and when I returned home, the Mexican furniture I was having made started arriving, piece by piece. Finally, my dream house was finished and furnished—and so lovely it was featured in several magazine layouts and TV interviews.

Oh, and during the summer of 1990, I flew to Dallas to accept an award for clothing design.

Hello, Laverne? Eat worms.

CHAPTER TWENTY-FOUR

"Show me someone who's fearless in the face of danger,
and I'll show you someone who doesn't grasp the situation."
—WOODY ALLEN

*T*he Greek musical farce Norman Hartweg and I had written together and noodled on for years was finally ready for try-outs, and a friend suggested the ideal title: *Oedipus, Schmedipus, As Long As You Love Your Mother*.

We decided to get the play on its feet at the Golden Theater, a ninety-nine-seat house in Burbank, and engaged their temperamental but talented choreographer/director, Gregory Scott Young. His conductor, Jay Bradley, and I came up with a blockbuster opening number. I wrote a song to open Act II in a feverish rush, sitting spread-eagled on the carpet in my walk-in closet one night after I got home from taping *Golden Girls,* and the next day, Jay put it in professional musical shape. I called in Rosalind, the witty, talented costumer from *Mama's Family,* who concocted forty Greek chitons and capes and whatnot for the cast of twenty. The sets and costumes were gorgeous and practical, and the talented young performers left me in awe.

Opening night of *Oedipus, Schmedipus* was a smash. We had full houses every performance, standing ovations at the end of every show, and mostly favorable reviews. Norman drove me home after a

Saturday matinee, and as he let me out in my driveway, commented, "Good show."

"Yes," I agreed. "I think we pulled it off."

"*You* pulled it off," he answered. "I suggested we write a play just to get you writing."

"But, Norman," I said in amazement. "I only agreed to write a play with you to get *you* writing! *You* are the one who should be writing."

He just grinned and backed out of my driveway. The old smarty.

⁓

As we neared the end of our six-year contract on *The Golden Girls,* Bea, Betty, Estelle, and I had the option to call it quits or sign for one more year. Of course, I wanted to continue, but I assumed Bea wouldn't. She didn't seem very happy on a daily basis, and remembering her decision to lay *Maude* to rest, I knew she would never agree to keep a show going if she wasn't happy with the artistic integrity and caliber of the writing, or if the production values were not what she felt they should be. Much to everyone's delight, Bea did sign on for a seventh year. "Slats" (my pet name for Estelle) also signed on. Now Betty and I, the only two who counted the precious weeks that melted away so quickly every season, could look forward to one more glorious year. And I would be earning well over a million for season seven (look, Ma! I'm a millionaire!), which meant I could stay a little longer in my chichi Encino digs.

Late in the season, we did a segment in which Blanche is competing in a singing contest against Dorothy at the Rusty Anchor, a neighborhood bar. Blanche is determined to gain back her star status, which Dorothy has wrested from her by singing at the piano, and devises a spectacular number to sing *atop* the grand piano. I chose the song "I Want to Be Loved by You," Marilyn Monroe's sultry number from *Some Like It Hot,* and asked Gregory Scott Young if he'd choreograph it, knowing he could come up with some smashing comedy moves.

Greg, who'd been a temperamental tyrant in Burbank, was a lovable lamb in Hollywood, a little awed by the surroundings, and very cooperative indeed, creating a perfect routine for Blanche. Dressed in a red-spangled tight dress, singing sexily into the mike, she proceeds to make an absolute shambles of the song, accidentally kicking off a shoe, which barely misses the pianist, sliding down onto the keyboard with a bang, slinging the mike cord out of control, and finally running off in tears. The precise choreography had to be perfectly executed, which it was, if I do say so myself, and this turned out to be my favorite segment of the whole series.

Boop-boop-ee-doop!

Ever since that night in 1976 when Brad Davis showed up in a taxi at our house on Doheny Drive, he'd been steadily employed in movies and TV, doing everything from *The Twilight Zone* to big-screen successes like *Midnight Express*. I was utterly staggered to receive a call from one of Brad's friends in September of 1991, saying, "Susan wanted me to tell you that Brad died last night."

"What? Wait—I don't understand."

How could that be? Brad wasn't yet forty-three and had seemed perfectly fine the last time I'd seen him, as young and vital as that day we were caught with our Levi's down in my yard.

"He's known for a few years that he was HIV positive," his friend said. "He kept it under wraps to protect his career."

"He had *AIDS?*"

"Yes. From an infected needle years ago."

As I tried to absorb this information, Brad's friend asked if I would be willing to speak at the memorial service, and, shaken, I murmured, "Of course. Of course I'll speak."

I called Mark, who was shocked and devastated equally, and got out of rehearsal for an hour the day of the service. At the lectern, shaking and weeping, I said Brad had been an angel in disguise. Yes, he'd been a long time growing up, but had become a good husband and father and had built a solid career on extraordinary talent.

I have a photo of Brad on my office wall, young and healthy, costumed for his brilliant starring role in *Midnight Express,* the movie that kicked off his career and became a cult classic. In the film, Brad's character, Billy Hayes, says, "To the Turks, everything is *shurla burla,* which means 'like this, like that.' You never know what will happen."

God. That had been some shurla burla year.

⟶

The seventh season of *The Golden Girls* neared an end, and Bea declined to sign for another season, so the producers opted to marry Dorothy to Blanche's uncle and have her move away. Then they called Betty and Estelle and me into their offices to propose a spin-off of *The Golden Girls* to be called *The Golden Palace.* Blanche would sell the house and buy an old hotel, which she and Rose and Sophia would run, assisted by manager Don Cheadle and chef Cheech Marin. Our salaries would all be the same, a "favored-nations" agreement. And we'd have the same crew of writers.

"Candidly? It doesn't sound so hot to me," I said. "I think we should get a new roommate to replace Dorothy. There are a lot of wonderfully talented comedy actresses out there."

"That's not an option," I was informed, and I understood the reason behind their decision: *The Golden Girls* was already in syndication, which is where the producers make the megabucks. This new show only had to last three seasons to go into syndication. More megabucks. But it was too big a gamble in my opinion—which, of course, counted for a flea's fart. So Betty, Estelle, and I accepted the offer. At least we'd have one more year of steady employment, and I could count on one more year of living in my amazingly beautiful estate, with its amazing $8,000 monthly mortgage payments and the amazingly expensive yard.

"And hey, who knows?" I told the other girls with true Blanche bravado. "Maybe it'll be fun working with Don and Cheech. Maybe the show *will* survive three years. Maybe *The Golden Palace* will be a big hit!"

And maybe next July it'll snow in Wambusi.

Before we started taping the new show, I bought Mark a Toyota Forerunner and we drove across the desert toward Oklahoma and Texas. My high school class was having a reunion, and Mark wanted to investigate Austin, Texas, a hot music town, as a place he might like to live. In the middle of Arizona we drove up a long dirt road to the Hopi Reservation, a small collection of one-story adobe homes with a dusty parking lot and a gift shop. As Mark and I shopped for pottery and art, we chatted with the employees and shoppers. After maybe half an hour, we returned to the parking lot, where a sizable crowd was gathered around the Forerunner. Here in the middle of nowhere were Hopis who recognized me and wanted my autograph. This blew my mind. Just didn't compute. Then I looked at the adobe houses, and they all had TV aerials sprouting atop them like weeds. What a country.

The reunion was fun. Keel was there, and it was good to see him. He and I drove up to Turner Falls with an old classmate, Sandra, and her husband, Lou. We rented inner tubes and floated down the river to the falls, laughing ourselves silly. Then I flew home, leaving Mark in Austin, which he found to be lovely, artistic, liberal, and definitely to his taste—and does to this day. Keel and I kept in touch. He was studying a course of self-discovery, uncovering valuable revelations. For starters, he'd decided after much introspection to abstain from sex while he continued soul-searching. I was surprised, but had a lot of respect for that kind of commitment. I was celibate, too, but not by choice! I was still hot to trot, just didn't have a horse. Certainly not a rocking horse.

We started taping *Golden Palace* in early July and learned, to our dismay, that the show would not be aired on Saturday nights at nine on

NBC, our former successful slot. No, it would air on CBS on *Mondays* at eight. On CBS. Mondays. At eight. And there was hardly any publicity or hoo-ha to let people know where we'd disappeared to. Now, there's a recipe for roadkill if there ever was one. A large share of our loyal *Golden Girls* audience never even knew *Golden Palace* existed until the reruns popped up on the Lifetime television network fourteen years later. If our producers were mining for syndication megabucks, they weren't using very big pick axes. We limped along in the ratings. Thank God CBS had bought an entire year, because the real estate market was drooping down around its argyles, and it looked as if I wouldn't even break even if I had to unload my swanky address any time soon.

On the bright side, I was right about one thing—it *was* great working with Don Cheadle and Cheech Marin. Even though Don was striving for a serious film career and didn't really want to do comedy, he threw himself into the role with the heart of a real actor and was quite funny. As was Cheech, who became a good pal. And here's a remarkable thing—Estelle rarely needed cue cards, handling her lines without panicking! Had she been subconsciously intimidated by Bea (who could do that to some actors), or was it a remission in that damn dementia that had played such havoc with her mind? Impossible to say, but it was great to have Slats back.

While we were taping the new show, the 1992 presidential campaign was in full swing: Governor Bill Clinton of Arkansas was running against President George Bush (no, the other George Bush—the one who doesn't have his picture on my toilet seat). Finally! A Democrat with the marbles to take back the White House! I was eager to help out and did an appearance in New Jersey, introducing the New Jersey governor, who would then introduce Governor Clinton. Waiting offstage, I looked up at Governor Clinton standing close behind me and was awash in that extraordinary charisma. He was dazzling but down-home, friendly as a speckled pup. I attended his inauguration and took videos of the party, everyone exuberant, the president himself offering me a terrific spontaneous close-up. I also became acquainted with his mother, Virginia Kelly, later recording the audio edition of her book, *From the Heart*.

And being a properly raised Southern boy, President Clinton wrote me a sweetly sincere thank-you letter. Now framed.

⌐

Jackie Mason says, "Getting old isn't hard, you just have to find a disease you like."

I honestly didn't think of my father as getting old, but one night Melinda called and said, "Rue, Marie says Bill has been dragging his left foot and not using his left arm for weeks, and he doesn't seem aware of it. I told Marie to take him in for an MRI right away."

Now, while we all nervously pace, waiting for the test results, let me bring you up to date on my miraculous baby sister. Melinda, you will recall, married Sheridan Kinkade when she was a mere babe in arms and earned her B.A. during the five years she was birthing their four beautiful children. Once when Mark and I were visiting the Kinkades, I noticed Melinda's biology book propped against her sewing machine so she could study while making clothes for the kids. She also baby-sat three neighbor children to earn extra money, made gingerbread houses for Christmas, cooked three meals a day, and was homeroom mother for both Marci and Brendan. She went on to earn a master's and then a Ph.D., becoming a professor, then a dean—managing to look fabulous throughout. After Mother died, she divorced Sheridan, married a Louisiana good ol' boy eight years her junior, eventually divorcing him. You might say we McClanahan girls are superachievers, but as of the mid-nineties, neither of us had had much luck with marriage, not to put too fine a point on it.

Okay. The test results.

"The MRI shows a large blood clot on Bill's right brain."

Melinda and I arranged for him to have surgery in Oklahoma City, but she had to fly on business the day before the operation. That night, I slept on a cot in Bill's room, taking the opportunity to talk to him without the ever-present Marie. I needed to talk to him, as I'd needed him that night Melinda was born and Bill and I had stayed in the boarding house together. I decided to ask him some questions that had weighed on my heart all these years, and this time he was willing to talk with me.

"I've always been sad that I never got to see you much when I was a child," I said. "Where were you all that time?"

"Oh, honey, I had to be at work in the oil fields before you were up in the morning, and didn't get home till after you were in bed."

"I don't remember you playing with me, though. Even when you were home."

"I carried you around town on my shoulders when you were a baby, showing you off to everybody! I was proud of you, Frosty!"

I had no memory of that. But it was a helpful conversation, the first time I'd ever tried to clear up the lifelong yearning for him that had fostered my dusk panics and in some ways set the stage for my not-so-guido relationships with men. The next morning, while Bill underwent brain surgery, I waited with Marie, who harangued and kvetched the whole time. The operation was a resounding success, both with the safe removal of the blood clot and the fact that I had been able to sit for several hours on a sofa with Marie without killing her. Knowing Bill was going to be fine, I flew back to Los Angeles with some darling snapshots of us taken the morning I left, big grins on our faces.

While *Golden Palace* was on hiatus, I was offered the lead in *Lettice and Lovage,* to be done at the Vienna English Theatre in May. *Wow, Vienna!* I thought. The marvelous Nan Martin, who'd spent her career doing everything from Broadway to *Star Trek,* was playing the second lead, all the smaller roles to be filled by English-speaking actors living in Vienna.

Before rehearsals for *Lettice* began, I went to The Ashram, a health retreat nestled in the Santa Monica Mountains and run by the Scandinavian munchkin who inspired Shirley MacLaine's book *Out on a Limb*. She noticed I was taking estrogen pills and demanded, "Vy are you putting dees *sheet* in your body, baby?"

"It's to counteract the effects of menopause. Hot flashes, mood swings, and all that," I said. (It's been said that they call it menopause because "mad cow disease" was already taken. And frankly, "spontaneous human combustion" doesn't do it justice.)

With unwavering assurance, she growled, "Dees is poison, baby. T'row eet away!"

She only came up to my shoulder, but she had the authority of a drill sergeant and a formidable reputation as a healer. So what did I do? T'rew deem away, baby!

I hadn't realized The Ashram was a hiking retreat. The first day, three miles up the steep hills. Second day, nine miles. Third day, sixteen miles. Don't even think about the next four days. My feet were a garden of blisters. Every morning after breakfast, the other lodgers and I met in the anteroom to cover our tattered feet with Vaseline before setting off up the hills. I didn't stick around to find out how many of them made it through to the last day. This place was *way* beyond my stamina. The munchkin sent me to the Optimum Health Institute in San Diego to cleanse my system with colonics and raw food—make me strong like bull! I went. And she was right: After three days of nausea and flulike symptoms, normal for a newcomer, I experienced a surge of energy I hadn't felt since I was thirty!

Rehearsals for *Lettice and Lovage* began in L.A., then moved to Vienna, and the afternoon we arrived there, I noticed that the ominous, heavy gray sky was hanging too low. Much too low. It made me uneasy. That night around midnight, walking through my spacious suite in an ornate nineteenth-century hotel, I suddenly found myself gripped in a vise of panic.

What in the name of God? Black terror I hadn't experienced in years enveloped me.

I can't do this play! I can't learn it! I'm not capable!

It was a nutty reaction. I called my friend Jered Barclay, who helped me get a slippery handle on reality, but I was up most of the night. It was a bit easier during the day. I explored the city, enrolled in exercise and German classes, and found a Turkish café down the street, which became my supper place of choice, an alternative to the typically heavy Viennese fare. Every time I turned around, someone said, "Hef you tried our famuz Black Forest cake?" and shoved a plate in my hand, so I shopped for fresh produce on market day each week. Distracting myself on trips along the blue Danube, I could keep the terror down to a dull roar during the day, but playing the show six nights a week— mind-numbing panic. I had a new empathy for how Estelle must have felt on tape days. I'd rather have a root canal.

Lettice and Lovage is a challenge under the best circumstances. I played a guide in an English museum, leading tour groups through long, dry seventeenth-century British history lessons that bore everyone into a stupor, until she begins sprucing up the recitation with spicier stories, growing more and more rococo and colorful. Each scene repeats some of the former dialogue, changing it just enough to challenge any actress's memory. If I had been well, I would have delivered those scenes with gusto, but under my heavy cloud of panic, I could barely keep my balance. It wasn't a question of acting the role well—I was fighting for basic survival.

The audience was all smiles, throwing flowers, satisfied to be seeing Blanche Devereaux in person. Nan, who is a hoot and still one of my favorite people, was also struggling with her lines, which didn't help. I started drawing a large abstract picture—a woman on horseback on a winding path out of a gray city—and worked at it, wondering, *Will I ever get out of this hell?* My agent called the day before I flew home.

"CBS promised to pick up *Golden Palace* for another season," she said. "Look for the announcement in three days."

That was good news, and I expected the panic to disappear on the trip home, but when I arrived in L.A., it still gripped me.

"Maybe your estrogen-progesterone dosage needs to be altered," my doctor suggested.

"Oh, I stopped the estrogen replacement about ten weeks ago," I said.

"*What?* Rue, get back on it at once! You have to be weaned off hormone replacement slowly, or it's a terrible shock to the system. No wonder you're having panic attacks."

I went back on the hormones and within three days was fine and dandy, wondering what on earth women did before the days of synthesized estrogen. My doctor said they often wound up in insane asylums. By then, I had been on the estrogen-progesterone pill for ten years, unaware of the havoc it could play. Apparently, mine is one of the longest menopauses in recorded history, beginning when I was forty-four and just now waning away. I've become unusually hot-natured. And that ain't a joke, son. I step out in fifty-degree weather with no jacket or socks and love it.

Ah, womanhood.

Three days after I got home, CBS announced it had dropped *Golden Palace*.

Ah, television.

Within a week, I was offered the role of a tough bartender in a new Valerie Bertinelli sitcom, set in a Paris restaurant, guaranteed for a full season. I would be paid a little over a million dollars. I read the script. No creative challenge whatsoever. The bartender had eight lines. The writing wasn't funny. Valerie Bertinelli was . . . Valerie Bertinelli. But I would be guaranteed over a million dollars, which meant another year in my fairy-tale house in Encino. Network salaries had started to drop. This could be my last chance to make real dough. Shall I play the bartender and run away with a mil plus? Supporting *Valerie Bertinelli*? What shall I do, behave as an artist or a businesswoman?

This struck me as a reprise of my butt-naked, two-bucks-an-hour decision.

I turned it down this time.

Good-bye, fairyland. Hello, dignity.

CHAPTER TWENTY-FIVE

~~~

"God does not play dice with the universe."
—ALBERT EINSTEIN

"There's no way to tell which alternative will occur."
—QUANTUM THEORY

"P-p-personally, I disagree with b-b-both theories."
—PORKY PIG

B ack in our salad days in California, Norman had once become terribly discouraged with auditioning and told me he was giving up his attempt to be an actor.

"Oh, Norm, you can't give up!" I said, because I certainly never could have, but he shrugged and said, "What's the point? I'll never be anything but a warmed-over Franchot Tone."

Franchot Tone was ahead of my time, but I'd seen him in films when I was a kid. (Those in the know pronounced it "Fran-show," but Mother called him "Fran-shot.") He was usually cast as the handsome leading man's friend or rival, never getting the leading lady, but sometimes getting the other girl. He was graceful and charming and looked smashing in his tux, but rarely got cast as the big leading man. Unlike Clark Gable or Tyrone Power or other square-jawed he-men, Franchot Tone was slender and fine-featured, with a soft, sensitive jaw.

Norman and I went to see *Harry Black and the Tiger,* a movie starring the terribly square-jawed Stewart Granger as a bigger-than-life hero wrangling a man-eating beast, and later Norman said to me, half seriously, "But you know, my dear, I *am* Harry Black!"

And he proved it. In 1964, John Patrick Hayes directed a World War II movie, *Shell Shock,* in which Norman played an American soldier scaling a rocky hill. Upon reaching the top, he gets strafed with machine-gun fire and tumbles ass-over-teakettle back down over the dirt and rocks to the bottom. It was really a job for a stunt man, but Norman insisted on doing it himself. We shot it in one setup, without a rehearsal. It was quite realistic to watch, and God knows how he managed to land at the bottom without breaking several bones.

Yep. Norm had a face like Franchot Tone, but inside, he really was Harry Black!

One day not long after *Golden Palace* had been dumped, I was at Norman's, checking in on him, bringing him groceries, taking some time to visit with him as I often did. I saw him looking across the room at me from his wheelchair, and I said, "What are you thinking?"

As he rolled away, he answered, "Trying not to wish."

⌒

In October of 1993, I was offered the role of the Mother Superior, an ex–circus acrobat who'd embraced the dedicated life, in an A&E special of Danny Goggin's hit stage musical *Nunsense*. I read the script, listened to the tape of Mother Superior's songs, and decided to do it for one reason: a scene in which she sniffs a mysterious bottle found in a nun's locker, and gradually gets stoned silly. What a delightful—and challenging—little bit! I played the hell out of that nun, pardon the pun, and became lifelong friends with both Danny Goggin and Terri White.

Tom Keel made a brief but spectacular guest appearance in my life that fall, inviting me to join him on a visit to a friend's B&B in New Jersey. We hadn't seen each other since the high school reunion, and it sounded like a lovely spot to enjoy a pleasant respite in the country. After a nice long dinner with the owner, we went up to share the only available room and both fell asleep on the spot. The next day, as we explored the area, Tom told me about Joel, the Dallas woman he was in love with. She refused to go out exclusively with him, having other beaus as well. And who could blame her? He was still doing that abstinence thing, you know.

That night a glorious rainstorm blew in. After a late dinner, I went to bed, leaving Tom and the owner drinking together downstairs in the dining room. Some while later, I was roused out of a deep sleep as someone clambered on top of me. It was Keel! Thunder roared. Lightning flashed. And the storm raged outside, too. Being drunk didn't slow that guy down one whit. And neither did being abstinent! I was surprised, but not upset, and when it was over, we both fell asleep without a word.

The next day, never mentioning the night before, we parted on good terms and flew our separate ways. Over the years, Keel has kept in touch with me and gone out of his way to do many kindnesses for my family. In Bill's waning years, Keel visited him regularly and equipped the house with handholds and other special needs as Bill became frail. For my money, Tom Keel is one of the most decent men walking. And he's still as sexy as can be.

I bet you a nickel he doesn't remember that stormy night we spent together, which is too bad, because the memory still makes me smile.

～

On January 19, 1994, at 4:19 A.M., I was awakened by a deafening roar accompanied by violent shaking, side to side and forward and back, along with the shrill tinkling of shattering glass.

Earthquake! Get under a doorway.

I stumbled out of bed but was instantly knocked off balance, falling with my ribs against the sharp corner of my bedside table. I'd been in a few earthquakes, but nothing like the unceasing intensity and duration of this one. Stumbling for the doorway, I gripped it firmly for what seemed like forever. As the quake finally died down, I stayed where I was, expecting aftershocks, my heart pounding. Within seconds, two flashlights came through my bedroom door.

"Are you all right, Mum?"

"Yes, Celi, are you?"

"Yes, mum. I'm going to the car to listen to the radio. All our electricity is off. Alma, you help Mum see about the animals."

My ribs stabbing at every step, we checked the cat room and dog run. All fine. All accounted for except for my favorite cat, Gracie. We gathered in the kitchen as the faint dawn rose, made tea, and listened to the portable radio. Water and gas mains were broken. Electric and phone lines were down. Businesses along Ventura Boulevard in Sherman Oaks were shattered and flooded. Many houses had fallen. Sherman Oaks, between Studio City and Encino, fared the worst in our vicinity. My house, recently and sturdily rebuilt on Encino granite, suffered only minor damage. Furniture had traveled around, some of it perilously close to toppling over. It could have been much worse had it gone on another five or ten seconds. That Northridge earthquake measured 6.7 on the Richter scale, but ground acceleration was the highest ever recorded in an urban area. Fifty-one people were killed, almost nine thousand injured.

After the sun came up, I drove to Norm's apartment in Studio City, taking detours to avoid the worst flooding, and found him characteristically unflappable.

"Not much I could do but lie there in bed, waiting for something to fall on me," he said.

"Is there anything you need?" I asked. "Anything I can do for you?"

"Nah. Go find Gracie."

There were numerous aftershocks all day. And still no Gracie. I had to fly to New Mexico the next afternoon to help Melinda, following facial surgery.

Worried sick, at 2:30 the next day, I noticed Angie and Belle, my sheepdog, pointing like statues toward a far corner of the living room, where there was a built-in bench against the wall.

"Gracie?" I called.

A meow. The poor dear had been wedged for thirty-four hours into a tiny crawl space behind the bench. Greatly relieved, I left for New Mexico. Sis and I made a dandy pair—me daubing alcohol on her stitches, she doing the cooking because I could barely move with my bruised ribs.

⌐

Back home, that April I went by Norman's. He had a light flu, so I took him several half-gallons of fruit juice and other goodies.

"I'm off to Austin early tomorrow," I said. "Tom Keel offered to help Mark with some carpentry and electrical work. Mark's old house actually *leans*. I'm telling you, you can *move* it if you push hard enough on the outside. We're going to build him a new front porch." I laid my hand on Norm's forehead. "You're warm. Is there anything else I can get you?"

"I'm fine," he said. And I knew the cleaning woman came twice a week and could shop for him if necessary, so I wasn't worried.

Keel drove down from Dallas and started to work on Mark's house, the three of us working together but Tom doing the lion's share, bless his manly heart.

On the last day of work, Mark came outside and said, "Mother . . . Jerry Hartweg called. Norman died."

There's an Emily Dickinson poem that speaks of "the hour of lead" and the great silence that falls in a moment of profound loss. I stood without moving. Mark's SUV was parked next to me in the driveway. The sky was clear blue up above us. The house leaned in the breeze.

And Norman was dead.

"I . . . I need to . . . to fly home," I stammered.

Norm's landlady let me into his empty apartment, brushing aside the coroner's yellow "Do Not Pass" banner.

"I didn't see him for a couple days, so I thought I'd better look in," she said. "And he was there in bed. Looks like he'd been sick. They said he must've got dehydrated."

She left me to wait for Norm's brother and sister, and I stood in his apartment, which felt neutered and hollow without him there, like when you pierce a little hole in an eggshell and suck all the egg out. Standing by his letter file, I looked across the room, and there he sat in his wheelchair, grinning at me.

Relax, he said. *It's no big deal.*

First Lette, then Brad, and now, after forty years, my touchstone, my irreplaceable Norman, gone.

An era had ended.

⌐

I am not one to dwell on roads not taken, but I am fascinated by history, and I have a hard time letting go of personal artifacts, as you may have noticed. Once when I was visiting Melinda in Washington, D.C., I noticed an old blue vase embossed with flowers on a shelf.

"Oh, Mother's vase from Durant!" I said. "What memories that brings back! She loved that vase."

That Christmas, I opened a package from Melinda, and there was the vase. Of course, I still have it. My dear little sister, the unemotional Virgo. She has no trouble letting go of things for love.

Once when I, the oversensitive Pisces, was about ten, I accidentally stepped on a beetle, killing it, and burst into tears. Poor little beetle! That moment is another sort of artifact, one of many—some as small as bugs, some as big as mountains—which I carry with me. Not to torture myself, but because they've become part of me. Sometimes, honoring the memory of what we've lost is the only redemption we have.

Just recently, Norm's sister, Joyce, was clearing out her mother's keepsakes and came upon a letter Norm wrote to his parents when he returned to Fitzsimmons Army Hospital after his Christmas visit to Ardmore in 1958, when he was twenty-three.

"I thought you might want this," Joyce wrote. Of course I do, even though every time I read it, it breaks my heart all over again.

Jan 5th, 1959

I am back at the ole job, and I wish to hell I wasn't. My two weeks of civilian life have so spoiled me that putting on my uniform this morning was so traumatic as to be sickening. The Army is a dreadful place that holds in it only dreadful people, and 20 months is one hell of a long time. Six months until my next leave is even longer. I will get through it, by gritting my teeth and persevering. Yet what do I do? I bitch. I want out. Out out out!

I must admit that a good deal of the reason I want out is Eddi-Rue. She is such a darling I can't stand it; Mark is a perfect jewel—he has these huge eyes and stares in rapt wonder at the world and laughs and has a good time and almost the only time he cries is when he gets sleepy, because he hates to get sleepy and miss out on things; other than that, I have never seen such a good-natured baby. And, of course, he is doing things ahead of when he is supposed to be doing them, which, considering his mother is Eddi-Rue, is not surprising. As I mentioned on the phone—Eddi-Rue and I are where we were in New York again. The week was great. And I miss Rue much.

I love her, people.

It is now a question of waiting a few decades until Tom is good and clear and she can see the trees and then sees if I'm a tree she'd like to nest in. Way too early to tell now, and besides, here I am. Laws.

Patient? I do beat all.

Love, Norm

CHAPTER TWENTY-SIX

"From birth to 18, a girl needs good parents.
From 18 to 35, she needs good looks.
From 35 to 55, she needs a good personality.
And from 55 on, she needs cash."
—Sophie Tucker

I do not ascribe to the belief that "you can't teach an old dog new tricks." Not only is that not true with human beings, it's not true with dogs. I *have* taught old dogs new tricks. I've also taught a few old men some new tricks. I've even had to teach some old men some *old* tricks, and in almost every case, they learned just as quickly as puppies. It's all about providing the proper motivation. A little kibble here, a little nibble there. You'd be amazed. I don't know why people continue to buy into that "old dog" idea and other myths about aging, but when a myth is embraced as truth, it becomes a Belief System, or as I like to call it, "BS."

Another popularly held BS is that after a certain point, "the horse is out of the barn," which is to say that in old age—or even firmly established middle age, which is always about fifteen years older than you are at this moment—it's too late to reverse the effects of too much liquor, fatty foods, cigarettes, and lack of exercise. The truth is, nature is very forgiving, the human body resilient. That horse may be headed out of the barn, but a few good rope tricks can lure it back in. If a middle-aged smoker packs off for more than two years, she's at no greater risk for stroke than her pristine friend who never smoked at all. Eating habits are hard to change, but it can be done, and with some added exercise, you can change your weight, which matters a lot more than your age. Regular sexual activity is excellent exercise. So is lifting weights. It all depends on what's available. Dumbbells are pretty easy to come by, but since many of them are married, I suggest lifting weights.

Youth is not a time of life, it's a state of mind. It's not a matter of rosy cheeks, red lips, and supple knees, it's force of will, quality of imagination, and vigor of emotions. It's the freshness from the deep springs of life, and the idea that every day is God saying to you, "May I have this dance?"

There are two things to aim for in life: First, get what you want. Then, enjoy it.

⟶

The time had come to put my Encino Fairyland on the slumped real estate market, and after a few exciting offers fizzled (real estate attracts crazies like a bundt cake attracts flies), I managed to unload it for a million six. I had a mil nine in it. Notzo guido, but—oh, well. I had lived like a movie star for six glorious years, and I figured the $300,000 loss could be thought of as $50,000 worth of enjoyment per year. Or $4,166.66 per month. Or $138.88 per day. Or $5.78 per hour. But who's counting? (9.6 cents a minute.) Hey, those homegrown tomatoes were a bargain at just $87.50 a pound!

After looking for several weeks, I found a place to my liking in Hidden Hills, a small horse property adjoining untold acres of hills with an old partially renovated house, a nice backyard with a pool, a pretty gazebo, and even a vegetable garden, plus a tennis court and stables that were used by two women in exchange for their keeping all the fences repaired. Celi and Alma helped move me out of Fairyland into Horse Country, and I helped them find a little house about an hour north of L.A.

The fall of 1994 brought two intriguing stage offers: *After-Play*, by Anne Meara, to be presented by the Manhattan Theatre Club that winter, closing early in March, and Mary Chase's *Harvey*, to play in London's Shaftsbury Theatre beginning rehearsals in mid-March. Rather fortuitous timing, eh what? I accepted both.

Now to find a place to stay in Manhattan.

"You'll stay with me," said my friend Marty Richards, and he didn't have to twist my arm. Marty lived in the River House on East Fifty-second Street, employing a live-in married couple, a full-time chauffeur, and various assistants. His wife, Mary Lee (remember the heiress of the Johnson & Johnson dynasty?) had died of cancer in the eighties, leaving Marty the inheritor of untold millions. I'd be earning Off Broadway minimum, so his place would be pretty swanky digs for me. In late December, I exited my cab in the River House's circular drive and stepped into the foyer, where the butler intoned, "Please remove your shoes."

Well, my God, yes! Shall I also remove my clothes?

There was a party that night, given by Marty in a midtown restaurant, full of celebrities. I put on my best black dress and one of my Viennese evening capes, feeling quite lah-dee-dah, hobnobbing with Gloria de Haven, Rex Reed, and other swells. After a couple of heady hours, I left, accepting a ride with Joan Rivers. Also in the limo happened to be an older man on crutches.

"Actually, we've met," he reminded me. "I was one of the producers of *Jimmy Shine*."

I piped up, "Oh, it's so nice to see you again! Maybe we can have a cup of tea sometime and discuss old times."

There was a noticeable freeze in the limo. Oops. I think I had just made a pass at Joan Rivers's boyfriend. Hey, who knew?

Marty's chauffeur took me to rehearsals in the grungy West Twenties and brought me home to Marie Antoinette's palace after. Yes, Marty actually had Marie Antoinette's private writing desk among his crystal chandeliers and plush rugs and fabulous furniture! ("Mary

Lee would hate all this," he told me. "She was very unpretentious.")
After-Play was an engrossing play about two couples having dinner in a
little restaurant, where Raziel, the Angel of Mysteries, is tending bar.
We got good reviews, and Anne got investors to move *After-Play* Off
Broadway, where it ran for a year, and it's since played all over Europe
and Australia.

Annie, go braugh!

I popped by Hidden Hills just to check on things, then flew off
to Heathrow and *Harvey*. The producers put me up in the only hotel
in the Westminster area, a few blocks from Trafalgar Square, which
introduces pedestrians to SoHo and Shaftsbury Avenue, known as
The West End, where the theatres begin, the Broadway area of London. At the far end of Shaftsbury, totally out of sight behind a building,
is the Shaftsbury Theatre, in which we were to play. Hardly a location
to catch the eye of strolling tourists, thirteen telephone poles past the
standpipe from all the other West End theatres—the first of several
major gaffes on the producers' part. Besides housing us in the out-of-
the-way Shaftsbury Theatre, they'd set our opening for "low season"—
the chilly vacation period when Londoners traditionally go to the south
of France but the tourist trade hasn't yet begun. As I walked over the
Waterloo Bridge to The Old Vic for rehearsal each day, gypsies were
everywhere, sending their kids out to beg.

Harvey is a broad comedy, brimming with delicious dialogue. The
first days of rehearsals, I was shocked to find nobody chuckling at their
fellow players' scenes. Not a peep from anyone. I played Veta, the pro-
tagonist's older sister, who is chagrined at the dent her brother Elwood
makes in her social life when he begins talking to a six-foot-tall rabbit
only he can see. At the end of her rope, Veta takes him to Chumley's
Rest, a mental clinic, where a hefty intern mistakenly rousts her
upstairs for treatment, letting Elwood go home. After a couple of
hours, Veta returns home from the clinic, staggering into the library,
her stockings below her knees, her hat askew, carrying her corset.

MYRTLE: What happened to you, Mother?

VETA: As I was walking along the path—this awful man stepped out. He was a white slaver. I know he was. He had on one of those white suits. That's how they advertise.

Come on, people! That's hilarious! In rehearsal, we got *not one snicker* from the director, the stage manager, our fellow actors, nobody. This unnerved me. I was a stranger in a strange land, up the crick as far as getting a handle on the character. Well, I thought, maybe the audiences will laugh and help me find Veta. We opened in Wimbledon. No laughs. Oxford. No laughs. Over to Belfast. A few laughs. And last, Bath. A titter or two. Quite disconcerting. I wondered if London would be more of the same. If so, God help me.

We visited a Scotch distillery on the northern tip of Ireland, and although I had never cared for Scotch, I tried their little samples laid out on the greeting table, and oh, my Lord, they were *good*. I bought about eight mixed-sample packages of different blends for family and friends and a fifth of a remarkable malt for myself. During our London run of about six weeks, I polished off the malt, as well as all the gift packages. Every drop.

One night, in the scene at Chumley's Rest, Veta is told by the nurse receptionist to wait while she gets the doctor. As written, the nurse goes offstage, returning at once with Dr. Sanderson, but on this particular evening, the nurse was gone longer than usual, leaving me alone onstage. When she returned, she said, "Dr. Sanderson . . . uh . . . he'll be with you shortly."

Excuse me?

We started ad-libbing. And we ad-libbed and we ad-libbed for over three interminable minutes. I was considering singing a song, maybe doing a little soft-shoe, perhaps a few jokes, when Clive Carter, who played the doctor, finally burst on stage.

"Sorry to keep you waiting!" he said, out of breath, and we resumed the scene.

Clive had been on the phone with his agent and missed his cue! By the time the show closed, I was ready to be admitted to a mental clinic for real.

We attended an award event at one of the West End theatres. Raquel Welch was also a guest, and standing next to her, I was truly amazed at her youthful beauty. She was setting off on a tour of Shaw's *The Millionairess*. Raquel Welch doing Shaw. My, my. And his worst play, to boot. I wished her luck but felt she might be in for disappointment. Which she was. She did even worse business than we did, if that's possible. With ticket sales too low to keep running on income alone, the producers asked us actors if we'd donate our salaries to keep the play open. Most of the younger actors were eager to donate at least part of their salaries, but the unanimous decision among us old farts was "Not one farthing!" We'd been down that road before.

A year or so later, Bea Arthur mentioned to me that she'd been offered a play in London.

"Oh, that's wonderful," I said. "Are you taking it?"

"God, no," said Bea. "I didn't want to read in the paper: *Second Golden Girl Flops in London*."

Well, bust my britches, Bea, that wasn't very nice. But as Winston Churchill once said (between mouthfuls of Boodle's Orange Fool), "Success is going from failure to failure without loss of enthusiasm."

So onward I forged.

⟿

Hidden Hills looked mighty good on my return. Mark got a gig doing guitar music for *The Guiding Light*—an innovative switch from the sonorous soap opera organ—so he packed his Forerunner and came back to L.A., moving in with me and Melinda's son Brendan. He transformed my party room into an English pub, with a pool table, refinished furniture, and antique wooden plaques—bas-relief 1890 British cricket players in knickers inscribed:

THE MANAGER'S WIFE WILL DEAL WITH YOUR DAMAGED BALLS.
PLEASE LEAVE YOUR BALLS IN THE FRONT OFFICE.
PLAYERS ARE RESPONSIBLE FOR THEIR OWN BALLS.

Mark and Brendan and their cronies spent many a jovial hour out there, drinking beer and shooting pool. Every morning I'd stand in the kitchen drinking my coffee, looking out at the backyard, thinking, *I'm happy!* A novel feeling. I liked it.

Work was a little slow, however. Early in January of 1996, I lamented to my Guatemalan housekeeper, "I don't know why I never get called in for movie auditions!"

"Turn a glass of water upside down in a saucer," she said seriously. "Light a candle and pray daily to the water goddess for assistance."

So I did, and say what you will, within a week, I was cast as the blinded, disfigured biology teacher in Paul Verhoeven's *Starship Troopers*. To create my disfigured face, I had to have a plaster cast made. The special-makeup people came to my house, and we did it in the kitchen, with me holding on to the edge of the cabinet for dear life, my nostrils and eyes plastered over, my lips all but plastered shut, with a straw to breathe through. Before the twenty minutes were up, I couldn't take it anymore, but they had what they needed. And that little role was a trip!

I did that job, relit the candle, and—hey, that little water goddess knew her business. I was immediately called to do Garry Marshall's new film, *Dear God,* playing the crotchety mother of Greg Kinnear in his film debut. In the TV movie *The Margaret Mitchell Story,* I played Mitchell's grandmother (her inspiration for writing *Gone with the Wind*). Shannen Doherty played Margaret Mitchell, and she was an experience. Fortunately, she liked me, and who better to play the headstrong, wild young flapper? After another candle, I agreed to play a farmer's wife in *Rusty, a Dog's Tale,* a talking-animal movie—but only if I could also do voices for two of the animals, so they gave me a loquacious, matronly cow and a fussy little duck. Such fun!

Late in August, the water goddess decided to test my mettle with a very dark film, *This World, Then the Fireworks,* as the insane mother of incestuous twins played by Billy Zane and Gena Gershon. Blasted in the face with a shotgun when the twins were children, she was another disfigured character. Not only disfigured, but crazy as a bedbug, a Bible-thumping lost soul. When the twins realize she knows about their affair, they smother her to death. Yeah. That's beyond dark. That's not even film noir—that's dismal, inky, stygian black, baby. At the audition on camera, I pulled out all the stops, going wild-batty hysterical. When I finished the scene, the director said, "Well. *Now* I know what this movie should look like."

After *Fireworks,* I asked my pal the water goddess if she could come up with a happier role, and she hooked me up with Martha Coolidge, who was casting *Out to Sea*, which would be Walter Matthau and Jack Lemmon's last collaboration.

"I can't offer you one of the love interests," Martha told me. "The producers have actresses in mind for those roles, but I'm going to ask to have the role of the cruise ship owner expanded for you. Are you interested?"

Interested? I left there floating on a cloud. As I recall, it was Cloud Number Nine.

Out to Sea was great fun. I got to rhumba with Walter Matthau, who dove under my chiffon gown in an effort to hide from Dyan Cannon. Walter never learned the dance, so I had to whisper to him, "Turn left and dip me after two more steps" and "Now dive behind me," while looking as if I'm being manhandled. He was wonderful to hang out with, full of unending stories and anecdotes. Jack Lemmon, whose love interest in the film was Gloria de Haven, was delightful but quiet off-camera. Brent Spiner was hilarious as the smarmy British entertainment director. Hal Linden and Donald O'Connor were also onboard, and I even got to do a bit of ballroom dancing with O'Connor.

Trying to negotiate the rhumba with Walter Matthau in Out to Sea.

The juiciest gossip on the set was born of the snarky rivalry between Dyan Cannon and Elaine Stritch, playing mother and daughter. That and Gloria de Haven's daily wardrobe crises. The wardrobe mistress went from trailer to trailer every morning, checking first on Cannon and Stritch, then de Haven, and ending up with me, bringing the day's tastiest gossip with her. There were various altercations on the set between Elaine and Dyan, but Walter—never raising his voice—would suggest we take a short break, and when we returned to the scene, he'd always worked it out with them. Oh, Lord, that movie was too much fun! One of the best experiences in my career. But I wouldn't be surprised if Martha Coolidge went straight home and had a nervous breakdown.

Meanwhile, *The Guiding Light* fired their new music producer, so there went Mark's job. In June he moved back to Austin, sleeping on friends' sofas while looking for a house.

I told him, "Turn a glass of water upside down and light a candle."

Hey, no stone left unturned. Or as a book on theatre critics says, "No turn left unstoned."

CHAPTER TWENTY-SEVEN

"Leap, and the net will appear."

—ZEN SAYING

*A*s of this writing, *The Golden Girls* is playing on television somewhere in the world at any given moment of any given day. It was a smash hit in sixty countries and remains popular throughout the world. DVDs fly off the shelf (and I get almost two cents for each sale, by God!). Internet fan sites abound. It's been almost fifteen years since I delivered my last line as Blanche Devereaux, yet she has made me one of the most recognizable women in the world, recently voted in one poll as the Fifth Most Beloved Celebrity Over Fifty-Five—after Mohammed Ali, Walter Cronkite, and I'm not sure who else. Mother Teresa and Shirley Temple, I would assume.

Ah, Fame! Celebrity! To be adored by throngs!

But wait a minute . . . who is really adored by throngs? Rue McClanahan or Blanche Devereaux? The throngs don't know Rue McClanahan. They only think they do, because if someone appears to you nightly in the privacy of your bedroom, you must be intimately acquainted with her, *n'est-ce pas?* But Rue McClanahan has also played witches and bitches, killers and drunks. It's the Fame of Blanche Devereaux, week after week for decades, that has laminated her to Rue until, to the public, the two seem inseparable.

My friends who knew me before Blanche love me for myself. And I love them. Most are "unknowns," and the few who are famous I still love for themselves, warts and all.

Not all important people are famous, and not all famous people are important.

Let's agree on that. Okay, little loves?

Late for my hair appointment one morning, I stopped at the bakery next door to get a fast bran muffin, then rushed outside and almost bumped into a guy who approached me, extending his hand. Thinking he was a panhandler, I pushed the bakery bag at him and said, "Here— it's a bran muffin!"

Whereupon he said, "Oh, no, Miss McClanahan, I wanted an autograph."

So a guy on the street thinks my name on a piece of paper is preferable to a bran muffin. If that's what fame is, then—hot cinders! I've arrived! But I'm still on the same mission I was on when I was Little Miss Nobody. I want to do good work and be rewarded for my effort. Back then, I was thrilled if acting paid enough to cover the rent and an occasional beer. I've since added a few amenities to my list of simple needs, but the work is still what matters.

One May morning in Hidden Hills, Barbara Lawrence, my manager, sent me the script for *Millions of Miles,* a play about an over-the-hill prostitute and a shy widower living in Queens, to be presented in a small theatre north of Manhattan. It wasn't very good, but I was interested in the role of the prostitute and wanted to work on her. I talked it over with Barbara.

"You wanna go disappear for a couple of months?" she asked.

"Heck," I said. "Sure!" And we accepted it.

The frugal producers rented quarters for me in a funny old theatrical apartment hotel in the West Forties. I checked in, saw a couple of plays, and reported for rehearsals on May 19, where I met the director, Barry Nelson, and his wife, Nancy, the husband-and-wife producers, the stage manager, Joel Vig, the leading man, Milo O'Shea, the playwright, and two younger actors who rounded out the cast. Nobody else, no assistants. The stage manager was also the costume department. A minuscule budget, to say the most.

On the third day of rehearsals, I was returning from getting coffee when I saw a tall, slender man in a blue blazer talking to the director and producers, and kids, that was one good-looking dude. Thick, wavy brown hair. Big hazel eyes. Full lips, quick to smile.

"Rue, meet Morrow Wilson," said Barry.

And Morrow Wilson shook my hand and said, in a low, mellifluous voice, "I saw you play Caitlin in *Dylan,* and you've never disappointed me since."

How refreshing! Caitlin in *Dylan* in 1972. One of my favorite roles. And not one word about *The Golden Girls*.

Mr. Wilson stayed for the full day of rehearsals, but I was never told why he was there. Next day, he returned, watched rehearsals, and had several little private conversations with Barry and Joel. Was he a possible investor? A play doctor? Just an interested friend? It turned out he was there to give any assistance he could, gratis, as a favor to his friends, Barry and Nancy.

At the close of rehearsal the second day, I announced to the room in general, "Oh, gosh, I'll never get all these lines learned without some help. Is there anyone here who could cue me for about an hour before rehearsals?"

After a moment, Morrow Wilson said, "I could do that."

Method in my madness, folks.

The next morning, Morrow arrived at my apartment at 9:30 sharp, as dapperly dressed as he'd been at rehearsals, and I knew I was going to like him right away when he candidly asked, "So. How did you get stuck to this tar baby?"

I laughed and said, "Oh, I thought the role had possibilities. How 'bout you?"

"Well, Barry and Nancy asked me to produce this piece of poultry a while ago with the idea that Barry would make a career change from hotshot Broadway comedy actor to hotshot Broadway comedy director, but I could see five good reasons this play was going to go over the falls, and I made the mistake of leaving a message on their answering machine listing those reasons. So I didn't hear from them for two years. Then Nancy called last week and said, 'Remember that play you said was the worst play ever written?' And I said, 'I couldn't have said it was the worst play ever written; *I* wrote the worst play ever written.' She said, 'Well, we're taking it to Broadway starring Rue McClanahan and Milo O'Shea!' And I said, 'Wonderful! Rue McClanahan is the best comedienne in the English-speaking world, and a surefire box office draw. Let me know if there's anything I can do to help.' Nancy said, 'What are you doing Thursday?' See, in show business, the only promises kept are the ones *you* make. So here I am."

God, I loved the zingy way he talked, the silver-tongued devil! And it was heartening to meet someone who felt the way I do about keeping one's promises. Yes, we eventually got around to running lines, but over the next several days, sitting with Morrow every morning, I was a lot more interested in the character on the sofa beside me than I was in the characters in the play. He was funny—no, *witty*. He had a gargantuan vocabulary, with which he spun interesting stories and raised thought-provoking questions. He had integrity and was decent in the rarest sense of that word. He could argue anyone into the ground and enjoyed verbal confrontations, but he never swore, never used four-letter words. He had more information in his head than any cranium should have been able to hold. He remembered every joke, every song, every piece of pertinent information he'd ever passed his eyes over, able to quote someone famous on any subject, but when I said something about his impressive intellect, he pointedly told me, "I am *not* an intellectual."

Well, I thought, *that's how much you know.*

Born in Manhattan, a direct descendant of one of the six men to sign both the Declaration of Independence and the United States Constitution, Morrow had grown up in Vermont and Arkansas (in itself a bizarre mix), the eldest son of a professional writer and Southern mother. He'd gone off to Putney, an offbeat, prestigious school in Vermont, then to Columbia to major in English, and then straight to work at twenty-one as the first associate producer for David Susskind's talk show. He'd spent his career in theatre, broadcasting, and advertising, always writing, always stirring things up. He'd been married to his first wife for sixteen years and to his second for seventeen years, and had now been divorced for almost seven months.

Good heavens, I wondered, *how old is this man?*

He didn't look a day over forty-five, but when he mentioned he'd lived in Manhattan during World War II, I figured he had to be at least fifty-two. He was actually fifty-seven. I was sixty-three. Okay, I could buy that. Even if he did look like a kid of forty-five.

Morrow and I continued to meet every morning, and at rehearsals he became overtly flirtatious. Shocking! Believe it or not, I'd never been pursued by such a blatant flirt. But then I noticed he also flirted with the younger actress in the cast, so I wasn't sure if he was making a play for me or just doing what came naturally. However, the more time we spent together, just the two of us, the more I saw a difference between the public and private playfulness.

Something I found sweetly odd about Morrow when we were alone together: He was shy. I found that terribly charming. I found *him* terribly charming. I'd almost forgotten what it felt like to be so fully engaged in conversation, to laugh like that, and think like that, and feel that deep-down frisson of *Hmm, now where might this be leading?* I liked the feeling of his lanky, six-foot frame striding down Broadway beside me. Those hazel eyes that didn't break away from mine when I was talking, because he was genuinely *listening* to me. And those Jimmy Stewart lips—you know those lips!

Begging to be kissed.

~

I found The Lump while I was getting a massage one night. Those of you—and there are far too many—who have felt The Lump know exactly what I'm talking about.

The fingertips stray across it: *Tra-la-la.*

Then return: *I beg your pardon?*

Then palpate: *What the hell . . .*

Then grope: *Oh, my God!*

The Lump, meanwhile, just sits there. Like a Lump.

"It's under my right arm, and . . . I didn't know who else to call, Morrow," I said. "I don't have a regular doctor here. Can you suggest someone?"

He said, "I do know someone. Dr. Steven Field. I'll make an appointment right away."

The next day, I had rehearsals upstate where the play was due to open in a week, so he made the appointment the following day, Friday, June 6, at 9:00 A.M. When I arrived, Morrow was waiting on the sidewalk outside Dr. Field's office. He opened the taxi door for me and gave me a firm, reassuring hug, but his expression was so solemn, his eyes so penetrating, I felt a twinge of anxiety.

The examination was brief.

"It's breast cancer," said Dr. Field without a shred of doubt.

The room—his voice in my head—that split second on the clock—everything seemed to slip off track, the whole world suddenly toppling.

"Breast cancer?" I echoed. "But . . . I'm a vegetarian. I exercise every day. I get regular mammograms. And in my family . . . *no one* in my family . . ."

Clearly, he couldn't be right, because cancer is something that happens to other people—right up until the moment it happens to you.

"How long have you been on hormone replacement?" he asked, consulting my chart.

"Seventeen years."

"Well. There you go," he said. And there I went. "The cancer is well into Stage Two. It's already metastasized to the lymph nodes. You'll need surgery right away."

I struggled to assimilate the information he was giving me, grateful to know that a deeply concerned but comfortingly practical Morrow was waiting for me in the reception area. The person you need with you at an event like this is a producer, not a director. Someone who will take action instead of telling you how to feel. When I told Morrow the news, he took it in, showing no surprise or fear.

"I suspected as much." He nodded, taking my hand. "Rue, you've had so much work to do on this play, I wasn't going to say anything until after you'd opened, but now I want you to know that I love you. Whatever happens, I want to be with you over the long haul."

The difference between the blackness of the examination room and the unfiltered sunlight of those words was almost too much. The thing I wanted to hear and the thing I most dreaded hearing had both landed in my lap in the space of fifteen minutes. For the first time in my life, someone was there for me with exactly what I needed, at the exact moment I needed it. I looked at Morrow and said, "I love you, too."

He took me outside, into the air, into the oxygen, and right away was working on what to do. We called the producers and told them I had to drop out of the play to deal with this emergency and spent the next days seeing surgeons and oncologists. Through the batteries of tests and procedures and decisions that immediately hit like a blizzard, Morrow helped me gather facts, weigh options, and weed out priorities. Dr. Larry Norton at Sloan-Kettering was the only one who didn't want to do a single or double mastectomy right off the bat.

"I think we have a shot at a lumpectomy," he said, "and if the borders are clean, we'll start on a stiff regimen of chemotherapy and radi-

During chemotherapy, New York City, 1997. Hey, a good lookin' woman looks good in anything—or without anything!

ation. The cancer's moving quickly," he added. "So we have to move quickly, too."

I said, "All right. Let's get started."

As plans for my treatment moved rapidly forward, the producers called early every morning, telling me how much they loved me—and how much they urged me to do the play first and *then* get the surgery.

All heart, those two.

～

One evening the following week, Morrow took me to see a revival of *Chicago*. Sitting there beside him in the dark theatre, I discovered I wasn't in the mood for the ol' razzle-dazzle. At intermission, I said, "Let's leave."

"Let's go to Sardi's," he said, "and have a glass of wine."

We sat across the table from each other, and I couldn't take my eyes off him.

"You know, I bought the sheet music for 'I'll Be Seeing You,' " said Morrow. "If you'd gone back to L.A. before I worked up the nerve to tell you I love you, I was going to FedEx it so it would get there before you did."

"Good grief, Morrow. I would've had to turn around and fly right back to New York."

"Well . . . that was the general idea."

I couldn't help hearing the song in my head when he told me that. The most heart-meltingly poignant song ever written, so full of longing and tenderness.

Over my second glass of red wine, I said to Morrow, "I'd like to marry you."

Such an expression on his face! His eyes grew wide.

"Will you *marry* me?" he said.

"Yes."

After a moment, he said, "*Will* you marry me?"

"Yes!"

I guess he believed me, because he didn't ask a third time. We'd known each other two weeks and five days, and while that might sound like the old *BA-RUMPH! BA-RUMPH!* to some, it was actually more like that time back in 1949 when I emerged from the subway on Forty-second Street, inhaled my first breath of New York City, and immediately realized: *I'm home.*

Christmas Day, 1997, Morrow and I were married at the Waldorf Astoria between my sixth and seventh chemo treatments. I was bald as a billiard ball. Morrow had bronchitis and a 102-degree fever. The wedding was ridiculous and the honeymoon was worse, but I've been Mrs. Morrow Wilson a lot longer than I was ever Mrs. Anybody Else. And without a shiver of panic.

With Morrow at Sardi's, June, 1997.
"I'd like to marry you."

⁓

I can only surmise that someone somewhere must have sneaked out in the dark of the moon and buried a new potato on my behalf. Ain't that Saint Dymphna a hoot and a holler?

⁓

The sun is streaming down on Manhattan's East Side, and across my back fence a children's tennis class is presently in progress. Every morning, we find chartreuse balls hiding in the foliage like Easter eggs. We figure they're ours, since they say "Wilson" on them. The exuberant voices of the instructor and kids come sailing past the fence into our lovely garden, along with the balls bouncing off the walls of the high-rise buildings around us. I used to say I wanted to die onstage after the curtain goes down on a play that I'm in. Now I think I'd be just as pleased to check out right here in the garden, listening to those kids' voices across the fence.

A writer friend of mine says there's no such thing as happy endings, only happy intervals and inevitable conclusions, and that an author must choose whether to follow a story to its inevitable conclusion or draw the curtain at a happy interval. And so, my dears, I'll draw the curtain here. On days like today, there is no ending. Perhaps there never is. All I know is that at this moment, I am happy. I love my life as it now is. I hate the madness going on in the world, but in my personal life, the beauty stays ahead of the ugliness, and in my professional life, good work hasn't stopped coming my way, bringing joys and challenges.

In my vast collection of memories and mementos, one of my proudest possessions is a letter quoting Tennessee Williams's reaction to my performance in *Dylan*.

"Your work has that rare combination of earthiness and lapidary polish," said Mr. Williams, "that quality of being utterly common and utterly noble. Frippery combined with fierceness . . ."

Oh, Lord, I wish I'd gotten to meet him! I had no idea he even knew who I was, but he certainly had me pegged.

Frippery combined with fierceness.

Even as a child I had the strong feeling that life was good. I had a passion for work, an openness to love, and a penchant for joy. In a word, I had hope.

I still have it.

One more thing . . .

"Thanks for noticing."

—Eeyore

S everal years ago, I did an event at Chippendale's, the popular male strip club in New York. Not my cup of tea, but I did it to help PETA, which was a new group at the time. People for the Ethical Treatment of Animals accomplishes courageous and compassionate acts on behalf of our animal friends who can't speak for themselves, and I'm proud to lend whatever support I can. I testified on PETA's behalf when they were sued by a trainer who'd been caught on film beating orangutans he used in his Vegas act. Initially, the bastard won, but PETA pushed the case to State Supreme Court and got the trainer and his act barred from ever appearing in Nevada again. Ingrid Newkirk, director of PETA for more than twenty years, is a true heroine. Dan Matthews and the rest of PETA's staff and volunteers bravely fight cruelty, work for the prosecution of those who cause suffering, and close down facilities not operating within the law. From time to time, I appear at events in order to encourage more people to attend, and it delights and amazes me that the bubble of celebrity actually has this powerful inside. To learn more about PETA and discover what you can do to help, visit their Web site at www.peta.org.

PHOTO PERMISSIONS AND CREDITS

Diligent efforts have been made to locate the copyright owners of all the photographs contained in this book, but some have not been located. In the event a photograph has been used without permission, the copyright owner should contact the author, c/o Broadway Books, 1745 Broadway, New York, NY 10019, Attn: Editorial.

TEXT

Page 6: (three photos) Author collection

Page 23: Author collection

Page 29: Author collection

Page 130: Photo by Dick Bowen

Page 134: Author collection

Page 159: Photo used by permission from NBC Universal

Page 250: Author collection

Page 277: Author collection

Page 290: (two photos) Author collection

Page 322: OUT TO SEA © 1997 Twentieth Century Fox. All rights reserved.

Page 331: Author collection

Page 333: Author collection

BLACK-AND-WHITE INSERT

Page 1: Author collection

Page 2: Author collection

Page 3: Author collection

Page 4: Author collection

Page 5: (top) Photo by Judy Cohen; (bottom) Courtesy of The
    Cereghetti Agency
Page 6: Author collection
Page 7: (top) Photo by Martha Swope; (bottom) Author collection
Page 8: (top) Photo by Bert Andrews; (bottom) Author collection

COLOR INSERT

Page 1: Courtesy of Stuart Studios
Page 2: Author collection
Page 3: Author collection
Page 4: (top) Photo used by permission from The Walt Disney
    Company; (bottom) Author collection
Page 5: Photo used by permission from The Walt Disney Company
Page 6: Author collection
Page 7: Author collection
Page 8: Author collection